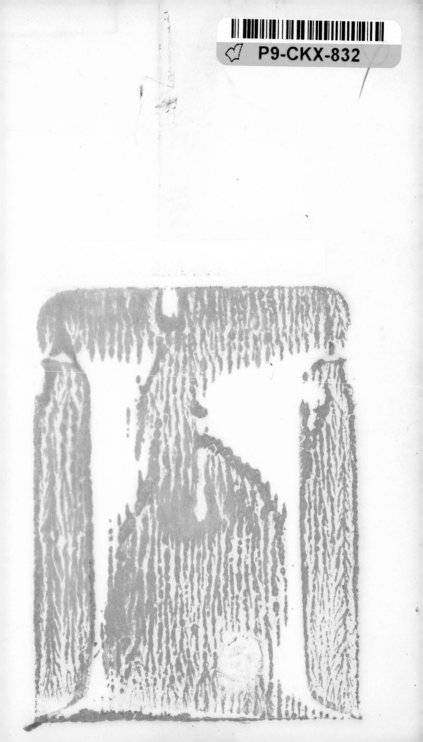

The French Novel from Gide to Camus

THE FRENCH NOVEL

from Gide to Camus

BY

Germaine Brée

&

Margaret Guiton

x

A Harbinger Book

HARCOURT, BRACE & WORLD, INC.

NEW YORK AND BURLINGAME

CONTENTS

AN AGE OF FICTION

Foreword

This book, published early in 1957, was written for the most part in 1955. Written at the present time it would be a different, not necessarily a better, book. World War II and the immediate postwar years loomed larger on the horizon then than now. The years between the two wars were nearer to us. The middle 1950's were still fairly closely involved with what seemed a recent past. It was, on the whole, a backward-looking time. In the 1960's we are looking, with mingled hopes and apprehensions, towards an uncertain future.

The change of perspective, common to both novelists and novel readers, corresponds with our original view of Gide and Camus as recognizable demarcations in the development of the French novel, of the period bounded by these two writers as an appropriate subject of investigation. Were we to revise the book a number of changes would be in order, particularly in the chapter on Camus. It is not merely that the whole chapter would have to be recast in the past tense. A literary career which had seemed full of promise must now, unfortunately, be seen as a completed whole.

The first two volumes of Simone de Beauvoir's memoirs, in our opinion her most interesting work to date, has brought valuable information about her immediate contemporaries, in particular Sartre. A more recent study of Sartre's early novel, *La Nausée,* would profit from her account of his hallucinations under the influence of certain drugs. Sartre himself has announced that he will not

1

attempt to finish his ambitious novel cycle, *Les Chemins de la liberté,* so intimately connected with the intellectual and emotional climate of the last war. Céline's *Voyage au bout de la nuit,* that most "disengaged" of novels, is meanwhile becoming an increasingly important influence.

A number of novelists have written new books which have reached the American public. Aragon turned from his chronicle of the "real" present-day world to a vast, historical pageant, *La Semaine sainte.* Queneau gave his linguistic experiments a more popular form with *Zazie dans le métro.* Aymé surveyed Parisian youth with his usual contempt, but somewhat diminished verve, in *Les Tiroirs de l'inconnu.*

None of these recent events or developments, however, changes our basic conception and evaluation of the novelists considered here, and we believe that the studies would lose more than they would gain from occasional scattered revisions and interpolations. The last chapter of the book, which anticipated certain new directions in the novel, has been completely rewritten. Writers just appearing on the literary horizon when the book was first published have produced work of sufficient importance to permit a clearer picture of their aims and their achievements.

Germaine Brée
Margaret Guiton

MAY 1962

AN AGE OF FICTION

To the question, What should the man of letters be in our time? Allen Tate has answered: "He must re-create for his age the image of man, and he must propagate standards by which other men may test that image, and distinguish the false from the true."

This definition explains the particular prestige of the French novel of the period between the two wars. If the names of Gide, Proust, Bernanos, Saint-Exupéry, Malraux, Sartre and Camus have become familiar to so wide a reading public in so many different countries, it is because these novelists effectively created a new image of man for their age. The same is no doubt true of all the major nineteenth century novelists. What strikes us in contemporary France is, first, the extraordinary number of major novelists appearing in one country within so short a span of time and, second, the fact that these novelists were highly aware of their role as propounders of a new conception of human reality.

It might seem more accurate here to speak of "conceptions" rather than of "conception." What common grounds, the reader well may ask, can one find for forms of existence so diverse, at times so antagonistic, as those suggested by the troubled adolescents of Gide, the hypersensitive and sickly narrator of Proust, the guilt-stricken Christians of Mauriac and Bernanos, Romains's Men of Good Will, Cocteau's poets, Giraudoux's mysterious young girls, Malraux's adventurers, Sartre's introspective Roquentin and Camus's Stranger?

It is true that some novelists, Colette among the best, remain aloof from the principal currents of the time, stubbornly resisting any attempt at generalization. But the new image of man is in itself

3

consistent with a great deal of individual diversity. It is that of a man who is dissatisfied with the various ready-made forms of existence that he finds around him and who deliberately attempts to create his own particular form of existence according to his personal convictions.

The French novelists often refer to this as a "conscious" existence. One of Malraux's characters states that his main object in life is to "transform into consciousness the greatest possible breadth of experience." Camus meanwhile asserts: "All experiences are similar in this respect. Some are useful to man, and some are not. They are useful to him if he is conscious." Whatever the scope or the quality of experience with which these different novelists are concerned, it is the conscious assimilation and utilization of the experience that forms the distinguishing characteristic of their new image of man. With Gide, consciousness is really an end in itself. With Proust, it leads to the discovery of the world of art; with Romains, to the discovery of the social organism. With Bernanos, it leads to God; with Malraux, to heroic action; with Sartre, to anguish; with Camus, to a sort of moral sensitivity to life.

This image of man as the creator of his own existence is directly and deliberately opposed to the view of the turn-of-the-century novelist: the so-called "bourgeois" attitude toward life wherein meanings and values are seen as something imposed on the individual from without, by family, church, society, state or nation. Both Bourget's *Le Disciple* (*The Disciple*) and Barrès's *Les Déracinés* (*The Uprooted*), novels still widely read in the 1920's, sought to illustrate the corrosive effects of individual reason and the moral necessity of habit, prejudice and convention as guides to existence. Even Flaubert, though he despised the narrow "bourgeois" world in which he lived, was extremely skeptical of the value of individual revolt.

To rediscover the ideal of conscious existence, one must go back to Laclos's Marquise de Merteuil, to Balzac's Rastignac, to Stendhal's Julien Sorel. Still, even though these are the very heroes and heroines to have been most enthusiastically rediscovered by twentieth century writers, they do not correspond to contemporary modes of thinking. The novel hero, as conceived by Laclos, by Balzac and by Stendhal, stands apart from, outside of, and very far above his age— one of a tiny aristocracy of the intelligence and of the will, intent, not on discovering the actual meaning of existence, but on creating a new esthetic of existence. With the contemporary novelists the ideal of conscious existence no longer represents an aristocratic attitude toward life. It has become an intellectual and moral obligation.

"I conceive myself both as totally free and as unable to prevent the fact that the meaning of the world comes to it from myself." This is Sartre's definition of the emotion of anguish, which in his mind is the inescapable attribute of any man of good faith. It also applies to the more general emotion governing the development of the contemporary French novel: a sudden and violent rejection of all external standards of reality.

As we look back on the interwar period, we can understand the origins of this emotion. Indeed, the most important fictions of the time were not those invented by the novelists. They are to be found in the newspapers, the military circles, the French Academy, the Bank of France, the Chamber of Deputies, the salons and the cafés—a series of purely verbal defenses against the onslaughts of historical change: technological revolution, social unrest, shifting power relations and increasing international interdependence. Some of these were incarnated in popular slogans, such as the "offensive à outrance" of World War I; the "Maginot line" of World War II; the "We will win because we are the strongest" of the final days of the Third Republic; the "neither victors nor vanquished" of Vichy; and the "France alone" of de Gaulle. Others existed, more intangibly, as a sort of moral sanctification of the *status quo*.

But if daily life during this period seems often to have been based upon a series of unconscious fictions, the art of fiction was meanwhile turning into a serious criticism of the fictitious as a way of life. It is no accident that Gide, the author of *Les Faux-Monnayeurs* (*The Counterfeiters*), was one of the most influential writers of his age.

This new awareness of the purely fiduciary nature of so many accepted concepts was an important literary stimulus. It forced each
novelist to discover his personal conception of reality and hence his
personal conception of the novel form. We can see this in the new
and persistently renewed vitality of the novel from Gide to Camus.
Indeed, whenever any literary innovation threatened to turn into a
perfunctory convention, the younger novelists were quick to sense
the danger and to find a new approach. Saint-Exupéry and Malraux
turned their backs on the surrealists just as Sartre has turned away
from Proust and Giraudoux; and Camus, away from Malraux and
from Sartre. Like the second half of the nineteenth century in Russia,
the first half of the twentieth century in France is particularly open
to criticism in the realm of social and political history; but it is one
of the great adventurous periods in the history of the novel form.

At the turn of the century it would have been difficult to anticipate this moment. Poetry and drama at this time were full of exciting possibilities. But fiction, which had once accommodated the
imagination of a Balzac and a Stendhal, had settled down into the
narrow rut of the "naturalist" novel, the "realist" novel and the
"problem" novel—a process which tended to discourage any serious
reconsideration of the actual meanings of the word "nature," the
word "reality" and the word "problem." Barring a few adventurous
spirits like Gide and Proust, neither the novelist nor the novelist's
reading public seemed to feel any need to do so.

It would have been equally difficult at the turn of the century to
anticipate World War I and the train of revolutions—political, social,
technical and intellectual—that followed in its wake. The French
reading public may have been slow to recognize what these violent
changes would mean for fiction, but the truth is that after 1914 the
novel had to change, or disappear with the safe, predictable and
somewhat stuffy world on which it rested. Neither the documentary
novel of the Goncourts, nor the psychomoralistic novel of Bourget,
nor the sociopatriotic novel of Barrès had any point of reference in
the postwar world. The signposts were tottering, the frontiers were
breaking down, and the novelist, alone again in the face of the

world, had to sit down and write his novel in much the state of mind that Descartes sat down to write his *Discours de la méthode*—on a perfectly blank page. But he was not writing a philosophical treatise; he was writing a novel.

This new vitality of the novel, with its function of investigating problems that generally fall into the realm of the philosopher—man's knowledge of himself, of the world he lives in, and of the impact of the one upon the other—is no doubt related to trends in philosophy itself. Philosophy, an important branch of philosophy at any rate, had been turning more and more from a study of outward reality to a study of man's inner consciousness of this reality as the only knowable quantity, the only ultimate truth. Husserl, at the turn of the century, officially labeled this "phenomenology," a word already used in much the same way by Hegel. German phenomenology did not become an important influence in France until the time of World War II, with Sartre. But already with Bergson and then with Alain, French philosophers had become dissatisfied with the positivistic systems of Taine and Comte and were turning back to the world of individual consciousness, a complex, fluid world whose laws, if laws there be, are strictly limited to consciousness itself.

It is significant that the age of Bergson, who has often been compared to Proust, of Alain, a serious student of the novel, and of Sartre, a novelist himself, should also be an age of vitality in the French novel. This indirect approach to life is perfectly adapted to the novel form. It is even better adapted to the novel, perhaps, than to philosophy, where it implies a sort of admission of defeat. In the epilogue to his one novel, *The Last Puritan,* Santayana puts this idea into the mouth of the narrator's friend, Mario. Mario, after criticizing the unreality of the narrator's novel, admits that he prefers it to the narrator's more ambitious philosophical writings. "In this novel, on the contrary, the argument is dramatized, the views become human persuasions, the presentation is all the truer for not pretending to be true."

This recognition of the make-believe quality of fiction, as contrasted with the conscientious realism of the turn-of-the-century novel, is a salient characteristic of the French novel of the past few decades. The novelist, as "conscious" in his approach to the novel as are his heroes in their approach to life, is well aware of the difficulties as well as the possibilities of the medium. Indeed, the whole problem of writing a novel is an important novel theme with Proust and Gide. The "conscious" novel makes no pretense of offering an accurate description of reality, a reality far too chaotic to be reduced to intelligible terms. This novel is no more than a point of view on reality, perhaps only a means of pointing out the gap between literature and life, mind and existence, the human consciousness and the world in which it moves.

In one sense this is a limitation, a limitation apparent in the irony of Gide, the style of Giraudoux or the despair of Sartre. In another sense it is a liberation. The novel is now governed, not by the commonplace realities of life, but by the intellectual or esthetic requirements of the novelist, who is free to indulge in any number of experiments in form and in technique, to embark on any number of adventures of the imagination and the mind. The novel hero, previously imprisoned in the closed, mechanistic world of determinist theory, becomes a free agent, capable of shaping his own life and choosing his own destiny. And the novel itself, which had threatened to degenerate into the expression of a series of pre-existing theories about life, becomes, as Alain has put it, "the poem of the freedom of the will."

The penalty of freedom is the loss of certainty. Without human liberty there would be no values at all—merely a set of mechanical rules. But given the assumption of human liberty, how is it possible to establish an objective hierarchy of values? The problem is one of the eternal sticking points in speculative thought. Such sticking points, if they are to be delivered from the cemetery of the textbook and again become a vital human problem, have to be personally rediscovered and experienced by each new generation of writers, as they were discovered by Gide and Proust, by Giraudoux and Bernanos, by Malraux and Camus and Sartre.

For men like Gide and Martin du Gard, novelists who remain

detached from their own works, there is no single answer. They are intent merely on formulating the problem and leave the reader to find his way in a world of relative values and provisional solutions. This quality of personal detachment, this ability to stand back and look at the world as it goes by, is not, however, typical of the times. The contemporary French novelist is generally committed to his own novel, which thus takes on all the urgency and gravity of a quest for personal salvation. And although the extreme emotional intensity of the quest may sometimes tempt a novelist to deceive himself with an overly rigid and narrow definition of the world, it will often quicken his apprehensions, sharpen his sensibilities and thus prepare him for that moment of almost mystical illumination when the shell of outward appearances explodes before his eyes, revealing a hidden world of meaning.

There is an intense excitement, both for the esthetic imagination and the mind, in these moments of illumination and in the novels that are built around them—Giraudoux's revelation of unincarnate forms, Saint-Exupéry's revelation of his civilization, Sartre's terrible revelation of existence, and, most important of all, Proust's revelation of the world of art. We too, the readers, feel that we have participated in the quest and in its triumphant or, occasionally, disastrous outcome. Our whole experience of life is deepened, widened, intensified.

Yet, even when these novels are concerned with problems that touch us closely in our daily lives, they cannot and should not be interpreted as practical guides to living. If Gide, in the early thirties, and Sartre, more recently, have been branded as "corrupters of youth" and "moral nihilists," this is due in large part to the misinterpretations of a naïve reading public, unwilling to recognize that one of the principal advantages of fiction lies in its ability to indulge in some of the perilous experiments and uncompromising attitudes that are so impractical in life.

At certain times, however, it is the novelist himself who is tempted to overstep the bounds of his novel form, to stretch a personal intuition into a dogmatic statement, to fit his personal needs and aspirations into the framework of a rigid cult. We can see this in the literary evolution of Romains, of Aragon and, more clearly still, of Sartre. In a world where practical problems of behavior have become so urgent it is a fairly natural evolution. If Proust and Gide observed the rules of their own game better than certain of their successors, they were also better insulated from the practical necessities of contemporary life.

There may be times when these problems become so pressing as to break through the limits of the novel form. Jules Romains, in his role of political prophet, continued as a prolific novelist. But Sartre, the political prophet, seems to be abandoning the novel for the political essay and the morality play; this, despite his eloquent assertion that contemporary fiction has an important social function. We can see the same movement away from fictional forms in Saint-Exupéry's later writings, in Malraux and in Camus.

The novel, meanwhile, has entered a period of transition. To the generation that grew up during the physical and moral cataclysm of World War II, the problem of conscious existence is overshadowed by the more intimate and pressing problem of existence itself. The heroic and defiant attitudes of the thirties and the forties are no longer possible today, and, as in the period following the first world war, the novelist is again faced with the problem of creating a new image of man.

THE MASTERS

When André Gide and Marcel Proust started to write in the last decade of the nineteenth century, the French novel, as written by their contemporaries, was an object of open disdain in the symbolist and decadent groups that both these young men frequented. The theory of the French novel, as it had developed out of the reaction against the romantic movement, was a direct product of the prevailing assumption that men lived in a closed, intelligible world. Nature, history and society were the only true artists, or more exactly, technicians, and an inhabitant of this universe could do little more than imitate their efforts. Novelists in general—the ones currently read until the 1910's—were still working on the assumption that art is an imitation of reality. These imitations took various forms: documentary, exotic, psychological. The expression "realist" was generally reserved for imitations of the lives of ordinary people, preferably the poor, but the idea, if not the word, is the principal key to the prevailing theory of the novel at the time.

To be sure, the major novelists of the nineteenth century were not realists as this word was understood by the writers of the nineties. Balzac's apparent aim of making a complete inventory of the social structure of early nineteenth century France is simply a pretext for the creation of the extraordinary hyperbolic universe inhabited by monsters like Grandet or Vautrin. Even those writers most fettered to theory made surprising escapes. Zola, the best-known of the "naturalists," merely paid lip service to the greatly simplified "scientific" theories he chose to adopt, while adventuring in the powerful and elemental universe supplied by his own imagination.

But the new generation of writers rose up in conscious revolt against the whole theory of literary "realism," proclaiming that the apparently objective universe of the realists was really an imaginary universe made up of dull, abstract conventions. Symbolists or decadents, they withdrew into the more fertile domain of subjective consciousness.

From a practical point of view, this attitude raises as many difficulties as it resolves. The revolt against nineteenth century forms of rationalism had the important advantage of breaking through the barriers of material and logical necessity. Man was no longer a helpless part of the universe but, in a sense, the creator of his own universe and destiny. "To be or not to be, oneself and all things, one has to choose." Alain, one of the masters of the generations growing up between 1910 and 1940, never tires of quoting this cryptic observation of his own revered Professor Lagneau. This advantage, a great advantage for the novelist, was purchased at a heavy price—objective standards of judgment. Although human consciousness had ceased to be a prisoner of the closed universe of determinist theory, it was now an exile in the alien and largely unintelligible realms of outer reality.

It is perhaps the failure to recognize this problem that explains the weakness of both the speculative and political thinking of the period: Bergson's attempts to use what seems to be a purely subjective intuition of reality as an objective standard; Sorel's attempts to exploit the romantic myth of "syndical violence" as a practical political program; Péguy's unrealistic rejection of the practical "politics" of republican government in favor of a *mystique,* a pure ideal. The real contribution of the *fin de siècle* revolt against nineteenth century rationalism lies neither in the field of abstract speculation, nor in the rather disastrous social and political attitudes it fostered, but in the field of creative writing. Indeed, the despairing and heroic attitudes conveyed in the philosophical and political literature of the time reflect the difficulties and aspirations of the artist rather than of ordinary men and women. In the nineteenth century the artist had often served as handmaiden to the philosopher. He was now to have his revenge.

Unlike the philosopher or the political thinker, the artist can safely push the contradiction between man and the universe to the confines of nihilism, because he has a good escape: He can reconstruct the universe in terms of his unsatisfied esthetic demands. Making the subjective objective, the impossible task that has so long evaded the philosopher, can be at least approximated by the artist. This is the positive discovery that men like Mallarmé, Valéry, Proust and Gide were to wrest from the doubts and negations of their time.

The conception of art as a reconstruction rather than an imitation of reality has almost always applied to the plastic arts, to poetry and to the theater. What is new in France during the first years of the twentieth century is first the *conscious* formulation of this principle as an esthetic theory and second its extension to the novel.

This development is, in some respects, related to the thought of Bergson. Bergson had attempted to pierce through the thick arbitrary crust of everyday discourse to the real nature of things. But he had been satisfied with a vague apprehension of this reality, a mystical identification of subject and object that evades the real problem of esthetic creation. This glorification of the unstable, incoherent forms of the imagination, more apparent, perhaps, in the Bergsonians than in Bergson himself, is indeed fundamentally antiesthetic, as the symbolists had already discovered. It created literary attitudes and literary styles but not great works of art. What produced the great artistic activity of the 1910's was the conscious rediscovery that art is neither an imitation of the intellectual concepts which we project outside ourselves nor a direct expression of the chaotic reveries which we apprehend within ourselves; rather, it is a creative effort arising out of the interplay of the two. The question, however, inevitably arises: Can the novel be a work of art?

Behind the debate there lurks the imposing negative of Valéry, the poet who had carried the ideal of conscious creation to its extreme limit. The novel, according to Valéry, is not an esthetic medium, for it is a bastard medium. A poem, which is wholly contained in the structure of language, affects us directly as a single entity; but the novelist, in order to establish a bond between the fictitious existence of his personages and the real existence of his reader, has to incorporate recognizable elements of reality into his novel. "While the poetic universe is essentially closed and complete in itself, being the pure system of the aspirations and accidents of language, the universe of the novel, even of the fantastic novel, is tied to the real world." And thus tied to life, the novel inevitably partakes of the arbitrary, nonesthetic quality of life itself.

So strong is Valéry's antipathy to the novel form that he cannot admire a novelist without at the same time lamenting that so great a talent should have gone astray. What a loss to the world of letters is Proust! Why did not Stendhal write for the theater! These lamentations betray a certain misunderstanding of both Proust and Stendhal—who are essentially novelists. Yet, however mistaken Valéry may be in his conclusions, there is an important element of truth in his diagnosis of the novel form. Reality, in a novel, is not simply a subject but, like the paint in a picture, the words in a poem or the actors a play, the raw material out of which the novel is made. This material has no special requirements or conditions of its own. The special limitations of painting, poetry and drama are not merely an aid to esthetic unity; they force the artist to transpose his subject into the powerful metaphors of color, shape, sound and movement. Whatever esthetic unity and whatever transpositions of reality can be put into the printed pages of the novel must be put there by the novelist himself.

Valéry's criticism of the novel undoubtedly had the salutary effect of obliging certain of his contemporaries, his friend Gide in particular, to reconsider the whole problem of the novel form. This intense preoccupation with the problem of the novel as a work of art can of course have a rather paralyzing effect, particularly in a country like France where esthetic theory tends to reflect the classical ideals of purity, brevity and clarity that limit the novel form. The great, the unforgettable novel, that acts strongly on the imagination, is seldom devoid of formal imperfections, as Proust observed. It would appear that the latent power of the great novel derives in large part from the fundamental characteristic that Valéry denounced as a flaw: the complex interplay in time of a subjective consciousness and its external environment.

This reintegration of the two different realms of reality was the main problem confronting the generation of Proust and Gide. Small wonder that they turned to the novel, but to a novel that they were obliged to rediscover, to re-create and to justify esthetically. Both men had to wrest their worlds from the double danger denounced by Valéry: the insignificance that threatened Gide and the formlessness that almost engulfed Proust's great work. Both felt impelled to justify their choice of the novel form and incorporated into their work a theory of the novel. Both used the form as a means of discovering and stating the real nature of man's relation to society, to the universe, to himself.

André Gide: In Search of the Novel

No writer seems less attuned to the temper of the mid-century than André Gide, and since his death in 1952, many attempts have been made to bury this former "master of three generations." But his work has held its ground even in the realm of the novel, where the attack has been most vigorous.

Gide's tales appear simple, deceptively simple. They are suffused with light. Harmony of structure, restraint—even parsimony—of language, clarity of line, clarity of form, a story impeccably told concerning a few characters abstracted from any definite time or social reality—such are the marks of Gide's talent. Gide is first and foremost a master of French prose. This in itself sets his novels apart from those of many of his contemporaries. The quality of his writing often eludes and even irritates certain critics who tend to seek for values in the substance of the novel rather than in the more elusive qualities of form.

In a sense the simplicity and clarity of Gide's tales are traps deliberately set to catch the unwary. Gide belongs to a generation of writers, painters and composers who boldly experimented with traditional art forms. He has sometimes been called a "cubist." The term, as applied to literature, is vague; but here it refers to Gide's tendency to organize his material according to an esthetic idea of his own. Through all Gide's work runs a certain detached humor concerning the nature of that work itself. He carefully stresses his own freedom as an artist: Given certain materials, what shall I make of them? he seems to ask. What Gide "makes" of them is literature. No fiction writer ever saw more clearly that a novelist constructs an imaginary world which he presents as if it were a real world but which is in fact only a means of approach to the real world. Gide constantly reminds his reader, though indirectly, that such is the case. He will not let us sit back comfortably and enjoy his novel as an absolute. "I am telling you a story," he warns subtly; "what do you make of it?" The story is told for the benefit of the reader as well as for its own sake. But it raises many questions.

A disciple of the poet Mallarmé, Gide never questioned the axiom that a work of art is the expression of some great fundamental human experience. To what extent, however, is the novel a form of art? Mallarmé and his disciples had little consideration for a genre which so grimly "imitated" the disorderly chaos of life; in their eyes, the artist was the organizer of a serene universe of chosen images that transferred transitory human impressions into the realm of the eternal.

Gide, however, wanted to be a novelist. His first work was a novel, a neoromantic novel, *Les Cahiers d'André Walter* (The Notebooks of André Walter), published in 1891, though written before he was twenty. "Mallarmé for poetry," he wrote Valéry at that time with disarming candor, "Maeterlinck for drama—myself for the novel." Gide at twenty-one obviously had set himself quite a task, that of reshaping the current forms of the French novel. He wanted his own approach to the novel to be as revolutionary as Mallarmé's approach to poetry and Maeterlinck's to drama. It took him many years to find his approach; his fictional works are experiments with the novel, experiments that finally culminated in *Les Faux-Monnayeurs* (*The*

Counterfeiters). By that time Proust, Joyce, Kafka, Thomas Mann and Virginia Woolf, along with other, lesser novelists, had completely transformed the genre; in Paris, the surrealist revolution had already shaken existing literary concepts. Gide's slow development of the novel form, carried through a quarter of a century, between the publication of *L'Immoraliste* (*The Immoralist*) in 1902 and that of *Les Faux-Monnayeurs* in 1926, seemed very cautious in comparison with these new ventures.

What Gide first found was a new approach to the novel reader. Gide likes to introduce a novelist into his story, and when this novelist is absent, one of the main characters steps into his role. Michel, the hero of *L'Immoraliste,* tells the story of his three-year experiment upon himself; Jérôme, in *La Porte étroite* (*Strait Is the Gate*), recalls his long-drawn-out love affair with his cousin Alissa; the clergyman in *La Symphonie pastorale* (*The Pastoral Symphony*) relates the story of his relationship with the blind girl, Gertrude, whom he has adopted. They are all temporarily novelists engaged in building a coherent story out of circumstances which they experienced as a series of successive incidents. Gide, playing with the technique developed by Browning in his dramatic monologues, is pointing out that an ordering of events makes sense only in relationship to the narrator of these events. Jérôme's story is not necessarily Alissa's, and in the later trilogy, *L'Ecole des femmes* (*The School for Wives*), *Robert* and the unfinished *Geneviève,* Gide develops three distinct points of view on the same situation.

This fictional quality of any story told is very clearly described in one of Gide's shorter tales, *Isabelle,* 1911. A young historian who is writing a life of Bossuet goes to an isolated château to study unpublished documents on the topic. There he meets a strange cast of characters—the owners—and senses that they are entangled in a drama centering on a young woman, Isabelle. He sees a portrait, observes certain scenes, finds a letter and, just as he might do with Bossuet, "relates" them all and imagines a plausible chain of events leading to the present dramatic situation. Later he meets the real Isabelle, and his coherent little tale collapses. She has nothing in common with his Isabelle. What had knit his tale together was his own personality, his own youthfully sentimental approach to reality. Out of fact and observation, interpreted according to his individual sensibility, he had woven a fiction. All Gide's tales are similar to this, and all his characters are fabricators of fiction—counterfeiters—but only insofar as they are dealing with two distinct elements which they endeavor to weave into one fabric: their inner motivations and emotions and an outward context of events, each element acting and reacting on the other. This accounts for the errors they inevitably make and the inevitable disappointments they incur when Gide eventually brings them face to face with a reality as puzzling and as uncompromising as Isabelle herself.

What is Gide himself if not a more complex, more penetrating storyteller of this type? Gide will not accept the role assumed by many novelists in their own universe: that of God the Father. By the very way he writes his novels he constantly suggests that each is the story of only one of many possible "relations" with life. It evolves out of a certain number of experiences, facts and reflections. It is a possible tale, and a convincing one too, but only one out of many, one that arises out of some aspect of Gide's own personality. The reader in the end finds himself face to face with Gide, but always indirectly, since the tale is objectively told and the teller inscrutable.

Like his own characters, Gide, when he writes, has a certain point of view; it is inherent in his relationship to the world in which he moves. This relationship is intellectual as well as emotional—and that is one of the most original aspects of the Gidian novel. Starting from a certain emotional confrontation with the limited circumstances of his individual life, he evolves an idea and thence an ethics, a "way of life." This, again, is like his characters. But whereas Michel and Alissa are irrevocably set in one direction and definitely committed to one set of values, Gide makes no such final decision for himself. He commits his characters for life, and their life is the novel; he commits himself only for the duration of the novel. The naïve reader can take the fictional tale at face value. It is the story of the fictional characters, not Gide's. Gide has only pulled the strings to make it end a certain way—generally disastrously—and no other. Gide's own story, the total novel, goes beyond theirs. Its significance lies precisely in the ironic interplay between what the characters thought would happen to them and what in fact did happen to them as revealed by the characters themselves.

Gide builds this subtle interplay into his novel very consciously. It may seem tiresomely complex to the casual reader but is actually an essential element of the Gidian novel, a source of much intellectual pleasure for a detached but active reader. What, in fact, took place? Where do the responsibilities lie? Are the characters at fault? or is it the "way of life" they chose? What, exactly, is Gide's own position? On the higher level of psychology and ethics, Gide's appeal to the reader is much the same as that of a detective story writer, but his tales carry no definitive solution tucked away in the last pages. They merely raise questions.

To a great extent the questions raised through the complexities of structure compensate for the obvious narrowness of the world Gide explores. Gide seems to have had no great imagination for either plot or character; nor, in terms of his own conception of the novel, had he much need for either. From the very outset of his career, he approached the novel self-consciously. He was never able to use the medium with the careless ease of a Balzac or with the painstaking but unquestionable esthetic assurance of a Flaubert, for whom "style" was the great alchemy transmuting the banal into art. Gide's dedication to literature was real. It was in a sense the very fabric of the man. He never thought of literature, though, in the Proustian manner, as a means of salvation; he seems rather to have considered it as a profession requiring very high standards of professional integrity. He thought of literature, in another sense, as a game, a game played with words; but he was far from thinking of it as nothing but a game. Like many of his contemporaries—Proust among others—he felt that the material selected for a work of art must be of unique significance to the artist himself. And there Gide's

difficulties as a novelist began. His own peculiar personality isolated
him from much that might normally go into the making of a novel.

In spite of many sincere attempts, Gide was never able to grasp
political or economic problems or take them seriously. This was a
real lack, no doubt, in a world where collective historic events of
great scope were to affect so many millions of lives. He himself remained free from economic pressures. His austerely Protestant education stressed spiritual and moral values excessively, and he carried
these preoccupations into the domain of literature. He was an om-
nivorous reader, familiar with all the great works of literature, whatever their origin in time and space. Their timelessness, however,
was what he admired, forgetful, as were the symbolists of his youth,
that this timelessness had its source in a vigorous relation with a very
definite historical time. In a sense Gide was almost as imprisoned in
the world of books as was Proust in his cork-lined room.

Unlike Proust, Gide conscientiously acted out the role of an active
member of society, assuming, at least to all appearances, the responsibilities of a normal life. He married; for a short time he was the
youngest mayor in France; he traveled widely in Western Europe,
North and Central Africa, Russia, Greece and the Near East. He
took sides in political and social controversies. He was, rather hesi-
tatingly, for Dreyfus in the Dreyfus Case; in his *Souvenirs de la
Cour d'Assises* (Recollections of the Assizes), 1914, he described
the inadequacies of criminal law. *Voyage au Congo* (Travels in the
Congo), 1927, and *Le Retour du Tchad* (Return from the Chad),
1928, exposed the abuses of the powerful commercial companies that
brutally exploited native populations in North Africa. For a short
time in the early thirties, Gide, prodded by his younger friends,
seemed genuinely interested in the Communist "adventure." *Retour
de l'U.R.S.S.* (Return from the USSR), 1936, and *Retouches à mon
Retour de l'U.R.S.S.* (Afterthoughts on My Return from the USSR),
1937, describe both his naïve enthusiasm and his subsequent disenchantment, with an almost childlike incomprehension of what it
was all about.

But none of these questions ever so much as raises a ripple on the surface of Gide's novels. His *Journal* clearly tells us why. He here analyzes his incapacity to feel life as real and stresses the inner fissure between his consciousness of life and his awareness of himself as part of it. His outer commitments were apparent, not real. In his novels he could not honestly use materials which seemed inconsequential to him. Because of this peculiarly marked detachment from life and because of his high idea of literature, the problem of sincerity and artifice in writing was always foremost in his mind.

There was one kind of experience which broke through the closed circle of his life and motivated him strongly enough to send him into somewhat hazardous adventures. This was his homosexuality, experienced in one of his first journeys to Africa. Married to his cousin, Madeleine Rondeaux, "the one great love" in his life, he found himself nonetheless living a strange, restless existence over which he seems to have had little control. The ambiguity of his position, reaching deep into his personality, gave him a penetrating insight into the complexities of the human psyche. The disconcerting elements in his own life were of great importance to Gide the novelist. He was only too well aware of the wayward ego hidden beneath the surface of the most apparently conventional being. Before he had ever read Freud, he set out to explore the one significant domain, for him at least: the game of hide and seek played within the individual, and often at his expense, by the limiting circumstances of life, the limitations of one's ideas about life and one's "way of life," and the many unknown inner forces that derive their power from their very obscurity. This is Gide's constant preoccupation, and it stemmed from his own encounter with himself.

One need only to turn to the *Journal* and to Gide's autobiography, *Si le Grain ne meurt* (If It Die . . .), 1926, to see how enigmatic, how inexplicable, Gide's own life appeared to him. It was the one great problem with which he had to contend, and only in his novels did he feel entirely free to give full scope to his disturbing self-knowledge. "It seemed as if my own thinking frightened me, hence the need I felt to lend it to the heroes of my books, so that I could more easily stand away from it." Gide's heroes are given the task of bridging the gap between Gide's thought and his life. They are, in a certain sense, subversive; not content with accepting the somnolent "normal" order of existence, they experiment with other "ways of life." For Gide, always an optimist as regards the many possibilities of the human being and the many positive values of life, there are innumerable possible ways of living and therefore innumerable potential novels which can be written with much the same material as their starting point.

Basically creative though they be, these ways of living are fraught with danger. At first they reveal hidden forces in the individual, create new types of human beings; then their efficacy dwindles as they impose their limitations upon life; finally they become empty mental forms, essentially destructive, that leave no room for the development of other forces latent within the human being and necessary to his welfare. It is clear that as far as Gide is concerned the significant adventure in any human existence is this recurrent and never decisive interchange between the individual's actual development as he moves through life and his understanding of what he is about. Character is precisely what develops in a human being in the course of such an experiment with living. The creation of a personality is the outcome of what takes place in the course of a story; it is not given at its inception. If Gide seldom goes outside his own small circle or even outside himself when he picks a set of characters for a novel, it is because he constantly reworks his material in depth, not scope.

It is hardly astonishing, given their origin, that all his characters have a strong family likeness. They belong to the intellectual French bourgeoisie and are almost all Protestant. They enjoy the same leisure as their creator or pursue only liberal professions, as men of letters, lawyers and judges, clergymen and professors. They live in Paris and Normandy and travel in Italy, Switzerland and North Africa. From book to book they reappear—the same yet different—stealing traits from each other. Young Jérôme is not very different from young Michel, nor are the women ever very different from each other at the outset of the tale. Almost all Gide's characters are frustrated in marriage. They pry into each other's secret correspondence, and, without the slightest animosity—indeed with alarming gentleness and good will—they precipitate each other into dramas that end in murder or suicide. Their interests are narrow; their lives are singularly aimless; they are amazingly free from financial needs and professional obligations. In contrast, their relations with themselves and with others and the inner momentum that impels their lives are ever-varied, dynamic and challenging to the reader, whose life, regardless of its circumstances, necessarily has the same enigmatic quality.

Gide's understanding of the relation of character, destiny and environment to the mental forms that we build around these forces has a strong analogy in his understanding of art. The writer, if he is to go beyond the trivial, must first, like the individual, break through the barriers of convention. He too must be stronger than his environment. Just as some adventurous individuals mold their lives in terms of an intellectual concept, the writer molds the raw materials of reality according to an esthetic concept. He attempts thereby to control that part of reality which he perceives at a given time. Each novel is an esthetic experiment, an attempt to bring to light one hidden aspect of human life. The novel thereby loses its triviality. Its very pattern reproduces an essential mode of human experience. Whereas in life no ethical experiment is definitive, in art it can be carried through to its outcome—a probable, not necessary, outcome—held in check by the stern discipline of form.

Gide published his first important novel, *L'Immoraliste,* in 1902. The French novel, at that time, was treading well-worn paths. The naturalist approach to the novel was being decried, though naturalist novels continued to appear. The psychological novel and the *roman à thèse* were also flourishing. Romantic exoticism à la Loti was fashionable. Barrès and Anatole France were using the novel as a form of philosophical disquisition. The symbolists, who despised the novel, had turned to the short story or conte, a genre which Gide himself had used. *L'Immoraliste* passed without notice when it was first published. Yet it was a new departure in the novel, written by a man who had reached maturity.

Behind Gide lay ten years of varied and abundant production. Except for a slim volume of verse, a few critical essays and three plays, all that Gide wrote in those ten years was a preparation for this novel. After his neoromantic novel, *Les Cahiers d'André Walter*, an idealized and highly dramatized account of his love for his cousin Emmanuèle, Gide never again approached the genre with such candid directness. The "treatises" that followed are tales told in the symbolist manner. The adventures they describe are vague and mysterious. They are supposed to convey a hidden spiritual significance, or so young Gide suggests; they "translate" the inner life of the soul and disdain the material world of outer reality. As such, they do not bring much to the novel. The really significant works of this period came with *Paludes* (*Marshlands*), 1895, and *Le Prométhée mal enchaîné* (*Prometheus Misbound*), 1899, two burlesque little tales which Gide later called *soties,* borrowing a medieval term designating satirical plays directed against church dignitaries, judges, nobility—and other powers that be.

In both these tales Gide is obviously experimenting with a form and hugely enjoying it. He has almost done away with narrative and in its stead uses conversations, diaries and speeches. The *soties* give the impression that they are being spoken, not written. The events take place in the present, right under our eyes. The juxtaposition of different and quite incongruous forms of speech, from the matter-of-fact to the solemn-emotional, gives the *sotie* its semiburlesque, semiserious atmosphere. Gide uses the same procedures that Laforgue was using in poetry, those that Eliot used later in some of his early poems.

Paludes is told in the first person. The narrator discusses an anguished week during which he unsuccessfully tries to write a story entitled "Paludes." Trivial occupations, banal meetings and inane conversations keep moving in a circle around him as he struggles to write his story about Virgil's Tityrus, a man who possesses nothing but a marshy plot of land, but is content because it is his own.

The author, on the other hand, is not at all content with his own marshland; he is weakly dismayed by the stagnation he sees all around him. As Tuesday follows Monday and Wednesday follows Tuesday and the same people appear and reappear saying the same words, doing the same things, he stages a mild revolt. Tityrus becomes a symbol of stagnation, but his creator turns into a prophet of adventure—travel, everyone must travel; and he himself leaves for a miserable weekend with his friend Angèle. As the book ends, the hero is again seated at his desk, writing.

Gide's story is an amusing satire on the monotony of salon life in Paris, but it is much more than that. *Paludes* is a small masterpiece of humor, and the seemingly nonchalant and episodic patterns of composition are one of the elements of that humor. Its light and airy structure reproduces the outer patterns of unrelieved futility by the simple procedure of repetition. Everything goes in a circle— the ventilator, the horses in the ring, people, their words and gestures. The inner revolt of the author wells up within that structure, suggesting the image of the marshland and its hero Tityrus, according to symbolist methods. It follows, too, its own trivial and helpless patterns. Gide creates his effect through the interplay of two motifs: the objective patterns of reflection, the subjective patterns of emotional anguish. His hero-author is both comical and touching as he talks himself into an impossible adventure, impossible given the limitations of his personality. The idea that a human being necessarily draws around him a world that to a great degree reveals his personality is not a new idea among novelists. What is new and amusing is to build just such a correspondence into the structure of a story.

Le Prométhée mal enchaîné is more complex both in theme and structure; it is in fact too cleverly put together to be more than a *divertissement*. But it is a gay little tale which gives a good deal of insight into Gide's point of view on human beings, their vagaries and what we call their "fate." It sets the fundamental pattern of all Gide's future novels.

The principal episode of the story takes place on the Paris boulevard that goes from the Opéra to the Madeleine, a familiar spot. But the characters we meet there are really unexpected: Zeus, Prometheus and his eagle; two ancient Romans, Damocles and Cocles; Virgil's Tityrus and Angèle, who both previously appeared in *Paludes*. A café waiter serves as a link between them all. The dialogue, often as fantastic as the cast, is brilliant and witty, though on first reading there may seem to be no sense in the succession of episodes, no relation between them. Yet there is an over-all design, and a purpose in the design itself.

Gide is projecting before us a fable that describes the "human condition." Two powers, Zeus and Prometheus, preside over the fate of the two human beings, Damocles and Cocles. Zeus distributes blows and bank notes at random, for no reason at all, and enjoys watching the strange effects of his irresponsible acts. Prometheus is deeply interested in men; he perpetually suggests to them what Zeus denies them—incentives for action, ideas, "eagles," like his own, that carry men into the skies upon their backs or, by turn, prey upon them. Clearly, Prometheus is the source of the human personality and also the creator of human difficulties. The problem of Cocles and Damocles is to find some kind of modus vivendi between those two forces. One abandons them to trivial trickery, leaving them to wander helplessly and undirected; the other suggests a destination, not just one, but several possible destinations, each one as likely as the other, each one as deadly in the end if accepted exclusively.

Gide's domain as a novelist is here clearly marked out. He sees man as a being thrown into a world without any divine guidance or revelation, but with innumerable possibilities for "becoming." The individual's adventure starts when he discovers within him the needs and potentialities that are stifled by the conventional order in which he moves. He then assumes the responsibility of ordering his own life; the outcome gives the measure of his strength. All Gide's novels present a search for integrity; while the characters are caught in the meshes of their own limitations, self-delusions and blindness, the Prometheus in them drives them toward an absolute which,

Gide suggests, is what a human being will always conceive and must always eventually relinquish.

What Gide describes in his novels is the incongruity of any human being's position. Thrown into a web of random relationships by the purposeless actions of Zeus, he tries obstinately to impose upon events, in which he is only a minor figure, an absolute meaning built out of his own very limited apprehension of what is going on. Only in the human mind could there be a universe ordered as the Christian universe or as the rationally structured deterministic universe of the naturalists is ordered. Hence there is a constant discrepancy between what exists and what human beings think exists. Gide's peculiar humor arises out of a full enjoyment of that discrepancy. His difficulty as a novelist is to give the reader the inner climate of a life seriously lived and felt in all its baffling pathos and at the same time to give its "measure," the sense of its limitations and of its incongruity in terms of the ferocious playfulness of Zeus.

Gide's two *soties* are simple experiments in setting up these two dimensions. When he turns to the full-fledged novel, he gives only one dimension explicitly, the inner dimension of the hazardous Promethean adventure; the flat reality contained in an objective view of the adventure is implicit in its outcome. Gide called this form of the novel a *récit*—or "tale." In one case alone, *Les Faux-Monnayeurs*, did Gide attempt to recombine the two points of view in the novel. This came much later, after a further and more ample experiment with the *sotie* in *Les Caves du Vatican* (*Lafcadio's Adventures*). *L'Immoraliste* is the first of the Gidian "tales" and, in spite of some shortcomings, perhaps the most successful. *La Porte étroite, La Symphonie pastorale,* the less successful trilogy, *L'Ecole des femmes, Robert* and *Geneviève,* and the somewhat precious but delightful *Thésée* (*Theseus*) are all variations on the same form.

L'Immoraliste is a word-by-word account of a long confession. Michel, the hero, has, like Job, called his three friends to the African oasis where he now lives to tell them his tale. The confession, rather oddly, is taken down by one of the friends and sent as a letter to a brother with the query: Is Michel doomed? can he be saved? The question gives a dramatic intensity to Michel's tale.

Michel tells his story with cold objectivity and contained emotion. He does not explain it or comment upon it. He gives an account of the facts—subjective and objective—that led to the death of his wife Marceline, a death for which he feels responsible. When Gide created Michel, he borrowed from his own life; but he carefully selected what he borrowed, and he and his hero soon part company, largely because his hero has become a victim of Prometheus. Michel had an idea, made of it an absolute, and molded his life according to that idea; hence his present disaster.

The Michel to whom we are introduced is a young professor who married a charming young woman, Marceline, because his father so desired. He takes her to Africa for their honeymoon and there falls ill with tuberculosis. In spite of his wife's devotion, he almost dies. One day, as he watches young Arab boys at play, Michel feels, for the first time in his life, the beauty of pure physical existence. His nonchalance gives way before a "will to live" so intense that it becomes a moral force. Michel transforms this urge into an ethics, an "eagle." Everything that favors his physical well-being he calls "good"; anything that opposes it he calls "bad." At this point the "Immoralist" is born in Michel and very rapidly supersedes the weak and innocuous young professor. He moves out of the debilitating atmosphere of his former life, pushed by a growing and soon ferocious egoism.

From then on *L'Immoraliste* is the story of a man who leads a double inner life. He harbors within himself a sensuous, unscrupulous, cynical person who will not allow any obstacle to stand in the path of his desires. At first the "Immoralist" in Michel is a source of strength: Michel becomes strong physically, responsible and active. Very soon, however, his new personality becomes brutally destructive: Michel's professorship, Michel's estate, Michel's wife and child, are all sacrificed. Michel is not an "Immoralist" merely because of the unconscious homosexuality Gide suggests in him. Homosexuality is only one of the inner urges that Michel's simplified ethics releases; there are others more powerful and more dangerous. Whatever was stifled in Michel before, reasonable or unreasonable, is now liberated. Having relinquished the artificial constraints of convention, Michel eventually finds himself prey to sinister and trivial impulses. At what point did he lose control of his own creation?

The theme of *L'Immoraliste* is interesting in itself. Even more interesting is the fact that Michel's story reveals Michel's weakness without his being aware of it. The character in a sense is blind; blind at every point, blind to the direction he is taking, blind to the disaster he is preparing. There is something a little diabolical in the way Gide controls Michel's progress toward disaster and in the irony of the fate he metes out to him, though never seeming to intervene at all. The underlying theme of the novel is simple: Michel chose a path toward self-fulfillment and guided his life according to an idea. The idea, beneficial for a while, soon proved dangerous, taking Michel where he did not want to go. The eagle became stronger than the man. The reader can draw his own conclusion, and Gide, having tried out the idea, can now move on to another.

In *La Porte étroite* he varies his technique somewhat. The tale is told from two points of view: first by Jérôme, several years after the death of Alissa, the cousin whom he loved; then, in part, through Alissa's own diary. Michel had attempted to attain integrity through an egoism which eventually destroyed a whole aspect of his life and his personality. Alissa tries another road to fulfillment—the Christian road of fulfillment through self-relinquishment. Her experiment also ends in disaster, in the same betrayal of the values of life. Here too the tale is ironic, for in spite of the desperate grandeur of the baffled heroine, she is drastically punished for her whole-hearted allegiance to the high values of self-sacrifice. In *La Symphonie pastorale* the unfortunate clergyman tries the path of disinterested charity; eventually he kills the girl he set out to save. Only in *Thésée* does the hero come triumphantly through the test of living, for he does not live by an idea but according to a certain instinct of what each situation requires of him, Theseus, at a given moment. He has not set his course once and for all but charts his life as one might chart a voyage with no predetermined end, according to the events that occur. Theseus is the Gidian hero par excellence who accepts his own relativity and matches Zeus's game of chance.

Gide follows a similar basic pattern of construction in every one of his tales. In the first part of the story some inner or outer impetus carries the character beyond the trivial and establishes new relations between him and the very ordinary situation in which he finds himself. At the very center of the novel the force that motivates the character loses its creative power; the novel pauses, as it were, and the values are questioned, examined. The third part of the story, except in the case of *Theseus,* contains the defeat of both character and idea. Though the outcomes are usually tragic for the characters involved, the Gidian tales are not tragic in themselves. They are, as Gide points out, ironic. They come very close to being parables; in fact one feels behind most of them the figure of the Prodigal Son so dear to Gide—a Prodigal Son who sometimes returns, taught by experience, and sometimes persists in his erroneous course.

This *récit* form is stimulating to a certain type of intellectual imagination that goes beyond the outer, commonplace routines of everyday living and considers the mysteries of personalities; but it is nonetheless a limited form. Its carefully controlled development tends toward monotony, and however skillfully Gide dissimulates his presence, we cannot but detect him behind the scenes, stacking the cards against his hapless characters, aiding them all too enthusiastically in their many self-delusions. Gide's later tales lose the dramatic intensity of *L'Immoraliste* and *La Porte étroite.* The problems they raise are less deep. Gide, who was conscious of these weaknesses, became crucially aware of the limitations of his medium in the years 1909 and 1910. With *Les Caves du Vatican,* 1913, and *Les Faux-Monnayeurs,* 1926, all Gide's previous works came into focus.

Les Caves du Vatican, which goes back to the *sotie* form, is a highly amusing invention. Once again it appeals for its effect to a play of the intelligence. The stage is set in 1893. The rumor is abroad that the Pope has been secretly imprisoned in the cellars of the Vatican by a joint conspiracy of the Monarchists and the Freemasons. A false Pope is officiating in his place. The theme is obviously full of implications that delight Gide, for what better symbol of absolute truth can there be than the Pope, the representative of God upon earth? The very notion of a "false Pope" raises a dizzy set of questions and creates every kind of ambiguity. Gide never raises the question of the Pope's authenticity. He is merely interested in what happens when that authenticity is doubted.

The rumor is promptly exploited by a gang of crooks, led by one Protos, who are raising funds purportedly for the Pope's deliverance. The *sotie* at this level is a kind of detective story; the characters are divided into two camps. On one side are the crooks, the "Centipedes" led by Protos. On the other side are the people, all members of the same family, who have some conviction with regard to the Pope. Of the three most important, one is Anthime Armand-Dubois, a Freemason and atheist scientist; the second is a Catholic novelist, Count Julius de Baraglioul, author of the most conventional of psychological novels; the third is the simple and naïve provincial, Amédée Fleurissoire, into whose mind no question as to the order of the universe has ever penetrated. What happens to each of these characters when he is touched by a temporary doubt concerning his own inner Pope is one of the most hilarious sides of the novel. Each will move along his own line of interest and develop his own type of adventure. From the outside, however, comes a new element: Lafcadio, an illegitimate half brother of Baraglioul, handsome, healthy, poor, free of all ties, all obligations. He saves a life for no particular reason, by chance. Why not take a life for no particular reason, by chance? By chance, he runs into Fleurissoire and deliberately, for no reason, throws him out of a train window. His irrelevant act suddenly rebounds from character to character, and the question of the true and false Pope reappears in full force. If there are no absolutes, no conventions, that limit our freedom of action, what then can direct our actions? The problem here is the age-old problem of freedom and determination.

Unmotivated though Lafcadio's action may be, it is not inconsequential, for it delivers him into the hands of Protos and touches every character in the tale. The other indirect victim of Protos is Fleurissoire, who, unable to distinguish between the lies of Protos and the real facts in the case, had started off on a crusade to deliver the Pope. At the time Lafcadio threw him out of the train Fleurissoire, in all innocence, was earnestly working for Protos and his gang of swindlers. Lafcadio with his notion of irresponsible action, Fleurissoire with his moral simplicity, are both swindled in their dealings with Protos. What is Protos if not the perpetually ambiguous aspect which reality assumes as soon as a human being comes to grips with it, confronts it, acts in accord with some idea he has as to its nature. Lafcadio is obviously an immoralist like Michel, and Fleurissoire is the grotesque brother of Alissa, the heroine of *La Porte étroite*. The other characters in the *sotie* are only masks. It matters little to them whether the Pope be true or false; their ideas remain theoretical. Unlike Lafcadio and Fleurissoire, they never put them to the test of action. Baraglioul the novelist, tempted for one moment by the thought of creating a new type of hero, abandons the idea as soon as it threatens to reveal too disturbing a reality. He can imagine a fictional hero who, like Lafcadio, would step out of the neat patterns of psychological analysis and perform a gratuitous act; but he will not accept the living counterpart of such a character. Neither the Pope nor Protos will ever pull him out of his mediocrity.

Les Caves du Vatican departs completely from Gide's earlier, linear type of novel. It sets up separate sequences of events which accidentally yet fatally converge toward one event, the murder of Fleurissoire. It projects through farcical characters, ironically witty conversations and situations, a problem implicit in the very structure of the story and symbolized by the False Pope–True Pope alternatives. At one point Gide calls the novel a "fable." It is actually close in spirit to a philosophical conte. It got away from Gide a little bit, as he himself admits. His characters, originally conceived as masks, tended to become human. But its underlying schematic design is all-important.

To the extent that it introduces drastic simplifications in characters and situations this design is a source of comedy. It is amusing to watch the absolute seriousness with which these characters, completely unaware of the circumstances in which they are entangled, consistently take a given attitude or draw ethical conclusions that reveal nothing about reality, although quite a lot about their personal idiosyncrasies. Nevertheless, Gide is playing with a serious theme. Here again he is pointing out the basic discordance introduced into life by human consciousness, even the most elementary, and the pathetic absurdity of its quixotic attempts to "unify" a protean reality and introduce a rational pattern of cause and effect into the accidental sequences of events in which men are involved.

If we consider all Gide's characters up to and including those of *Les Caves du Vatican,* we realize that they are all like players engaged in a football game who persist in playing by the rules of basketball and who, though baffled, play scrupulously to the end. The *récit* is the tale of one of these players as felt by him. The *sotie* shows the figure he cuts in the middle of the football game. In both cases he is pathetic and absurd; explicitly pathetic and implicitly absurd in the *récit,* explicitly absurd and implicitly pathetic in the *sotie.*

What then are the rules of the game? Gide himself qualified as "ironical" the works that precede *Les Faux-Monnayeurs.* The main question Gide raises in all these novels is really the question of his characters' destination, their direction and development over a period of time. This is essentially the domain of the novel. But he examines the problem in a negative mood. Gide's first hero, André Walter, had supposed that man's destination is God, reached through the ascetic victory of spiritual purity over the corrupt desires of the body. He dies wretchedly. In *Les Nourritures terrestres (Fruits of the Earth)* Gide asserts that man's destination is a plenitude of joy reached on this earth through the development of all the senses. But Ménalque, the exponent of the doctrine, appears a selfish, superficial man. *L'Immoraliste* and *La Porte étroite* further exploit these two themes. They describe how the exclusive search for either sensuous plenitude or spiritual plenitude fails and becomes corrupt, eventually destroying both Michel and Alissa.

Gide, through Michel and Alissa, indirectly asserts that man's destination is neither God nor immediate sensual pleasure but a human equilibrium that is neither self-destructive nor destructive of others. The two books have the same underlying theme. They describe a human perversion. Gide is primarily concerned with growth, which is a sign of life, and with equilibrium, which is a form of duration, both necessary to human happiness. But he cannot reconcile the two. With *Les Faux-Monnayeurs* Gide attacks his problem from a somewhat different angle. As in his previous novels, he is concerned with growth; however, his position changes, perhaps under the influence of Blake, whose thought had greatly intrigued him. He is now concerned with the positive principle of "virtue": the inner principle of integrity and harmony that gives form through slow growth, as opposed to intellectual formulas that impose a pattern from the outside.

Les Faux-Monnayeurs takes as its main theme the passage from adolescence to manhood, symbolized by the achievement of the baccalaureate. It is a period of formation, of an orientation that may well become a destiny. At the heart of the story is the Pension Azaïs, a private Protestant school whose task it is to form the young. The paths of all the characters lead in and out of the Pension Azaïs. The group of adolescents connected with the school are at various stages of development. With the exception of Boris, a lonely child who is practically without a family, they all belong to three bourgeois families: the Vedel-Azaïs, the Moliniers, the Profitendieus. The Vedel-Azaïs are clergymen and educators; M. Molinier and M. Profitendieu are magistrates. The first instill inner moral standards of conduct; the magistrates impose the legal penalties that society exacts for failure to meet these standards. Edouard, a novelist, who is concerned with values rather than with standards, is connected with all three groups by family ties or friendship. He is writing a book entitled *Les Faux-Monnayeurs*. Despite the pastors and the magistrates, we see all the adolescents caught in the meshes of counterfeit, for counterfeit is all around them: in the disunited families, in the self-delusions of the adults, in their general refusal to admit that they are not all purely moral beings living according to high ethical standards. In the dark, rather like Protos, operates Strouvilhou, who is at the head of a real counterfeit gang that uses adolescents to distribute quantities of false coins.

In one of its aspects, Gide's novel is the story of how Edouard's novel remains unwritten. Counterfeiters are people who deliberately fabricate false coins and put them into circulation. Edouard's theme could hardly be more Gidian. He is concerned, like Gide, with all the situations created by the circulation of mental or emotional false coins: inflation, devaluation, bankruptcy and their psychological accompaniments of doubt, suspicion, distress and fear. Edouard's conception of the novel is also Gidian. He sees it as presenting the conflict between a certain vision of life and the reality of life itself. In the central critical part of the novel, Edouard temporarily borrows—from Valéry perhaps—the idea of a "pure" novel, free of compromise with the ambiguities of life. When his secretary, Bernard, brings him a false coin, a "real" false coin, Edouard is disturbed. It does not tally with his ideas. He will not come to terms with reality. As the book progresses, this tendency becomes more and more apparent. The real significance of what is taking place escapes him. Gide's own novel is not "pure." It is composed of heterogeneous elements that Gide borrowed from reality: episodes observed in newspaper clippings that he collected and published in his *Journal des Faux-Monnayeurs*. Gide "composes" his novel out of these elements, organizing them with subtle care according to his point of view on life. This is a positive and complex point of view that necessitates a new and complex architecture, simple though the book may seem at first.

The novel is divided into three parts. The first and the third are exactly balanced in length and take place in Paris. The second, shorter part is set in Switzerland. The events are carefully timed.

The entire first part takes a little more than twenty hours between a Wednesday afternoon and a Thursday night in July. The third part describes events that happen in the two or three weeks immediately following the opening of school in October. Between these two parts stretch the summer vacation months. But through Edouard's journals, through letters and conversations, Gide evokes in restrospect events that go back to the month of October, one year before his story starts. It takes approximately one year for the pattern of events to take shape. As he had done in *Les Caves du Vatican,* Gide sets in motion a complex web of moving relationships, all of which converge, but invisibly and by illogical progression, to the semisuicide, semimurder, of Boris, a moving and terrible climax that Edouard refuses to accept and rejects as material for his novel. The death of Boris is thus presented as a consequence of the interaction of many sequences of related and unrelated actions, a consequence foreseen and intended by none and yet in which everybody participates.

The real meaning of Gide's book thus goes beyond Edouard's and encloses it. It is as usual implicit in the structure of the novel and latent in the development of the characters. There can be no false coin unless there is an authentic coin. The problem for each character is not merely to find the source of emission of the false coin, as do M. Profitendieu in the world of crime and Boris's psychiatrist in the psychological world. The problem is to find the source and nature of the real coin. All the characters in *Les Faux-Monnayeurs* emit, accept and transmit metaphorical or real false coins for a variety of reasons, all related to their position in regard to the authentic coin.

The two extreme positions are held by the Reverend Azaïs and the enigmatic counterfeiter Strouvilhou, who circulates invisibly through the book but whose center of operations, like old Azaïs's, is the pension where adolescents are being educated. Azaïs is blind and deaf to all that does not corroborate his concept of an innocent world, ideally ordered according to the laws of Christian morality. He ignores all the real aspects of life. He is a corrupter by ignorance, but his ignorance is based on selfishness; he will not have his intellectual comfort disturbed. He emits false values that have no coverage in life. He cannot prevent life from being ambiguous, but he obliges all around him to pretend it is clearly ethical and therefore to wall themselves up in solitude and deception. All his children pursue a form of depreciation of life in themselves: Rachel in self-negation, Laura in self-delusion, Armand in self-depreciation, Sarah in self-dispersion.

Strouvilhou is the corrupter by choice, by perversion. He sees the gap between his ideal of what should be and what is. Because of this discrepancy, he cultivates a form of inverted idealism and operates a reversal of values that leaves room only for what is destructive. He hates life and obliges life around him to masquerade as vice. Azaïs and Strouvilhou are counterfeiters, like Edouard, because they cling to a preconceived idea of what life should be.

Les Faux-Monnayeurs can be seen to some extent as a sort of Pilgrim's Progress describing the spiritual trials of young men as they confront the ethical ambiguity of life. Vincent, incited by Lady Griffith and flush with success, takes the path of self-realization through the negation of any moral law; he is the much more powerful brother of Michel and marks the extreme limit that can be reached by following Strouvilhou. Gide throws him unregretfully out of the human orbit, and out of the novel, into Africa, murder and madness. Boris, an adolescent drawn toward the purity of his young friend Bronja, is walled in by the hypocrisy of the Azaïs pension. He mistakes his path and becomes the victim of Strouvilhou's gang of schoolboy criminals. His mistake is a mistake of context. He gives an authentic value to what is nothing but a masquerade. But because of its reality, the pistol shot that kills him shows up all the counterfeit around him. Bernard, Olivier and George will mistake their paths, realize their error and return to their families, having discovered that the measure of authenticity is inside themselves: What they say and do rings true or rings false. They can control the inner currency they use in life; they cannot control life's outer patterns, the "devil's share," as Gide now calls it, in their lives. The "devil's share," as is clearly shown in the structure of the story, is the play of blind chance that Gide had earlier attributed to Zeus. The problem Gide raises is the problem of maintaining an inner integrity by "composing" honestly out of a double reality—one's individual self and the independent workings of the world around one, a self-evaluation that is never final and that is essentially a search for a true form of living, a "style," one might say.

With *Les Caves du Vatican* and *Les Faux-Monnayeurs,* the Gidian novel becomes an "imitation of an action" in the Aristotelian sense. Gide is not interested in describing life as it appears either from within or from without. He reconstructs it from materials carefully selected and organized according to an inner perspective. The casual reader may find it hard to grasp the full implications of a novel like *Les Faux-Monnayeurs;* it may seem to him merely the rather pointless story of a group of perverted adolescents interested only in literature and love affairs, homosexuality more particularly. Or, he may find it too self-conscious, too carefully constructed a novel to stir the imagination. It is nonetheless a great novel in its own way. Gide's search for a satisfactory form for the novel is closely related to the broad problem of establishing an order of values in an unordered world. He does not impose his order as Proust does, creating a *summa.* He merely suggests it as a temporary working hypothesis, much as certain modern scientists might do. When Gide's perspectives change, his novels change accordingly.

For many readers, Proust's work will appear greater, but Gide, one of the first modern novelists to consider the ethical and esthetic problems arising out of a non-Christian and nondeterministic view of life, seems to have exercised a deeper influence on the contemporary novel. The problems of freedom, action and human significance in a world impervious to human values, problems which dominate the thinking of younger novelists such as Malraux, Sartre and Camus, are the problems that shape the destinies of Gide's characters and their world. He conceives the destiny of his characters as in the making, working out of the present into an unforeseeable future, thereby reversing the movement of a novel like *Madame*

Bovary. The Gidian novel tells the story of an adventure whose end cannot be calculated beforehand.

Gide's vision is essentially optimistic. Life with all its strife and suffering seems to him—as it does to his Theseus—a never-exhausted source of adventure. The "tragic sense of life" is not entirely absent from his work, but Gide sees in it the Promethean illusion par excellence, the illusion that deters men from playing the game of life fully "with the cards they have" and with no delusions about it or themselves. As far as he is concerned, the reward will be our liberation from the fictions that cramp our lives. Therein no doubt lies the continuing power of his work: He is the last of the prophets of serenity. In search of the novel, Gide found that the only novel worth writing was always one and the same—the novel that reveals the inadequacy of all fiction when it is confronted with life. Gide is not a creator but a destroyer of fictional worlds.

Marcel Proust: In Search of Lost Time

A la Recherche du temps perdu (*Remembrance of Things Past*), Proust's vast novel, slowly envelops the reader, as he falls under the spell of the voice that carries him out of the night into the sunshine of Combray. We stand back from the Gidian world at Gide's own bidding and look into it from the outside according to perspectives cunningly contrived by the author, though he himself is conspicuously absent from his novel. Proust, in contrast, substitutes his universe for ours and gradually immerses us in a time that is past, yet becomes plainly visible.

His novel was published between the years 1913 and 1927. In all probability the most remarkable literary work produced in the first half of the twentieth century, it raises all the fundamental questions latent in the intellectual climate of France since the last decades of the nineteenth century and offers its own solution to most of them. Proust literally gave years of his life to the work; and it is a far more complex achievement than the word "novel" generally suggests.

A la Recherche du temps perdu introduces us into the private world of a single individual, the narrator, who speaks throughout the four thousand pages of the book. It thus reflects the new interest in the workings of subjective consciousness that was characteristic of the time. Proust, whose father and brother were distinguished doctors, had had some contact with scientific thought, and this influence is apparent in certain aspects of his work and in his general conception of the novel. The Proustian universe is one of flux, of changing human perspectives, relationships and proportions, set within a rigid framework of "laws," both physical and psychological, that preside over its seemingly inexhaustible phenomena. The novel in which this universe takes shape has no real plot and does not seem to offer a coherent sequence of events; but it has a central theme. The narrator is telling the story of a spiritual quest: a journey from the magically ordered world of childhood into an adult view of life as an inhuman mechanism of senseless laws, and thence to the recognition of a new and completely satisfying ordering of his experience which contains and synthesizes all the knowledge life has brought him.

Du Côté de chez Swann (*Swann's Way*), the first of the seven parts of *A la Recherche du temps perdu,* was published in 1913, a crucial year for French letters, sometimes designated as the *annus mirabilis* of the first half of the century. That same year André Gide with *Les Caves du Vatican,* Alain Fournier with *Le Grand Meaulnes* and Valéry Larbaud with *Barnabooth* all broke with traditional patterns of the novel. Apollinaire's volume of verse, *Alcools,* showed that poetry too was following new paths. No one at the time thought of Marcel Proust as one of the great writers of the day. Even the forward-looking *Nouvelle Revue Française,* on the alert for new talent, would not accept Proust's manuscript. For a literary group still ignorant of Joyce and Kafka, its approach to fiction seemed too far removed from any known model.

Nothing in Proust's life, or even in his published work, could prepare his readers for the novel he had conceived. His first publication *Les Plaisirs et les jours* (*Pleasures and Regrets*), 1896, was definitely *fin de siècle:* a collection of rather vacuous short stories, poems and character sketches, many of which had already appeared in the current "little magazines." Translations of Ruskin and a few articles in *Le Figaro* had added little to his reputation. Proust was better known as a social figure and a rather strange one at that. In 1913 he already had his legend. As a young man, he seemed above all self-seeking: a young snob intent on making his way into the aristocratic circles of society. Even then, he apparently had two unusual qualities that endeared him to his hostesses. He was a brilliantly witty conversationalist with a gift for imitation that revealed a dangerous insight into human character. Though over-sensitive and prone to create endless complications, he had a talent for making and keeping friends of intellectual distinction who fell under the fascination of a powerful intelligence, unmanifest as yet in any actual accomplishments. Bad health soon ended Proust's career as a playboy. His delicate health, the asthma which had afflicted him since the age of nine, served as an escape from the absorbing demands of social life. We now know that Proust had never ceased to write. Several bulky manuscripts, which he had carelessly abandoned, were found after his death: a three-volume novel, *Jean Santeuil,* published in 1952; critical essays collected in *Contre Sainte-Beuve* (*Against Sainte-Beuve*), 1954.

Proust's gradual withdrawal from society was hastened by his mother's death. He then became a semirecluse, an invalid or *malade imaginaire* according to some, who shut himself up in a cork-lined room from which he emerged only at night. Proust unquestionably lived under the strain of a great inner disturbance. Until her death in 1905, when he was well over thirty, he seldom left his mother, whom he loved and wished to please but against whom he nevertheless waged an insidious war. His affection for her was marred by a sense of guilt arising out of his apparent lack of achievement as well as sexual abnormalities, not only his well-known homosexuality but also, apparently, sadistic and masochistic tendencies. Proust's asthma, his semiwithdrawal from everyday living, the complications of his sexual life, are all involved in the creation of his novel. If we consider *A la Recherche du temps perdu* in relation to Proust's life, we can measure the cost and profit of his pitiless lucidity; the roots of this work lie deep in his unusual personality.

It took Proust many years to find an adequate pattern for the formal organization of his work. It came to him in a flash of illumination, but this illumination was prepared by long meditation on the problem, since, as *Jean Santeuil* shows, Proust was working on his novel as far back as 1896. At the time he wrote *Jean Santeuil*, he had found most of his main themes, but they lacked significance. The book as a whole is banal in form and rather incoherent. Proust belongs to the line of French writers who, after Baudelaire, were concerned, in their approach to art, with the conscious creation of form. When he actually started to write *A la Recherche du temps perdu*, Proust had a theory of the novel, of his novel at least—a theory which the narrator formulates in the last pages of the final volume of *Le Temps retrouvé* (*Time Regained*). These pages contain a real essay on the novel and an explanation of the book Proust was finishing. As the reader looks back over the preceding volumes, he may question the necessity of this device, so clearly is Proust's intent apparent in the structure of the novel itself. This is a sure sign that the theory was not entirely an afterthought but directed the gradual composition of the novel.

Proust wanted his work to appear in one large volume, not piecemeal as it did. World War I imposed a gap of five years between the first and second parts, and Proust died in 1923, before the last three parts were published. His critics, understandably enough, failed at first to grasp the over-all pattern. They praised or blamed the intricacies of his style or the complexities of his psychological analyses. The beauty of the childhood world of Combray was attributed to the spontaneous charm of personal reminiscence. Proust insisted, but to no great avail, that the book was one whole, rigorously composed. The last pages of *Le Temps retrouvé* are a final and rather desperate attempt to prove that this is so.

The central theme of the novel is that of a spiritual odyssey: the narrator's initial sense of the futility of his existence, his search for fulfillment and his final triumph. This theme—better conveyed by its literal title, *In Search of Time Lost*, than by the English title, *Remembrance of Things Past*—is closely related to the over-all composition of the novel. In the last volume of *Le Temps retrouvé* the narrator finally reaches his destination. He becomes a writer because he discovers what he has been seeking: the spiritual form that his experience of life has taken unknown to him, a form that will determine the structure of his future novel. He must first go through the long and heartbreaking process of discarding all the established patterns of experience. Until he discovers his personal pattern of experience, the "wasted time" that constitutes his life is "lost"; with its discovery, time is restored to him, "regained."

For Proust, this search for a satisfactory form in art is more than a purely esthetic problem. It involves the artist's whole being: his feelings, his intelligence, his will, his memory. There is a pre-esthetic preparation for the work of art, an inner activity of a complex spiritual nature. It involves a sustained inquiry into the relations of the self with the universe, with other human beings, with itself. Proust carefully studies the quality and nature of that activity as experienced by a future writer, the narrator.

The crux of the problem for the narrator is the antinomy of subjective and objective reality, the intricate games they play with one another, the precarious balance they sometimes achieve. From the very beginning, the material Proust works with is entirely contained in a human consciousness. All the questions raised by the narrator are sifted through the mediums of sensation, emotion, dream, memory and thought. But the existence of an objective reality is never questioned; because it resists all the narrator's attempts to impose upon it his subjective interpretations, it forms an important part of his experience.

This interplay of the inner and the outer worlds is shown in the opening pages of the novel by a device that could hardly be further removed from the techniques of the naturalist novel: an internal monologue which takes the form of a meditation. It is neither conventional narration nor uncontrolled stream of consciousness. The narrator describes the fluctuations of consciousness as he has experienced them in innumerable nights of semi-insomnia. "For a long time I used to go to bed early. Sometimes almost before I had put out my candle my eyes would close so quickly that I had not even time to say 'I'm going to sleep.' And half an hour later the thought that it was time to go to sleep would awaken me; I would try to put down the book which I imagined was still in my hands, and to blow out the light; I had been thinking all the time, while I was asleep, of what I had just been reading, but my thoughts had run into a channel of their own, until I myself seemed actually to have become the subject of my book: a church, a quartet, the rivalry of Francis I and Charles V."

The reader never knows from what point in time the narrator is speaking as he recalls the great reaches of the past behind him. Slowly the personality of the man emerges and, with it, a whole world of people, objects and events.

The narrator is a cultivated, middle-aged man living in a time which is no longer ours, a time of carriages, oil lamps and candlelight. He is a sick and meditative man whose weary voice seems to rise out of the night, the inner and outer void of which he speaks. As he speaks, he remembers incidents, people, the rooms in which he slept; himself as a child, his grandfather and Mme de Saint-Loup; places—Combray, Balbec, Doncières, Venice, Tansonville. The shadowy inner stage is set. Its dimensions will merely grow until they accommodate a world. Among the vague and disconnected memories of the past, one incident always stands out, remaining distinct and clear in the mind of the awakened narrator. It is a childhood drama set in Combray, the little provincial town where he used to spend his summers.

The scene is always the same. It is evening at Combray; the family are seated in the garden; the bell rings, and the curtain goes up. Swann, a friend, comes to visit, and the child is filled with anxiety. Because Swann is there, he must go up to his bedroom alone; his mother will not come up to kiss him goodnight. One night, in a moment of despair, he stays up, makes a terrible childish scene, and his mother, to comfort him, sleeps that night in his room. The incident is told with a great wealth of detail. It introduces us to the very heart of the narrator's universe: Combray, the narrator as a child, the family. But it is also something more. The tinkling of the bell that announces Swann's entrance is recalled in the last pages of *Le Temps retrouvé*. It marks the beginning of the child's long journey away from the goal which he must reach.

The bedtime scene is the only part of his life in Combray that the narrator ever recalls. Where, he wonders, is the rest of Combray, the days for example? Is all that part of him "lost," "dead," "past"? The narrator then recalls a certain day fairly late in his life when he stumbled upon something which momentarily illuminated his existence. He remembers himself as a weary, middle-aged man who one afternoon drops in to see his mother. She hands him a cup of tea into which he dips a little cake, a madeleine. A feeling of joy sweeps over him: "I no longer felt mediocre, contingent, mortal. What was the origin of so powerful a joy? I felt that it was linked to the savor of the tea and cake but that it infinitely surpassed them and was probably not similar in kind." He makes an effort of concentration, and slowly, from a great distance within him, something comes to life: Combray, the peaceful, beautiful Combray of his long childhood summer days. The overture to Proust's novel is finished, and the narrator sets out to re-create the world of Combray, now seen as a completed whole.

This introductory monologue, formless though it may seem as the narrator follows his stream of reminiscence, is carefully composed and directed toward a complex end. It poses, by its very nature, the problems that the narrator will investigate during the whole course of the novel. What is the nature of the self? its relation to time? its relation to the outer world? to the inner world? to others? to its past selves? All these questions arise in the prelude and are pointed at the central enigma: What is the meaning of the word "reality" in terms of actual human experience? In addition the monologue simultaneously introduces us to the central character of the novel, its décor and its principal themes.

This double function of the I, at once the scene of inner dramas and the narrator of outer dramas, continues throughout the novel. The hero is the central figure of the novel through whom we can follow the fluctuations of an inner world; he is also the sole "narrator," who creates, through his narrative, the objective world in which he lives. In the course of the novel the focus and the proportions of this narrative are frequently changed. From his vantage point in an infinite present, the narrator can objectively consider his past or even past events that he has heard of indirectly. The whole incident of Swann's love for Odette, which forms the second part of *Du Côté de chez Swann,* took place before the narrator, who relates it, was born. The incident is seen from the point of view of Swann, not from that of the narrator, but the opening pages of the novel allow us to accept the change of focus.

The narrator lives in a fairly well-defined period of time which corresponds roughly to Proust's own life, although Proust opens vistas into the past and even into the future. Proust's very conception of the unbroken flow of time carries his novel well beyond the span of any individual life, either his own or his characters' lives. His world is rooted in a past to which he put no limit. The novel continuously refers as far back as medieval France, and we can discern in it the lineaments of a future which he projected even beyond his own death. The society to which the young man belongs is shown first in the seventies and eighties; the novel then moves imperceptibly into the twentieth century, then in and out of World War I. The narrator is the chronicler of two different generations, his own and the one to which his parents belong, generations that have now disappeared, they and their "time." They lived through the Dreyfus case, the Boer War, World War I; they belonged to the "horse and carriage" days, saw the first bicycles, the first cars, the first airplanes, used the first telephones. Proust sets up the décor with meticulous care, though indirectly—the fashions in clothes, in manners, in speech, in entertainment, the whole social pageantry of the time.

His narrator belongs to the wealthy and securely established world of the nineteenth century "grande bourgeoisie"; but he moves on into both aristocratic and avant-garde intellectual circles. The two centers of his rather narrow social world are Paris and the fashionable seaside resort of Balbec on the coast of Normandy. The people he frequents are either social or intellectual snobs, or both. Receptions, dinners, witty conversation, concerts, gala openings at the theater, are the fabric of everyday living, the very fabric of external reality from the somewhat limited perspective of the narrator.

The narrator himself is an overly sensitive, delicate child who grows up in the hothouse atmosphere of a small, closed family circle. He is nurtured on literature, art and the sound moral beliefs of a highly principled bourgeoisie. He becomes an aimless youth, floating in a private world of unformulated emotions and dreams; he desperately wants to become a writer but is always diverted by other, more immediate pursuits: love or social success. One disappointment follows another until, very gradually, he loses all interest in life and withdraws into a sanitarium. The narrator has reached a dead point in his life, and Proust, the part of his novel that immediately precedes *Le Temps retrouvé*.

When he was a child, the narrator lived in a magic world where people and things, words and places, seemed to promise the most exciting and mysterious adventures, particularly if they were just beyond his reach: the Swanns and the Guermantes, Balbec and Venice, beauty and love. Later it was the Combray of his childhood which seemed to him to hold the secret of all enchantment. But one by one his "magic casements" have closed. He now returns to Combray and finds nothing but a dull little town. Ever since his childhood, certain impressions had had the power to fill him with tremendous joy: a hawthorn hedge in bloom, apple trees in an orchard, the reflection of a roof in a pond. Elusive though they were, they seemed to hold a promise that the universe of art was not based on the artist's lyrical imagination but signified something concerning man's relation to the world. The time comes, however, when the narrator can see beauty in a row of trees but can no longer feel it; it brings him no joy. He is a prisoner in his own subjective universe.

Within the closed circle of consciousness he had sometimes enjoyed a sense of freedom and of power; there, objects, people, time and space lent themselves, as in dreams, to metamorphoses of all kinds. As he grows older, he loses his hold on these formless fantasies, which remain discontinuous and baffling. And his contacts with the outer world bring him sharp reminders that this world has escaped his hold, that its impersonal patterns have no relation to his inner ones. Reality now seems shapeless; or else monotonous and dull. What then is the meaning of art? Why become a writer if art is a lie, something the artist puts up like a screen between himself and the void of life?

At this point Proust's novel pivots upon itself. In a few quick flashes of revelation the narrator finds what he has been seeking. Through an illumination, long prepared by his experience, he realizes that he is endowed with the power to relate and unify the two incomplete and conflicting worlds he knows. He has never one instant ceased to be a creator. Somewhere, deep within him, a creator had been at work, selecting, ordering, preserving, the things that held a particular significance for him. The narrator sees that he carries with him, miraculously preserved from the inroads of time, an ordered, unique and beautiful world, the world to which all art refers.

This discovery frees him from his despair. It is a testimony to the permanence and significance of the human personality and of the universe in which human beings move. The narrator now becomes the artist; he will communicate the world he has discovered by creating a work of art. His work will have an important human meaning, for it will give the full content of a human being's unique experience of reality. That experience, in its totality, is fraught with a strange, mysterious beauty, the beauty of an individual life developing in a given time.

The form that Proust elaborated in order to transmit both the narrator's progress and the quality of the world he discovers is an ambitious form, so ambitious that Proust found it almost unmanageable. He was not able to finish the novel.

The history of its writing is enlightening. In 1912, Proust tried to find a publisher for a twelve-hundred-page novel in three parts, *A la Recherche du temps perdu*. The three parts were entitled *Du Côté de chez Swann, Du Côté des Guermantes (The Guermantes Way)* and *Le Temps retrouvé. Du Côté de chez Swann* was published in 1913. When publication was resumed in 1918, the book had grown, and it continued to grow until Proust's death in 1923. Proust had added about twenty-five hundred pages to a novel which now had seven parts. Often, particularly in the last volumes, the text shows signs of rather hasty interpolations: repetitions, grammatical errors and factual discrepancies which Proust would have eliminated had he had the time. But it was in the very nature of the novel, as he conceived it, thus to grow and remain unfinished. He insisted nonetheless that in its growth his novel had remained faithful to its original underlying pattern. This assertion needs qualification.

In its first stage, as it can be reconstructed from proofs and chapter headings, and also from *Du Côté de chez Swann* and certain parts of *Le Temps retrouvé* which were written at the same time, Proust's pattern of composition was relatively simple. In 1913 the entire novel was constructed around the theme of the two different walks the narrator used to take when he was a child at Combray. The one, Swann's Way, led past Tansonville, Swann's estate; the other led toward the historic castle of the feudal lords of Combray, the Guermantes.

The Swanns and the Guermantes fascinate the child: the Swanns because Swann, although a friend of the family, has made a "bad" marriage and Tansonville is therefore a "forbidden" world; the Guermantes because their castle is too far away to be reached during the Sunday walks and because this family moves in too high a social sphere. What Proust proposed to do was to show how the narrator, leaving his own real world of Combray behind him, explored those two other worlds and, having measured their vanity, returned to his own inner world where he could grasp the Swanns and the Guermantes in their reality. All the themes of the novel are bound to the Swanns and the Guermantes: art, love and homosexuality to the Swanns; the historic past, the pageantry and values of the social world to the Guermantes.

In the novel as it developed, the beautifully proportioned and symmetrical pattern disappears. The narrator's quest is longer and his experience more painful. Undoubtedly in his later years Proust's vision of life became more somber. He transformed his novel accordingly. The technique he had adopted allowed him to expand the book without basically modifying its structure.

Proust used the mechanism of involuntary memory in the first pages of *Combray* as a prelude to the creation of the inner Combray preserved in the subconscious reaches of the narrator's being. But a man's memory is inexhaustible, and there is no limit to the great blocks of the past that Proust could resurrect. As we follow the narrator's slow and nonchalant progress from his childhood days in Combray through his adolescence and manhood, we feel that Proust and his novel with him might well have fallen victim to the double chaos of internal and external reality that Proust was exploring were it not for the initial conception which ordered the book.

In the last analysis, Proust attempted to pour into his novel a veritable *summa,* a complete record of the world as he saw it and experienced it through the many different perspectives established within a lifetime. What saved his world from falling apart under the mass of what it tried to encompass was the superhuman and on the whole successful effort he made to express his intellectual concepts in the organization of his novel and not merely to expound these concepts in the novel itself, although he did this as well. His concepts became criteria governing an art form.

Although the whole novel is based on the narrator's efforts to transcend the rigorously deterministic views of many of Proust's predecessors, this in itself implies that Proust accepted these views up to a certain point. His novel is so organized as to emphasize the fundamental similarity of apparently diverse phenomena—an important source of social comedy. Human beings and human groups, in their physical appearance and behavior, are constantly repeating themselves. They demonstrate the existence of implacable "laws."

All Proust's characters are part of this kaleidoscopic aspect of the world. They are made of separate fragments, the same ones over and over, which by chance juxtapositions make a limited number of successive patterns.

As a child, the narrator already observes—with amusement—the peculiarities that recur in the behavior of the grown-ups in his family circle. During the long journey he later undertakes in search of "la vraie vie," he discovers and often formulates the laws that are implicit in Proust's technique of composition. These laws govern the variations of Swann's love for Odette and the narrator's love for Gilberte, then for the Duchess of Guermantes and then for Albertine, just as they govern the grotesque and grandiose loves of the homosexual Baron de Charlus. They become progressively more imperative as the patterns reappear implacably. The laws governing the evolution of social cliques are easily discernible as Oriane de Guermantes's salon loses its ascendancy and Mme Verdurin's rises amid myriad other salons, all following the same path. When, at the end of the novel, we see the merging of social milieux which at first were poles apart, and the niece of the little tailor Jupien marries a nobleman, while Saint-Loup, a Guermantes, marries Gilberte Swann, Proust suggests that such patterns recur throughout history —under Louis XIV or during the Regency, for example.

The most important of these laws, in Proust's eyes, are those that the narrator will grasp completely only at the end of the book: the laws governing human relationships within time. The word "time" gives Proust's title its haunting appeal. We lose time, waste time, find time, give time, but who, before Proust, went "in search of time" and, what is more, "found" it?

In the mechanistic universe of conceptual thought that the narrator first discovers, time really does not exist. Nor does the individual, destroyed piecemeal by a timeless mechanism, really exist. There is no past, no present, no future. The narrator first considers time as a linear dimension along which he moves. The empty road of the future becomes the empty road of the past; there is no present. But in sleep or sickness, the narrator learns, time can shrink or extend immeasurably. An instant can span many years. In his dreams he can simultaneously live on several different levels of time. The narrator experiences time as a form of being in which what we call "past" is, in fact, present. The middle-aged man who tastes the madeleine at the beginning of the book is no longer the helpless plaything of the passing years. He actually possesses a certain dimension of time.

For Proust, all human beings, whether they are conscious of the fact or not, literally embody time. In the clothes they wear, the round of their daily life, their whole appearance, they are the outward signs of time, the only ones. When Odette Swann takes her triumphant stroll in the Bois de Boulogne, she puts the stamp of time on its alleys and trees, just as the draperies and changing bibelots of her successive salons embody time. In this respect human beings are perhaps no different from slowly shifting continents, but their embodiment of time is swifter, more dramatic and more perceptible to the watchful eye. Nowhere is the embodiment of time more evident than in the more fragile and apparently superficial human activities; hence Proust's fascination with them and the long and careful pages he devotes to them.

Time models human beings ceaselessly, but it also ceaselessly destroys what it has modeled. Proust does not, therefore, present his characters as consistent entities. He gives several portraits of each as they appear at various stages in their lives, and these portraits are not necessarily given in chronological order: Charlus the nervous and disconcerting individual whom the narrator takes for a spy; Charlus the insolent young prince, idol of the Faubourg Saint-Germain; Charlus, fat and middle-aged, whose powdered face and strange associations make him the laughing stock of the Verdurin set; Charlus, white-bearded, paralyzed and half-dead, abandoned by all but the little tailor, Jupien. Proust thus raises the question of the permanence of each character, his identity and his continuity in time. Eventually all the characters, with all their selves, are completely destroyed in death. Death, in a sense, is the enemy of time.

The narrator fully grasps this creative and destructive process of
time, and with dramatic suddenness, but not until the last pages of
the novel. He has come back to Paris, and he has given up trying
to find some sense in his life. He accepts an invitation to the Guermantes; almost all the people he once knew so well are there, although the social kaleidoscope has moved. The title "Princesse de
Guermantes" now designates the tottering figure of Mme Verdurin;
Odette Swann, once excluded from the Guermantes circle, is now
the Duke of Guermantes's mistress. The narrator knows them all,
yet they all seem disguised. Wrinkles, gray hair, semiparalysis, heavy
bodies—all the terrible ravages of time—are pitilessly detailed by
Proust. The narrator realizes that he too lives in "their time": He
is growing old. "His time" and "their time" constitute a medium
common to them all. It will disappear with them before long, as
they die.

Other and more complex thoughts distract him, setting off a play
of involuntary memory—the same which at the outset of the book
started him on his long quest. He steps on an uneven pavement, and
the blue sky and brilliant atmosphere of Venice appear, as real as
the pavement on which he stands. He raises a napkin to his lips,
and out of the inner depths of his consciousness Balbec arises with
its sounds, its colors, the people it contained. A red-bound volume
on a shelf arrests his attention; the title *François le Champi* calls
forth in its bulk the bedtime drama at Combray, the room, his
mother reading aloud to him. "A man asleep," the narrator had
noted in the opening pages of the novel, "holds in a circle around
him the fleeing hours, the order of years and of worlds." Now,
though the narrator is awake, he holds his life in a circle around
him, not lost, not past, but present, a beautifully ordered whole.

This selected world rests on the few intense moments of delight
which the narrator experienced at rare intervals and always in the
presence of natural beauty: flowers or trees, the sea, cathedral spires
against the sky. These "impressions bienheureuses" mark the moments of contact between a spiritual self and the world; they suggest

to him that he contains a being who is at one with the beauty of the earth. These impressions elude time, can be recaptured and will give the narrator's work the unique sensuous content which is the mark of the great work of art.

Proust seems to believe that the human being is inhabited by a spiritual essence. Of what nature he does not say. Its presence is manifest in the power to create works of art which both arrest and transcend time, giving the instant its eternity. In order to be intelligible to others, this spiritual existence is forced to seek a concrete form of expression, borrowing its material from the outer world. Throughout his novel, Proust establishes a vast network of relationships between the various arts and his own creation; art, as the narrator discovers, is the only form in which the spiritual essence common to all men can be expressed. Art in all its forms is represented in *A la Recherche du temps perdu;* artists such as Vinteuil the composer, Bergotte the writer, Elstir the painter, are not the least imposing of Proust's creations. Each poses the same enigma: apparently mediocre and vulnerable in his individual life, the artist, in his work, transcends mediocrity and death and opens for others the closed paths toward a full apprehension of reality.

Proust is a great artist in his own domain and could speak with the authority of intimate personal experience on the fundamental meaning of art. And in view of his unusual intellect, his sensibility to art in all its forms, Proust's reflections on architecture, music and painting are always interesting, though colored by a somewhat literary bias. His intense preoccupation with the relationships between the arts no doubt reflects the influence of circles he frequented in his youth. The symbolists, under the spell of Wagner and perhaps stimulated by Hegel, were greatly interested in a synthesis of all the arts that would express the whole drama of man's presence in the universe. There is evidence that Proust consciously attempted to create this synthesis in his novel. The cathedrals, musical compositions and paintings which he describes in such detail apparently correspond in his mind to different aspects of the novel itself. The cathedral seems to represent the outward appearance of human life; it embodies "layers" of time and yet is a unified whole. The sonata, septet or symphony evokes the invisible inner life of subjective emotions, perceptions and feelings. The paintings record the moments of ecstatic, almost visionary union with the outer world that Proust's narrator occasionally experienced.

Proust's efforts to create a synthesis of all the arts actually resulted in a series of beautiful literary metaphors. *A la Recherche du temps perdu* belongs to the domain of literature and particularly to the domain of the novel. Proust created an autonomous universe of related human beings, moving in time, living out their lives, happily unaware of the perspectives that Proust's vision of life brought to bear upon them. Swann, Odette, Charlus, Oriane de Guermantes—and the others in this vast assemblage of characters—mediocre and vacuous as they may appear to the disillusioned narrator, nevertheless retain, for the reader, the peculiar beauty, the fascination and the poetry of an exotic plant.

Proust explored more deeply than any previous novelist the shifting depths of individual consciousness. He created, within his own perspectives, an entire society, penetrating into circles that novelists before him had hesitated to describe: the circles of homosexuality. His world is at times curiously deformed by his peculiar temperament and emotional instability; it thus contains an element of the fantastic. It is held together, woven into an almost stifling whole, by the intricacies of a style unique in the history of French literature. Proust's long meandering sentences envelop and almost conceal the dry humor that pervades much of his work. Their arabesques are a heritage of the decadent period but carry a wealth of imagery which is often mistaken for mere descriptive detail. There are really few purely descriptive details in Proust, but analogies pointing to the autonomous internal organization and unity of Proust's fictional universe are endless.

With Proust, the novel reached one of its extreme limits. All other contemporary novels, interesting though they may be, dwindle in stature when compared to Proust's achievement. Yet it is almost with a sigh of relief that the reader turns to other forms of fiction, so stifling and so nearly desperate is Proust's struggle to disengage from the labyrinths of subjective consciousness the objective, fundamentally optimistic, courageous and human vision his novel embodies.

BRAVE NEW WORLD

To write the genuine history of present-day Europe; there is an aim for the whole of one's life." This ambitious literary task, which Tolstoi considered so important but which he never undertook, has tempted other novelists as well, and never more strongly, it would seem, than in the present century. Although the apparent chaos of the modern world has led writers like Proust and Gide to invent more coherent fictional worlds of their own, it has also presented the stimulating challenge of elucidating the nature of man's position in his twentieth century environment.

This problem was first explored by Georges Duhamel, Jules Romains and Roger Martin du Gard—three novelists who belong to the fertile generation of the 1880's. The medium used in each case was the massive, multivolume cycle novel that traces the history of an individual, a family or a group of friends in relation to the history of society, thus revealing a multitude of different perspectives on changing situations and events and showing their interaction over an extended period of time. Innumerable other novels of this type, many of them serious in intent and good in execution, were published during the thirties; even today they continue to appear and to win literary prizes. Only two of this younger group of novelists, however, are generally known: Louis Aragon, the most talented of those whose interpretation of history has been simplified by adherence to Marxist ideology; and Marcel Aymé, although his documentary novels form only a small part of his total output.

This return to reality of the erstwhile poets Duhamel and Romains, the ex-surrealist Aragon, and the Aymé of the fantastical

La Jument verte (*The Green Mare*) may appear as something of a counterrevolution. Does not the principal originality of the contemporary novel lie in its questioning of the habitual meaning of the word "reality"? In its proposed aim of seeking an autonomous existence in utter disregard of facts and events that lie without its sphere? It is true, certainly, that the novelists with whom we are concerned at this point are far less interested in epistemological or esthetic problems, far less inventive in their treatment of the novel than many of their contemporaries. The instrument that they have used was already perfected by Balzac, Flaubert and Zola.

Their material, nonetheless, is very different, and this in itself has affected the character of their novels. The nineteenth century, as we look back on it today, was the century of the individual. His personal life was influenced by the external events of his age, yet it was not determined by these events. The hero of a novel by Balzac could fling himself into the course of history if he so desired, but he could also return to the provinces and heal his wounds. Today the choice has been removed. The individual is irrevocably tied to his community, for this community has gradually come to include the greater part of humanity. We can celebrate these ties, as did Romains, or we can deplore them, as did Aymé; but we can no longer ignore them.

The gradual emergence of this new and close relationship between the individual and the collectivity is the principal theme of all five novelists. With Duhamel, Romains and Martin du Gard, the individual and diverse paths of the different characters depicted in their novels ultimately merge in the collective disaster of World War I. The same may be said of Aragon, who, though he belongs to a younger generation, is concerned for the most part with a similar period of time. Aymé, who covers the period leading from the Popular Front to the end of World War II, shows a somewhat similar pattern in a still harsher light.

History is thus no longer the external context but the central subject of the novel. Balzac, Flaubert and Zola presented as detailed and as exhaustive a picture of their times, but the picture itself is less central to their purpose. Whatever their original intentions may have been, we do not read these novelists primarily in order to understand the social structure of the Restoration period, the bourgeois classes of the Second Empire or proletarian conditions at the end of the century. In contrast, the novels of Duhamel, Romains, Martin du Gard, Aragon and Aymé are so intimately related to the history of the past few decades that they must be read, and to some extent evaluated, as fictional interpretations of their age.

To write a "genuine history of present-day Europe"—a history seen only from a slight vantage point in time—is a formidable undertaking. If even a literary giant like Tolstoi, living in what now seems the relative quiet of the nineteenth century, abandoned this ambition, how can we expect any of these lesser novelists, living in an extremely complex age, to succeed?

The most obvious pitfall is that of oversimplification, and three of this group of novelists, although men of unquestionable literary talent, have fallen into it. Duhamel, profoundly shaken by World War I, simply turned his back upon his age. Rather than attempting to grapple with social problems that conflicted so sharply with his personal ideals, he took refuge in a nostalgia for prewar times. Romains's mistake lay rather in his uncritical glorification of twentieth century life. This native optimism was only slightly shaken by World War I, which Romains interpreted as the end rather than the beginning of an era. Not until the actual outbreak of the second war did he perceive the catastrophic potentialities of the material and social forces that he had previously extolled with lyric enthusiasm. By this time it was too late; his major work was all but finished.

Aragon has had the advantage of greater historical hindsight. But then he is a Marxist—and the romantic, "bourgeois" type of Marxist at that; although a penetrating critic of his own social milieu, he has little firsthand understanding of the proletariat and, one would gather, a rather limited understanding of political and economic problems. His ideology provides him with a ready-made set of heroes and villains and a ready-made interpretation of historical events. We have only to change the labels to unbare a traditional nineteenth century melodrama. Romains occasionally reads like something out of *Amazing Science Fiction;* Aragon, at his worst, can come fairly close to soap opera.

Roger Martin du Gard is perhaps the most interesting of this particular group of novelists. Although he is a contemporary of Duhamel and Romains, his novels have on the whole survived the test of subsequent history, for he has been more cautious in his approach to the events of his time. Rather than trying to subsume these events under a convenient over-all theory, he has simply raised what he considers to be the fundamental problems of his age and has allowed his characters to draw their own conclusions. These characters, in consequence, are far more living people, his novel as a whole, a more penetrating testimonial than the works of Duhamel, Romains and Aragon.

If Aymé has avoided certain errors of his predecessors, this is not really due, as with Martin du Gard, to a greater depth of insight. Like Aragon, he has had the advantage of greater historical hindsight, but unlike Aragon, he carries a much lighter load of social idealism and is naturally inclined toward a satirical and negativistic view of modern life. Had he had more of the crusading spirit, he might, indeed, have become as narrow and as dogmatic in his defense of the good old-fashioned bourgeois as Aragon in his championship of the noble working man. We get a glimpse of this in his essay on "intellectual comfort." In his novels, however, he has assumed the role of a detached and occasionally ferocious observer. Aymé's attitude toward his characters thus lacks the warmth and breadth of Martin du Gard's objectivity, but it has permitted him to expose the hypocrisy, cowardice and inhumanity of certain socially conditioned mid-century types of human beings in highly effective terms. Whereas Romains's ideal of historical "engagement" to some extent anticipates the later novels of Sartre, Aymé's iconoclastic individualism, although on a much more limited scale, is comparable to certain attitudes expressed in Camus's *La Peste* (*The Plague*).

Georges Duhamel and Jules Romains: "Men of Good Will"

In the early 1900's, no two young men set out more enthusiastically to give a new direction to French literature than Georges Duhamel and Jules Romains. Prolific and energetic writers, they reached a wide audience in the twenties. During the thirties they were generally considered, both inside and outside France, as the most representative of French writers. Both men are members of the Académie Française. Today their novels seem dated and often quite tedious. The postwar generation of the fifties is on the whole politely indifferent to their work.

Optimism was in the air in the years immediately preceding World War I when Duhamel and Romains started on their literary careers. Poetry—and they both thought of themselves first as poets—was beginning the spectacular "modern" experiments that were to culminate in surrealism. The "futurists" were glorifying the new power of the machine. Cubism in painting was challenging more traditional techniques; music with Satie and Stravinsky was also making history. A new world was in the making. This was particularly true for the "petite bourgeoisie" to which both Duhamel and Romains belonged, a class that was rapidly rising as the Third Republic became more solidly established. It was coming into quick possession of its cultural heritage and was eager to make itself heard.

All around the two young men surged a new enthusiasm for the modern world. Modern life had created new objects—typewriters, telephones, transcontinental trains and ocean liners; its costumes and style of life; its large cities with the scope and power they give to human lives. The "open world" was there to be enjoyed, as the delicate and sensitive writer Valéry Larbaud suggested. New human problems also appeared as the working class slowly became articulate, voicing its claims and grievances through the young socialist party. A strong dose of social idealism accompanied the literary ambitions of Duhamel and Romains from the very start. Influenced by

Tolstoi, Péguy, Romain-Rolland and the socialist theories expounded by Jaurès, they were concerned with the relations between the individual and the community. Agnostics, they believed each man's destiny is achieved on this earth, not, however, as Proust and Gide saw it, by realizing a unique individual equilibrium, but by becoming a conscious member of the human community. It was the artist's task to live as one of the community and to speak for all its members. Long before Sartre launched the term as a *mot d'ordre,* Duhamel and Romains serenely "engaged" their lives in that of their time.

Of the two writers, who were fairly close friends in 1906-1907, Duhamel, the more sensitive, was more deeply concerned with the human problems of his time: the unbridged gap between the masses and the intellectuals; the essential solitude of modern man; his unsatisfied, latent ethical aspirations. While young Romains, a student of science in France's most difficult school, l'Ecole Normale Supérieure, was evolving his optimistic literary-philosophical theory of "unanimism," Duhamel, at that time a medical student, entered into a project for community living with a small group of friends. Artists all, they settled in an abandoned house near Paris, where they installed a printing press that was to be their means of livelihood—a function in which, needless to say, it failed. The experiment lasted only about a year, but the sincere and naïve evangelism of the attempt is quite characteristic of Duhamel.

It took the war of 1914-1918 to make a novelist of Duhamel. As a doctor operating in a field hospital, Duhamel was deeply shocked by the sum of human suffering caused by the war. He diagnosed the disaster as mechanistic in origin and set out to save man's soul and body from the clutches of mechanization, in his eyes the enemy of centuries of slow development in human civilization. Duhamel's fear and rejection of a whole facet of contemporary life is apparent in his *Scènes de la vie future* (Scenes of a Future Life), 1930, an ill-tempered attack on the ills of a mechanized world where man is a slave to the machine, a world typified by the United States. For satirical impact, the book can be compared neither to Aldous Huxley's *Brave New World* nor to George Orwell's *1984.* As Duhamel "scolds" the modes and rhythms of modern life, one wonders how he would have us make our way back to the European world of 1910. It is clear that, scientist though he be, Duhamel has been unable to grasp, still less to tackle, any of the great currents that fashioned the twentieth century.

Though his novels are mainly concerned with the adventures of individuals supposedly seen in terms of their situation in the twentieth century, the climate of Duhamel's work is clearly related to the traditional values and beliefs of a pre-World War I "petite bourgeoisie"; this may explain both its wide appeal and its fundamental insignificance in the development of the novel. Duhamel's humanism is sincere and his concern with the frustrations and joys of the man in the street is real, but the rather facile sentimentality of his approach, the naïve ethical evangelism of his attitude, based on vague spiritual values, hamper the creative artist he might have been. The long list of his essays and articles, their monotony and increasing self-righteousness, reveal Duhamel's intellectual limitations.

His two main fictional works are cycles that reflect the changing temper of those two strongly differentiated decades, the twenties and the thirties. In the twenties, the decade of individual "anxieties" and maladjustments, Duhamel published the five-volume *Vie et aventures de Salavin* (*Salavin*), 1920-1932. In the thirties, a decade of social restlessness, appeared *La Chronique des Pasquiers* (*The Pasquier Chronicles*), nine volumes of which were published between 1933-1939, and the last in 1945. Though certain volumes of the Salavin cycle still have considerable appeal, neither the Salavin nor the Pasquier cycle is entirely readable today, and large sections of the latter seem incredibly tedious. It is fortunate that Duhamel prudently conceived each volume in the two series as an entity that might be read separately.

Salavin—a new type of novel hero—is the central character of the first cycle. He introduces a host of lost and restless individuals, unimportant individuals, "strangers" to the world, voyagers "to the end of the night." They have nothing of the grandeur of the romantic

hero. Their mediocrity is the source of their distress. Salavin is a
white-collar employee who lives with his mother in a dismal apart-
ment in the populous section of Paris that stretches behind the Pan-
theon. The first volume of the cycle introduces us to Salavin in a
startling and moving overture. Ill-clad, unemployed, dragging out
a miserable existence in cafés, Salavin, like the Ancient Mariner,
stops a passer-by and in a "midnight confession" tells his sad tale.
La Confession de minuit (*Confession at Midnight*) is a monologue
reminiscent of Dostoevski's *Notes from the Underground*. Salavin's
account of his restless wanderings in Paris, of his mental torment
and helplessness, successfully conveys the senseless nightmare of a
life lived in physical and spiritual misery. At the origin of Salavin's
adventures is an apparently absurd and inadvertent gesture. Although Salavin is subjected to all the routines and servitudes imposed by society on a minor employee, he never consciously revolts
against them. One day, however, when called in to confer with his
boss, he gives way to an irrational impulse: He touches, ever so
delicately, the rim of his boss's ear. The reaction of outraged authority is violent. Salavin, ejected from his job, starts his life as one of
society's unemployed; poor Salavin, to whom society concedes not
the smallest grain of human irrationality.

The initial inhumanity of Salavin's relationship with his boss is
apparent in all the further encounters of Salavin as he gradually
becomes an outcast. The story of his wanderings through Paris in
search of a job, the terrible jobs offered him, his slow disintegration
as he lies on a couch in his mother's living room, unwashed, unshaven, pathetically human, are all well told and moving.

Yet Salavin, we feel, is a little unreal. His misery is rather artificially cultivated to serve Duhamel's intent, and is not too deeply felt.
His salvation will be assured at the end, for Duhamel must save his
unheroic hero for future adventures. Somewhat in the picaresque
manner, Salavin must explore other paths and give vent to other
aspirations. Duhamel has placed at Salavin's side two humble and
saintly women whose love will sustain Salavin in his adventures:
his mother and Marguerite, the woman he marries, a counterpart of

his mother. They embody Duhamel's gospel of salvation through love, the love he finds lacking in our impersonal society. A rather facile sentimentality—Salavin's perhaps, Duhamel's also one suspects —pervades the story, but Salavin is well launched on his adventures. Unfortunately these soon turn into a prolonged parable, the morality of which is spelled out in the last volume. How can Salavin, modern man, satisfy his human aspirations, enter into contact with his fellow men, feel he is one of a community of men, find happiness, transcend his pitiable and limited world? He successively tries friendship, saintliness and political action. But his failure is always foreseeable. His character remains unchanged. He is cut out for frustration.

At the same time Duhamel's project becomes clear. Not content to create in Salavin a living character and to tell the adventures of this character, he uses Salavin for his own ends. In the last volume Salavin is about to die, and we are rather glad of it. He has, he says, found himself, and he would now, he tells his patient wife Marguerite, know how to live. Salavin has found salvation in disinterested sacrifice. He has saved the life of a child and as a result dies—but dies regenerated, a new man.

Duhamel's message seems rather vague, pompous and too general to be inspiring. The mixture of humor and pathos with which he had enveloped his character disappears, but no powerful or tragic revelation takes its place. Obviously Salavin is struggling for his spiritual existence. Seen in this light, he is the Don Quixote of our times, a hero after all. Meanwhile the shiftless but touching outcast of *La Confession de minuit,* the excited, slightly ridiculous but very human enthusiast of *Deux Hommes* (Two Men) have disappeared. It is to them we must return to get the best Duhamel has to offer: a compassionate, humorous view of the narrow confines of a lower middle-class world that circumvents and conditions the aspirations of the man caught within its barriers.

The qualities that animate some parts of the Salavin cycle make all too rare an appearance in *La Chronique des Pasquiers.* Duhamel may have had in mind Zola's great cycle *Les Rougon Macquarts,* but he seems closer to Galsworthy. His account of the rise and develop-

ment of a lower middle-class family from the 1880's through World
War I has a certain documentary interest but is otherwise fairly
arid. This, perhaps, is because the Pasquier family is too close to the
Duhamel family to allow for the play of imagination, compassion
and humor that mark the best pages of Salavin. In the first volume
Duhamel presents the family, evoking the figure of M. Pasquier,
who is drawn from memories of his own fantastic father. We then
follow the Pasquier children as each one moves rather conveniently
into a niche in one of the different professions open to the middle
class: clerk, businessman, musician, actress, scientist; for the Pasquier
children are singularly gifted. They too, like Salavin, have a special
novelistic function. They realize the intellectual and artistic aspirations latent in a certain class of society. The scientist, Laurent, tells
the story and points the moral. As Laurent grows older, we begin
to find him something of a prig and feel only a perfunctory interest
in the family trials. The climax of the book, the war of 1914, is also
one of its weakest points. There Laurent, and Duhamel with him,
deep though their concern may be, deal largely in platitudes.

"Georges Duhamel or the Bourgeois Saved" is the apt title of a
critical essay on Duhamel. The bourgeois may or may not need salvation, but his salvation as a bourgeois is not a very potent theme
in a novel. Duhamel's faith in the values of honesty, affection, hard
work, art, selflessness and devotion to humanity is above reproach,
as is also his faith in the capacity of individuals to achieve ethical
and spiritual greatness. He wants to put his readers into contact with
those realities. But Duhamel's so-called realism moves out of the
realm of objectivity. Ethical judgments are given as facts and a personal moral view as an objective truth. It is actually a form of personal idealism that imposes its limitations on the novelist. It rejects,
a priori, whole segments of human experience, just as Duhamel rejects our mechanically conditioned age. Busily engaged now in putting old wine into old bottles, Duhamel becomes increasingly conventional. His books, after the Salavin cycle, lack that generous and
total involvement in life that characterizes the living novel. In a
sense Duhamel is the Anatole France of his generation, but a France

in whom earnestness has displaced whimsicality. The violence of the times proved too powerful for Duhamel to cope with.

Less sensitive than Duhamel, intellectually more robust, Jules Romains recovered more easily from the shock of the war. He was convinced that it would be the last one and that the optimistic vision of his philosophy of "unanimism" was still valid in the postwar world. "Unanimism," according to its creator, was not merely another label for a literary group. It was the key to the understanding of the modern world. It offered man a new psychology, a new ethics and a dynamic new code of action. "We were the children of the large modern city," he writes; "and I might say the first children it recognized and fully satisfied. The large city breathed around us and through us. Its streets were the lanes in which we took our walks. The deep courtyards of its buildings were the thickets in which we sensed the throb of life. The rumors of its densely populated sections, of its distant stations, the vibrations of its faraway suburbs opening out like a fan, were the constant music that accompanied our lives."

As a child of the "large city," Romains had always seen the individual, not as a separate unit, but as an integral part of a complex organism, be it a city street, the city itself or the entire nation. In general, however, he considered the twentieth century individual to be unconscious both of the existence of these organisms and of his place in them. Romains's function, it seemed to him, was to reveal to his contemporaries the exhilarating possibilities and all the poetry of such participation. In an anthropomorphic fashion, Romains thinks of human groups as monstrous, superhuman beings that centralize and concentrate all the power and emotions which they draw from their individual members. A city street, a funeral procession, an administration, an army, has a real physical individuality. As long as the human beings contained therein remain unconscious of this organism, they are barred from a whole zone of existence and confronted, moreover, by a strange blind Caliban that acts in unpredictable and disconcerting ways. The individual may then suddenly be carried away by something beyond himself. But the super-being can be detected, felt, and its latent powers can be directed. It can be penetrated by human consciousness and will. It then ceases to be a monster and becomes a conscious power with psychic unity, unanimity of will and purpose: it is a god, as Romains explains in his *Manuel de déification* (Manual of Deification), 1910, and so are the individuals who participate in its action. The artist and the statesman, more than other men, have the duty and the power to detect and efficiently direct the god.

Romains's view was formulated in the optimistic atmosphere of the early 1900's with absolute intellectual certainty. It has something of Whitman's enthusiasm—a broader "Song of the Open Road" for all humanity—and it reflects certain themes of sociologists like Durkheim. Still, it is essentially a personal, visionary interpretation of the dynamic world Romains felt was in the making. It is directed toward the future, deliberately "modern" in character and coupled with a somewhat naïve admiration for the technical achievements of modern man.

When Jules Romains's first novel appeared in 1911, it brought with it a breath of fresh air. *Mort de Quelqu'un* (*The Death of a Nobody*) is still considered by many as Romains's masterpiece. From the very start, Jules Romains boldly did away with the existing props of the novel: the conventional hero or heroine, the plot, the psychological analysis. *Mort de Quelqu'un* deals with death—a serious topic—seriously, but it has none of the overtones generally associated with the theme. Jacques Godard dies, and from his death there evolves a beneficial experience for a group of people. This throws warm new light upon his existence. He is "any man," a railroad employee, with almost no friends. He had been living a nondescript life in a nondescript boardinghouse. He is found dead, and the lodgers in the boardinghouse come to life. They join forces to offer him a wreath, a funeral. His parents come from the country, his colleagues from the railroad. They all set out in a funeral procession. The procession makes its way through the city streets. Traffic stops to let it pass.

The policeman waves it on; men take off their hats. An unknown young man joins the group, and Godard is buried.

That is the whole story. Its originality is directly connected with Romains's unanimistic theme. Godard may be just anybody, but his life is prolonged outside himself in all the people with whom he was in touch. The invisible extensions of Godard's being become visible in the funeral ritual, wherein Godard's expansion in time and space is manifest. Godard is part of the human *unanime*. On an outer boulevard in Paris the young man who had joined the procession thinks of Godard's funeral. "Traveling out toward him from an invisible center" come "beneficial waves," a living force emanating from the millions of human beings concentrated in Paris. "If I died now," he thinks, "I feel sure I would not disappear. I would become part of a great soul that does not die." That soul is not cosmic, nor divine in essence. It is the collective soul of the community of men made visible in a city like Paris. When considered in this light, Godard's death is not a sad event.

Mort de Quelqu'un was rapidly followed by a second, no less successful work, *Les Copains* (The Pals), 1913. *Les Copains* is light and gay, but here again Romains's theory successfully carries the novel beyond triviality. Romains tells the story of the spectacular escapades of a small group of young men who set out to awaken the collective consciousness of two small provincial towns, Ambère and Issoire. The action of the book, apart from the amusing youthful pranks that Romains invented, is contained in its refreshing description of the bonds of friendship that hold the group together. The group is an *unanime*, strong in affection, good humor and freedom. These short, unpretentious but successful novels were followed by more ambitious experiments.

In *Psyché*, 1922-1929, a trilogy, Romains uses the Psyche myth but transforms it by systematically exploiting the psychological implications of unanimism. Lucienne and Pierre Febvre meet and marry, thus forming that closely knit *unanime*, a couple. Because they are a couple, certain powers are available to them which they would not possess as individuals. They can thus transcend the laws of time and space by which human beings are normally bound. Although Pierre, a naval officer, is miles away on the ocean, Lucienne, by the concentrated power of her will, can join him and become visible to him in certain privileged moments.

Pierre's methodical account of this experience shows the particular form of Romains's imagination and certain of his techniques as a novelist. Like any writer of mystery science fiction, he turns a plausible hypothesis into a fact by building a fictional world that will corroborate it—a rather dangerous procedure when, later on, he takes it upon himself to write a fictional history of his time. *Psyché* starts with a realistic, carefully detailed description of a provincial setting, and then, little by little, although never departing from the same matter-of-fact and meticulous use of detail, carries us, rather pedantically, into the fantastic world of Lucienne. Romains's effort to give his abstract concept material content and logical coherence finally tires the reader, who is never deeply touched by so artificial a mechanism.

With *Les Hommes de bonne volonté* (*Men of Good Will*) Jules Romains courageously tackled the job of writing the great unanimistic novel of his time. Instead of describing the adventures of fictional individuals, he set out to describe the adventures of a collectivity, France. And it was no doubt true that the main adventures lived by individual Frenchmen in the early twentieth century were collective adventures. Jules Romains's approach was sound.

From his youth, Romains had been the poet of a powerful god, the city of Paris: Paris whose life goes far back into the past; Paris moving, flowing, changing, with its great body sprawled out for all to see; Paris, radiating an immense energy felt over a large portion of the globe. Paris is at the center of *Les Hommes de bonne volonté*. The quarter of a century Romains chose to portray in his novel stretches between 1908 and 1933. During those years in Romains's novel, Paris lives an adventure of its own, animated by "the harsh genius of the twentieth century," the "genius" of the "new men" with their vast industries, their machines and audacious enterprises. In this age, according to Romains, a new Eros also was born, "a lucid Eros," manifest in Paris. At regular intervals in his novel, Romains paints brilliant tableaux of the city, in 1908, 1918, 1922, 1928 and 1933. Powerful, accurate, richly detailed, they contain the various stages of an epic of modern Paris. Through the meditative and lyrical Jallez, a writer and one of his main characters, Romains also describes the poetic life of Paris, its affective life rich in signs, in "lost cries," related to the universal psyche.

The collective life of Paris contains many individual destinies. Romains describes the various "secret lines" that orient the individuals living in Paris: the line of business, the line of work, the line of pleasure, the line of thought, the line of eroticism. Through the activities of various characters, Romains presents the birth of new collective forces such as the proletariat, the persistence of other, declining forces, and their struggle as they seek some form of equilibrium. Jerphanion, the friend of Jallez and the most important character in the novel, stands one day on the roof of l'Ecole Normale and wonders what gigantic force would move, as one mass, the huge body of Paris. The "Men of Good Will" in the novel are there in search of the right lever with which to move, not only Paris, but France and beyond France, Europe.

The first volume of the series sets the stage for all the others. Romains introduces a number of individuals whose activities and thoughts on one specific day, October 6, 1908, are conveyed in a set of discontinuous tableaux juxtaposed so as to give an impression of simultaneity. There is no merging of themes as in Joyce or Dos Passos. The different individuals described are used somewhat artificially to represent the different strata of Paris society, the various groups that go into its making, its human geography.

Romains then takes us through the years that lead to the war of 1914, showing the awakening of the working class *unanime,* the conflicts it creates in older groups. As the danger of war becomes more apparent, a few earnest and deeply concerned men strive to act in some way upon the collectivity in order to avert the coming disaster. These are the Men of Good Will. Volumes XV and XVI, *Prélude à Verdun (The Prelude)* and *Verdun (The Battle),* are the pivotal volumes, the best known, too. Here, especially in the description of the long, inhuman resistance at Verdun, Romains convincingly describes the merging of the individual into the collectivity. The volumes that follow develop the theme of uncertainty that reaches its climax in the opening pages of Volume XIX. Romains describes the crowd strolling in the Champs Elysées in 1922. Where are they going? where? where? The small group of Men of Good Will anxiously scrutinizes the situation. Now they no longer think in terms of France: Beyond France lies Europe. From the East comes the reflection of a great light, a dawn perhaps, or perhaps a vast destructive fire—the Russian revolution. "We live in a world where there is no refuge for anybody," says Sampeyre, one of the purest of the Men of Good Will. Insecurity and confusion are the keynotes to a world that has lost its direction.

The last volumes of *Les Hommes de bonne volonté* are deeply pessimistic. They tell the tale of failure: parliamentary failure, the failure of the League of Nations. They analyze the appearance of a new danger in the form of organized gangs, united only in order to seize power for their own profit and ready to use any means to this end. In the closing chapter of the novel, Romains presents "Europe in 1933," Europe the home of the white man, who after struggling for more than a century toward the realization of two ideals, the ideal of social justice and that of European unity, now sees them wrecked on the reefs of the postwar world. Paris in its turn "moves into the night," following the rest of Europe, which "had itself been moving backwards into darkness." The symbol is clear.

One wonders, despite the author's assertions to the contrary, whether the same pessimism animated the original conception of the novel and how far the end, less convincing than the beginning, was affected by the events of 1940. In the preface written in 1932, Romains warned his readers that the novel was centered around the "ideal" line of a collective development. Beneath the apparent chaos of the book, the reader would eventually discern a direction, an orientation at least. "Everything takes place as though the collec-

tivity had spasmodically wanted to advance." The Men of Good
Will, Romains added, would also be recognized.

In 1946, through a note addressed to the reader at the end of his
novel, Jules Romains justifies the place given in his work to "political and social preoccupations," since "political and social anguish
has been our daily fare." There is no sign of anguish in the 1932
preface, but rather a disarming satisfaction with the obvious truth
the author intends to reveal, a truth conveyed in the title itself,
which as Jules Romains points out refers to the Biblical blessing addressed to Men of Good Will, ". . . on earth peace." It would
seem that the historical events that followed 1932, the date at which
Les Hommes de bonne volonté was entirely planned and conceived,
failed to concord with the vision Romains then held of the future,
the immediate future. The collective "super-being" Europe did not
follow the "ideal" line he had projected.

In *Comparutions* (*Offered in Evidence*), the twenty-fourth volume of the series, published in 1944, Jerphanion says: "My entire
life cannot be a battle against despair. . . . If I am not fairly sure
that human will, a good and reasonable will, is capable of influenc-
ing the destiny of humanity and, more or less, of orienting history . . . , I shall be forced to admit that I based my life on an
error. I am a priest who at forty discovers that his god does not
exist." In the light of the preface of *Les Hommes de bonne volonté*,
and many essays and articles as well, one has every reason to believe
that Romains's vision was deeply affected by the war of 1940.
Jerphanion's discouragement sounds like a personal confession, and
his friends, who have such an important role in the novel, are left
stranded in the last volumes like Romains himself.

As the novel comes to an end, Romains seems to waver between
two conflicting conceptions of man's fate in the modern world.
When he started the novel, Romains believed that within a community the best individuals could reach a dynamic equilibrium by
consciously acting in harmony with the vital tendencies of the group
and that these tendencies would, if rightly understood, serve the forward march of humanity. At the end of the novel, Romains's Men

of Good Will are rather like a group of shipwrecked people on a raft in a stormy sea. Europe is sinking slowly into the night. Perhaps, they think, man is after all only the toy of blind forces, and any hope to the contrary is absurd. But Romains cannot totally abandon his role as prophet of a "brave new world." "And yet," says Jallez as the book ends, "what a wonderful place our modern world would be if . . ." If? Romains does not tell us what.

The novel suffers from this change in mood, since its main originality and interest lay in Romains's personal vision, an optimistic vision of the movement of history as embodied in the *unanime,* France. Interesting and original as a personal vision, it was too schematic, too cerebral, too oblivious of the complexities of history, to sustain Romains's ambitious projects. The same simplifications and gratuitous systematizations dull his perceptiveness and efficacity as a writer.

One cannot attempt here to give more than a quick evaluation of the complex world of *Les Hommes de bonne volonté,* for it sets in motion "more than a thousand characters" over a period of a quarter of a century. Romains's theories, coupled with his ambition to "give as exact a picture of our time as the present resources of literary art allow," led him to set up a rather abstract group of "representative" human beings who belong to the various strata of modern society. Many represent these strata in their "becoming." Side by side are an artisan of the old type and a modern factory worker, old-time politicians and modern politicians. The same holds true in the realms of business, erotism, crime, research and literature. Delegated by the author to illustrate the fundamental characteristics of contemporary society, they are necessarily schematic. Even Jerphanion and Jallez, the most carefully developed and the most human of them all, do not reach full individual stature. All these characters seem to move like chessmen over the board according to the needs of the author. They are all terribly talkative; they think and even daydream discursively. One cannot help being struck by the insignificance of the actions to which they apply their incredible logic. No gesture seems to come to them spontaneously.

This universal trait, especially when applied to their excursions into the rather tiresome world of the "modern Eros," gives them the mechanical aspect that is at the root of Romains's particular form of humor.

Romains's characters are on the whole free from metaphysical anguish and sexual inhibitions. In every realm, from crime to artistic creation, they tend to work with the precision of an intelligent and high-powered machine. This effect is further accentuated by Romains's technique of composition. He presents his characters in short, juxtaposed scenes that lead to powerful syntheses in which all separate lives are merged, as though each were brought there by an assembly line. It is not, however, the individual that interests Romains but his participation in a larger sustaining group. Unfortunately, one rarely feels the link between the separate worlds of his individual and rather insignificant characters and the super-world of the group. In spite of the carefully marked chronological points of reference, Romains fails to give us the sense of a flux of time or to show the destiny of the whole through the individual.

Les Hommes de bonne volonté partially fails as a novel in the same way that Romains's conception of man's fate fails to meet the test of history. His conception of individual existence, like his conception of history, raises to the status of an abstract system what was at best an excellent novelistic point of view. This point of view is rich in such literary possibilities as inventiveness and humor and gives Romains's farces and less ambitious novels their special savor. But it is unable to sustain his more ambitious project of showing how modern man moves, thinks, feels and acts, still less of revealing "the shape of things to come."

Stripped of its literary trimmings, of its very individual and rather naïve unanimistic mythology, Romains's faith in the future reflects the less articulate faith of many of his contemporaries. It shows how strongly the conception of human progress was rooted in the best minds, how deeply, therefore, they felt the shock of the upheavals they witnessed, of a crisis all the more intense because it had been slow to get under way. Rather than a novel *about* a time, as it was intended to be, *Les Hommes de bonne volonté* is, in this indirect way, a document *of* the time.

Romains and Duhamel, in different ways, were both victims of early twentieth century optimism, attuned to the 1910's rather than to the 1930's, the period to which they attempted to serve as guides. It was consequently not to them the younger generation was to turn for guidance, either in the realm of thought or in the realm of esthetics.

Roger Martin du Gard: "The Corneille of the Bourgeois Novel"

Jean Barois (1913), the first of Martin du Gard's works to attract attention, carries on its title page a quotation from a contemporary, Suarès: "A sick conscience, such is the theater of the modern fatality." All Martin du Gard's main characters are victims of this sickness. According to their creator, it is caused by the simultaneous disappearance of the two beliefs that had sustained Occidental civilization until the end of the nineteenth century: the Christian faith, and faith in the progressive march of humanity toward perfection. Martin du Gard's two novels and his great novel cycle are an attempt to investigate the individual and social consequences of this moral drama, as it is played out from the early years of the century until the end of World War I. The theme is already present in the almost untranslatable title of his first novel, *Devenir!*—the process of becoming, how to become. What is the twentieth century becoming as it takes shape in time and in the consciousness of the people who are *of it,* not merely "engaged" in it as if it were a phenomenon that could be separated from them?

Martin du Gard's works, like Jules Romains's novel cycle, are set in a definite historical period. *Devenir!* belongs only vaguely to the first years of the twentieth century, but *Jean Barois* is painstakingly dated. It starts in 1878 and goes on to give a careful account of the crisis created by the Dreyfus case. *Les Thibaults* (1922-1940), Martin du Gard's most important work, begins in 1905 and ends on November 18, 1918, a week after the armistice. The milieu described is the solidly established French bourgeoisie, the class which over the centuries furnished the spiritual and political leaders of France. This is the milieu that best reflects the "sick conscience" of thinking Europe and to which Martin du Gard himself belongs.

The first and least interesting of Martin du Gard's characters is André Mazerelles, the hero of *Devenir!,* who is a living example of the sickness that accompanies the loss of the Christian faith. There is no crisis in André Mazerelles's life. The only son of a well-to-do bourgeois family, André is brought up according to rituals that no one questions, the rituals of the Catholic religion among others. His life has an outer form and continuity uncorroborated by any inner reality. André Mazerelles simply drifts away from Catholicism, yet he keeps many of the reflexes of a practicing Catholic: "Though he had lost his faith, he still carried within him intermittent Catholic 'selves' that were no longer coordinated but that still presided over some of his thoughts and many of his acts; and his life, oriented by the impetus of a dead faith, rested intact on a meaningless foundation." Though he vaguely attempts to "become" someone, his inner uncertainty foils all his endeavors. A rather pale precursor of Camus's Stranger, he has no vital contact with reality.

Jean Barois, the hero of Martin du Gard's second novel, is a strange figure whose life is a succession of crises, one of which coincides with a national crisis, the Dreyfus case. Barois too lives in a state of intellectual schizophrenia, but more lucidly and violently than André Mazerelles. His tragedy is inherent in a conflict that involves his whole generation. He carries within him two incompatible beings: the modern scientist and the Christian idealist fashioned by centuries of mysticism. Barois's scientific understanding of the laws that govern human life and the subconscious aspirations that condition his affective life cannot coexist.

Outwardly, Barois's life is a success. Born in 1886, the son of a doctor, Barois himself becomes a doctor and an eminent scientist. He abandons Catholicism and becomes a freethinker, the center of a small group of energetic men devoted to the humanitarian task of promoting social and moral progress, who battle successfully on the side of Dreyfus in the Dreyfus case. In his forties, Barois is a vigorous, disinterested and successful man, one of the intellectual leaders of France. He clearly states what seems to him the crucial problem of the time. The Catholic religion keeps alive a conception of the human being that science invalidates; it therefore hampers the adaptation of modern man and society to present conditions of living and has produced a civilization marked by uncertainty, fear and a costly, perhaps fatal, inability to face the future. "Confronted by an indifferent nature that surpasses him," man will carry his investigations further and further into the unknown and gain new, fantastic powers; but he must abandon his notion of a total and revealed truth, his belief in the individual destiny of the soul and the code of ethics based on these beliefs. He must forge a new human ethics based on a scientific study of psychology and on the needs of the community of men. So thinks Jean Barois when, in the full glow of his forties, he rather surprisingly formulates his intellectual credo as a last testament that is to be read at his death, whatever his actions in his later years.

The stage, somewhat obviously, is now set for the dénouement. The Christian Jean Barois in turn displaces the scientist. Barois cannot face illness and death without the consolation offered by the Christian religion. Martin du Gard does not describe a sudden loss of faith, followed by a sudden conversion. Barois's slow detachment from the Church and his return to it are typical of the slow spiritual movement of a whole generation. Around Barois, Martin du Gard groups a gallery of characters who are all more or less in the throes of the same experience, for it is at the root of the unrest of their time. In his old age Barois meets with bewilderment the next generation. Indifferent to the conflict his own generation embodied, they are either Catholics by deliberate choice, for the sake of convenience, or agnostics, quite naturally detached from the Church, who feel no mental torment. Weaker than Barois, they fail even to see that there is a conflict. The Christian faith, be it in one group or the other, is no longer a living force: It is an empty social form.

With *Les Thibaults,* Martin du Gard moves into the period of France's next great crisis, the period of World War I. The Thibault family around whom the novel is built are the representatives of a Catholic bourgeois dynasty, securely entrenched socially, morally and economically, which, by alliance with the Church, has taken out a solid insurance on eternity. The father, Oscar Thibault, has disposed of the problems of man's fate. He is merely concerned with the problems of man's conduct, and he believes that at no time should man deviate from the established social pattern. Man, according to him, is naturally evil and should be forced into the paths of Christian and social virtue by stern outer and inner disciplines. M. Thibault fulfills all his obligations as a member of a certain social order—at least insofar as he understands them. At school, his younger son Jacques meets the Fontanins, a Protestant family. Mme Fontanin's faith in God is coupled with an unshakeable belief in the essential goodness of human nature, and therefore in the values of freedom of choice and decision. Different as their attitudes may be, both M. Thibault and Mme de Fontanin live and think within the given Christian and social framework.

Against this background, Martin du Gard describes the younger generation as it grows out of adolescence: Antoine and Jacques, the two Thibault boys; a girl, the niece of M. Thibault's housekeeper; Daniel and Jenny de Fontanin. The novel opens with the charming and moving story, quite traditionally told, of an adolescent crisis involving the fourteen-year-old Jacques and his friend Daniel. In the next few volumes Martin du Gard seems intent merely on following the individual paths of these clearly differentiated and appealing characters. Antoine becomes a doctor; Jacques, always a rebel, leaves home and finally begins to write; Daniel becomes an artist. The terrible illness and death of the father, Oscar Thibault, brings the first part of the novel to its climax. With him a species disappears, and an era comes to an end.

When the next volume opens, the Thibaults and the Fontanins are carried away in a collective adventure that almost annihilates them and for which they are unprepared. In reality, war merely accelerates a process latent in their development. The first six parts of the novel show how, within the bourgeois fortress itself, the mental and moral structures set up for the intellectual comfort and perpetuation of the bourgeoisie have quietly crumbled. Before the war began, Antoine and Jacques, each in his own way, had spent the financial heritage amassed in two centuries of prudent management. The Fontanin children, meanwhile, live a most precarious financial existence because of the irresponsibility of their father, Jérôme. They are, in fact, moving away from the traditions of the past.

Antoine Thibault is an able doctor, a specialist satisfied to remain within the limits of his profession. At thirty, he is a typical representative of the reliable, competent scientist: open-minded but cautious as regards ideas; tolerant through indifference; liberal in his judgments of men. His scientific training has taught him to formulate problems only in carefully limited ways. His profession has familiarized him with human suffering and death, which he considers objectively. He practices no religion, nor does he feel the need of any faith. His brother Jacques is an adolescent in revolt against his father's rigid formalism. He is in search of a faith, a cause, and finds it in political action. He rejects the social order in which he has been reared. Unlike Antoine, he cannot accept as an inevitable fact the injustice and suffering of the human lot. He is attracted by the still uncertain doctrines of international socialism that seem to offer a means of serving humanity disinterestedly.

Daniel de Fontanin is a successful artist and a charming dilettante. He is not concerned with any problems; he is a happy-go-lucky sensualist whose moral code is drawn from the more superficial aspects of Gide's *Les Nourritures terrestres*. His sister Jenny, a tense young woman, moves in an inner world of her own. Not one of the four young people has any religious belief; nor have they retained the certainty passed on to them by their parents concerning moral values and rules of conduct. All four are divorced from the life of the community to which they belong and are even unconscious that it exists. Jacques is the only one who senses this lack, but his dissatisfaction and revolt carry him outside the social organism of which he is a part into the artificial and ineffectual group of social revolutionaries in Geneva. What all four young people will learn by violent experience is that the very existence of their individual worlds depends on the continued existence of a community that is in the process of being shattered. The nineteenth century atmosphere of *Les Thibaults* ends with the three-volume part entitled *Eté 1914 (Summer 1914)*.

The appearance of violent collective disturbances in the lives of the young Thibaults and Fontanins is disquieting. *Eté 1914* coldly presents a succession of factual, historical events. It reads like a "tale told by an idiot." War bears down upon Europe like a natural cataclysm, flicking aside all human prevision, logic and habitual activity. When it is over, it has destroyed the three young men: Daniel has lost his creative power; Jacques dies a fearful death at the outset of the war; Antoine, gassed, dies slowly as the war comes to an end. All that is left of the two families is the child of Jacques and Jenny, Jean-Paul. Oscar Thibault's only heir is an illegitimate grandson whose father died an outlaw and whose mother is determined he will be brought up in the cult of his father's ideas.

The last volumes of the Thibault cycle is the journal written by Antoine as he watches himself die in a military hospital. Antoine, Gide tells us, is very dear to Martin du Gard's heart. To a certain extent the young man gives us a clue to his creator's point of view.

Death for Antoine is natural disintegration, and beyond it there is nothing, no survival. His medical experience has taught him that this truth cannot be accepted by most human beings. As a doctor, he must continually lie to his patients about the imminence of death. The Christian ritual, he thinks, is one of many formulas that attempt to humanize death and to make it acceptable. Simultaneously, it rescues life from its essential senselessness by giving death a meaning. Like his father—whose death, a private death, is the subject of the entire sixth volume of the cycle—Antoine slowly moves from life into death, but unlike his father, he approaches death with a sort of indifferent lucidity. His experience of the war, the death of Jacques, his own fate, create in Antoine a feeling of human solidarity he did not have as a young and prosperous doctor. He now believes in the emergence, after the war, of a better society organized according to more human principles of peace and justice, the society heralded by Woodrow Wilson's League of Nations. In contrast with Romains's exaggerated confidence in the future, given as a historical prediction by the author, this illusory hope, is framed by a character within the novel itself.

Antoine sees clearly that the destiny of the individual is historically conditioned and that he must apply his will not only to the autodetermination of his life but also to the "becoming" of all men and, more immediately, of the community to which he belongs. He therefore gives meaning to his own pitiful destiny; along with the millions of other men caught in the war, he will have helped bring about a new era, the new era his brother Jacques had talked about so often.

As Antoine approaches death, these preoccupations disappear. November 11, 1918, is, for Antoine, merely a day of great physical suffering, a day when his decision to commit suicide becomes clear. Antoine's suicide is not due to revolt or despair. He knows that death is inevitable, and he wants to avoid the degradation and pain of a long-drawn-out agony. The last word in Antoine's diary is "Jean-Paul." Therefore, in the very last analysis, Antoine instinctively believes in a sort of survival through Jean-Paul, in a continuation that may compensate for the sterility of his own life. He has inherited his father's faith in the destiny of the Thibaults. Jean-Paul, ironically, would be twenty-five in 1940, the year in which the last volume was published. The irony is conscious. Martin du Gard implies that Antoine's hope is unsubstantiated by any fact. It is a tenacious belief in life, perpetually negated by the unpredictable fate meted out to human beings; a form of stubborn human persistence.

Although accurately and almost too meticulously documented as it moves to a climax in the three massive volumes of *Eté 1914, Les*

Thibaults is not a historical novel. It would seem that for Martin du Gard the significance of a period of social crisis lies not in any fundamental change in man's fate but in a change in man's understanding of his fate. What characterizes the society Martin du Gard evokes is the rapid change in its intellectual horizon. The change was accomplished within the lifetime of two generations and culminated at the time of World War I.

It is their continuing search for values, in itself an act of faith, that makes Martin du Gard's characters so human and endearing. Their search recalls the attitudes of Corneille's characters, though these, to be sure, are less deeply baffled. But the very stubbornness and stoicism with which Antoine and Jacques find their human way in an inhuman situation, drawing their values and their dignity only from themselves, is reminiscent of their seventeenth century predecessors.

Martin du Gard does not sacrifice the fundamental private experiences to which all human beings are subject, and all his characters are strong and convincing. Jacques's love for Jenny, Antoine's career as a doctor, his liaison, Oscar Thibault's battle with death, are especially moving. Behind this objectivity lies a warm imagination, an understanding of life fashioned by long meditation on the history of ideas as it evolves in each generation. Like Duhamel in *La Chronique des Pasquiers,* Martin du Gard has set his characters in the period leading up to the first world war. He goes more deeply into the vital changes of his time, however, and measures their consequences, not, as does Duhamel, in terms of right and wrong, but in terms of bafflement, strife and suffering. Like Jules Romains, he studies the interrelation of individual lives and historical events such as the Dreyfus case and World War I, but he does not inject a personal myth into his understanding of history. He is concerned with the problems the individual finds in his existence at a particular historical period. He is not interested in the collectivity as such.

Strictly objective in its form, meticulously composed according to traditional techniques, *Les Thibaults* is an achievement of stature.

And, within its limits, it is a far more probing document on the first years of the twentieth century than the novels of either Duhamel or Romains.

Louis Aragon's "Real World"

Born in 1897, Louis Aragon did not reach maturity until the end of the war of 1914. His experience was of its aftermath—the crucial events of the twenties. The consolidation of the Russian Bolsheviks, the rise of Fascism, the first signs of Nazism and the roots of the depression all developed in his formative years. As a result, Aragon became a militant disciple in the three principal "isms" of that decade. He was a dadaist, then a surrealist, and became a Marxist in 1930, promptly breaking with his surrealist friends.

In 1935 a manifesto entitled *Pour un réalisme socialiste* (In Favor of a Socialist Realism) explained that Aragon had abandoned poetry for the novel, a form of novel based upon observation of "the real world." "The real world," in obvious contrast to the surrealist world, was the over-all title Aragon chose for a series of novels, four of which appeared in quick succession: *Les Cloches de Bâle* (*The Bells of Basel*), 1934, *Les Beaux Quartiers* (*Residential Quarter*), 1936, *Les Voyageurs de l'impériale* (*The Century Was Young*), 1942, and *Aurélien*, 1944. Aragon's first stories, like the novels of Duhamel, Romains and Martin du Gard, are set in the period stretching between 1880 and the first world war. *Aurélien* takes place in the two decades between the World War I and World War II. A long novel, *Les Communistes*, the first installments of which were published in the Communist paper *L'Humanité* in 1949, covers the period of war and occupation that began in 1939.

Aragon, in his discovery of this "real world," somewhat resembles a pagan convert to Christianity who berates the pagan world to which he previously belonged. Nevertheless, the Marxist in Aragon has never altogether killed either the impertinent dadaist or the audacious surrealist who looks upon the world with new eyes. To these two discarded selves Aragon owes much of his literary success.

The basic pattern of his novels is simple. Aragon contrasts the corrupt bourgeois world and its efforts to maintain its *status quo* with the sane and honest proletariat struggling to establish a human order in the amoral bourgeois jungle. The history of our time quite naturally appears to Aragon as essentially the history of a class struggle. In his first four, and best, novels, the emphasis is on the jungle that Aragon, a bourgeois himself, knows all too well. His novels are one-man offensives launched against what is by his decree a socially unjust warmongering society that alienates men from their real human destiny. They give full scope to the verbal *condottiere* in him.

Aragon's fictional universe is thus divided into two simple zones somewhat similar to the hell and paradise of the Middle Ages, except that the line of demarcation irrevocably drawn for each individual by the circumstances of birth is less easily crossed. One is the bourgeois domain, the other the domain of the working class. Aragon's fictional chronicle is based on chance exchanges between the two, but, concentrating on the bourgeois domain, he merely opens sudden vistas on a working-class existence that the bourgeois habitually ignore. When they cannot ignore it, they attempt to destroy it. In *Les Communistes* the working class is the center of interest, "the immense working-class world, which stretches beyond all frontiers and above which all social comedies are played."

The bourgeois world in Aragon's novels is essentially venal. Everything in it is bought, sold or bartered—in particular the women, one of its main luxury products. The quick acquisition of money is the main concern of its members. This whole system is pictured as a vast gambling establishment connected with as vast an enterprise in prostitution. At the top are the tycoons, the Wisners, the Quesnels and their satellites—politicians, army and police officers, hangers-on, big and small, exploiters of the world at large. Allied to these are the "passengers riding on top of the bus," *Les Voyageurs de l'impériale,* as Aragon entitled one of his novels—the lower middle class, "fellow travelers" of the capitalist world. Women are the great victims of the system. Bereft of any other means of livelihood, they must seduce, win and hold men, and as age diminishes their powers of attraction, their security is threatened. When, through a man, they control money, they are also exploited. Quesnel, an aging millionaire, buys a young woman Carola; an ambitious and unscrupulous young man, Barbentane, will then exploit Carola's love to his own advantage.

Out of this hell, however, some characters wander in search of salvation. *Les Voyageurs de l'impériale* tells the story of the revolt of an honest middle-class professor, Mercadier, who one day disappears. His attempted liberation fails miserably. He squanders away his life and ends up in wretched mediocrity, the prey of a horrible brothel owner. Aurélien, the most pleasant of Aragon's bourgeois heroes, tries another path of escape. Young, unmarried, sensitive and handsome, with enough money to live on, he emerges from the first world war with no particular ambition. He is a "stranger" in society and views the world around him as if it were a moving picture. All the unused forces of his imagination crystallize around a woman, largely because of the name she bears, Bérénice, a name rich in literary associations. He lives in a kind of daydream, the dream of an impossible, great love which he believes to be the mark of an exceptional destiny. His love for Bérénice comes to nothing. Mercadier and Aurélien, for Aragon, are clearly typical bourgeois "escapists," unable to come to terms with reality.

There is a third way out of the bourgeois prison, and in each of Aragon's first three novels some one character, the hero, finds that way. In *Les Cloches de Bâle,* Catherine Sismondi makes a slow and difficult escape into the working-class milieu. She first becomes aware of its existence when witnessing a strike, and after losing her way among the anarchists, she is introduced into this milieu by a taxi driver, Victor, who saves her from suicide. Here people work for their living, and some, like Victor, are beginning to organize their fellow workers for a heroic struggle in defense of the vital rights of millions. In *Les Beaux Quartiers,* Armand Barbentane, in revolt against the hypocrisy of his milieu and abandoned by his elder brother, is thrown into the world of the proletariat by hunger and misery. He eventually reaches his full stature as a Communist leader in *Les Communistes*. As Pierre Mercadier dies his ignoble death in *Les Voyageurs de l'impériale,* his son, in the trenches, swears that men must find a more effective way than his father's to do away with the ills of a society that has led to such a catastrophe. Young Mercadier too will find salvation in Communism.

In all these novels the working classes are viewed by the bourgeoisie from the outside and felt as a menace; against the terrorism of the anarchists, against the growing strength of the organized unions, the bourgeois classes join hands. But as the reader, following in the footsteps of Catherine, Armand, or even Aurélien, discovers the proletarian world, he is clearly made to understand that this is the "real world," because, unlike the bourgeois world, it is sustained by a generous human ideal. It reintegrates the individual into the community.

Aragon's worker is united to his fellow workers by their common struggle against misery and by the history of the working class, with its heroes, its martyrs and its rituals that are not those of the bourgeoisie. He is united to his wife by simple bonds of love, class loyalty and common hardship bravely borne. Among the workers there is a knighthood: the Communist party. Adherence to the Communist party gives the worker an active feeling of responsibility and of faith in the future. Aragon's Communists are saints. A Communist in his novels always has the right instincts and is never wrong. Whatever the professed "realism" of this worker's world, Aragon, a bourgeois himself, becomes extravagantly lyrical whenever he enters its sphere. His worker has something in common with the "good savage" of the eighteenth century. He is strong, sane, inarticulate and naïve, but canny, with laughing, childlike eyes and an inexhaustible store of common sense.

Aragon's first novels are directed to the bourgeoisie—his readers— more than to the proletariat. In *Les Communistes* he is addressing the proletariat, to whose existing legend he is adding a new page.

The fictional chronicle he writes is shamelessly partial and its fictional value almost nil. And yet, as is not very apparent in *Les Communistes,* Aragon is a born novelist. He knows how to tell an ample, living story, full of color and movement; he is able to sustain unusual and strongly differentiated characterizations; his satire is often pungent. In addition, a holdover perhaps from his surrealist years, he has a fertile imagination that often carries him into the realm of pure fantasy. One can detect in Aragon a poet whose senses are alive to form and color, in particular to the charm of feminine beauty and fashion. One can detect the romantic writer of melodrama—and melodrama can make exciting reading. Unfortunately all these potentialities are hampered by Aragon's oversimplified Marxist dogma. He has an answer to all the questions of his time. This allows him to order his novels unhesitatingly according to a consistent point of view. But his novels lose in depth and honesty what they gain in certainty. As far as Aragon is concerned, the point of view in itself justifies the existence of his novels; the result cannot be expected to sustain the interest of the impartial reader who wants to read a novel for the novel's sake, not as a document.

In artistic terms, Aragon pays the price for his deliberate choice of point of view. A certain eloquent righteousness and maudlin sentiment, which are also typical of Aragon himself, creep into the didactic pages of his novels and disturb the pleasure the reader felt on becoming acquainted with the childhood of Pierre Mercadier's son, Pascal, for example, or with the Paris of the twenties that Aurélien, like Aragon, knew so well. We are willing to be shocked by the bad Wisners, Quesnels and Barbentanes and to take sides against them in favor of their victims, just as we do when reading Dickens. Nonetheless, we are ready to throw the book aside when the author solemnly calls upon us to accept his fictional world as an authentic picture of society. For social realism in the novel, it is better to turn to Aragon's near contemporary and intellectual antithesis, Marcel Aymé.

Marcel Aymé: Epilogue

A distinguishing characteristic of Marcel Aymé, when set beside other contemporary novelists in France, is the fact that he neither comes from nor has ever really been assimilated to the Paris bourgeoisie. Throughout his literary career he has remained an unreconstructed Jura peasant. The Paris whose mystery and excitement cast such a spell over Duhamel, Romains and Aragon, whose streets and cafés are so familiar a part of the Sartrian novel, has never stimulated his imagination—although many of his novels and short stories are situated there. Nor has he been attracted by any of the literary or ideological cults that have raged among the Paris intellectuals. He is not, on the whole, interested in ideas of any sort. He is interested in people, and in relatively simple types of people at that.

Like Duhamel and Romains, like Martin du Gard and the later Aragon, Aymé looks upon his characters as members of a social unit. Unlike his predecessors, however, Aymé has never attempted to fit these social units into the larger framework of contemporary history. He is most at home within the microcosm of the small provincial village, where peasants, animals and small-scale local powers achieve a healthy, if somewhat uninspiring, pattern of existence. This is the setting of his early novels and of his charming fairy stories for children, *Les Contes du chat perché* (*The Wonderful Farm*)— the adventures of two little peasant girls and their remarkable animal friends. When, as in his later novels, the scene removes to Paris, Aymé becomes suspicious; and when the scene is further complicated by political events, suspicion turns into downright misanthropy. Old-fashioned French individualist that he is, Aymé seems to be judging the complexities and corruptions of contemporary political society in terms of the simplicity and balance of tiny peasant communities.

This point of view, however limited in scope, can be extremely refreshing, as is already apparent in Aymé's first successful novel, *La Jument verte* (*The Green Mare*), 1933. This novel, which is concerned with the peasants of the Jura region where Aymé himself was born, might have been considered merely a humorous variant on the "regional novel" were it not for the astonishing presence of the green mare, an animal gifted with special insight into the sexual behavior of its owners, and whose comments recur at frequent intervals during the course of the novel. This equine Kinsey is, furthermore, distinctly attracted to the social sciences. Starting off from her restricted point of observation, she ultimately arrives at a complex and subtle systemization of the inter- and intra-family attractions and repulsions, religious convictions and political opinions of the inhabitants of the tiny village of Claquebue.

To begin with generalities, the mare informs us of a number of sexual taboos prevalent among the villagers at large. One is a belief, encouraged by the priest but typical of anticlerical as well as clerical factions, that continence is the secret of material success. This once established, the mare divides the population into families characterized by an unashamed, straightforward eroticism, who are anticlerical republicans, and families obsessed with hidden torments, scruples and hallucinations, who are church-going reactionaries.

Honoré Haudouin and his family are of the former variety; their neighbors, the Malorets, among whom unsavory incestuous practices are reputed to prevail, of the second. The long-standing hatred between the two is a consequence of their different sexual traditions. Honoré's brother, a socially ambitious veterinarian, provides an interesting variant on this general theme. Although consumed with suppressed desires and hence, on the face of it, an easy target for the local priest, he has, for reasons of personal advancement, sided with the anticlericals. His inner torments thus aggravated by the political impossibility of confession, he becomes something of a domestic monster, continually spying on his wife and children and finding erotic implications in the most commonplace events. The resulting antagonisms and rivalries—familial, religious and political—provide ample motivations for a plot culminating in the triumph of republican virility and the double discomfiture of the Malorets and the veterinarian brother. *La Jument verte* is a pure farce, but a farce shot through with a wealth of surprising insights into the mysterious, unspoken assumptions governing the collective life of Claquebue.

It is not difficult to see why this novel was, and still is, a best-seller in France. Aymé knows how to tell a story, to arouse our attention and curiosity in his very first sentence: "In the village of Claquebue there was born one day a green mare, not that bilious green that accompanies decrepitude in white-haired animals, but a pretty jade green." Aymé, moreover, is on extremely intimate terms with life, its material necessities, difficulties and pleasures. A man in full possession of his five senses, he, like his green mare, is gifted with a direct, almost physical flair for the elementary and generally unacknowledged motives of human behavior. He has a fertile and salty imagination. The supernatural, a frequent element in Aymé's early novels and his later stories, has none of the dreamlike, other-worldly qualities of the surrealists but is firmly planted in the terrestrial logic of everyday events. Finally, and most important, Aymé is a novelist who can make his reader laugh out loud.

These qualities—the functional plot, the concrete fantasy, a healthy taste for life and a highly developed sense of the ridiculous—are singularly lacking, if not deliberately suppressed, in the contemporary French novel. Aymé's sudden emergence in 1933 is thus something like a violent irruption of Sancho Panza upon a literary scene crowded with intellectuals, poets, prophets, and anguished rebels.

This does not mean that we can identify Aymé himself with the practical, earthy views of the peasants depicted in *La Jument verte*. His humor implies a certain degree of personal detachment. Still, we are fully aware, through the course of the novel, that Aymé and his mare stand firmly on the side of Honoré Haudouin and a straightforward republican virility. This position, which equates religious sentiment or intellectual complications of any kind with a sort of incapacity for life, is one-sided to the point of crudity. Aymé's indisputable crudities, in this novel and others, are an inseparable part of his sincere respect for life itself and for those who honestly and boldly come to grips with life. This attitude becomes more significant when he turns from the orderly routine of peasant existence under the Third Republic to the material and moral collapse of the French middle classes. The change of theme occurs at the time of the last war.

Two novels published in the early war years, although concerned with the Paris middle classes, are not too different from Aymé's earlier peasant manner: *Le Boeuf clandestin* (The Clandestine Beefsteak), 1939, the story of a respected vegetarian discovered by his daughter while privately consuming a juicy beefsteak; and *La Belle Image* (*The Second Face*), 1941, the story of a man who acquires a new and more handsome face. These novels, however, are somewhat strained as compared to the rich abandon of *La Jument verte*. One feels that Aymé has had difficulty in stretching his original plot mechanism out to the proportions of a novel. Later, at any rate, he tends to use the short story form for ingenious inventions of this kind. His novel, meanwhile, becomes increasingly independent of plot and of supernatural or farcical suppositions.

The special feature of the Aymé short story, as developed in collections such as *Le Passe-Muraille* (The Man Who Walked Through a Wall), 1943, *Le Vin de Paris* (Paris Wine), 1947, and *En Arrière* (Going Backwards), 1950, lies in a skillful combination of factual impossibility and convincing detail. The story is generally set in motion by some fantastic invention of Aymé's imagination: for example, a law rationing the monthly existence of the population in proportion to its social utility; or a law instituting a twenty-four-month year which, to the delight of those who are on the wrong side of forty and the chagrin of those in their teens and twenties, gives the entire population half its actual age; or a painter whose work is discovered to have nutritive qualities; or a marquise who gives birth to a centaur. Once set in motion, however, habitual social reflex moves these stories smoothly forward, sometimes to an ingenious and unexpected ending and sometimes not. For Aymé, unlike writers of the Maupassant–O. Henry school, is more interested in the original premise than in the final dénouement of his plot.

Some of Aymé's stories are written in a spirit of pure fun. Others arise out of the material rather than the moral difficulties of wartime and postwar existence. Seldom have the bare physical facts—lack of food, lack of wine, lack of heat, lack of space, the petty vexations and restrictions, the bleak comfortless boredom of it all—been brought home so forcibly. Others, and these are gayer, are concerned with the Bohemian world of demimondaines, writers, painters and journalists. Aymé has a good ear for language, as was already apparent in *La Jument verte:* the ritualistic dialogue of a peasant bargaining transaction; the involutions and irrelevant parentheses of a pointless peasant anecdote. Given the more varied subject matter of his later stories, he is irresistible and utterly untranslatable.

The enormous readability of these unpretentious stories does not, however, prevent a lurking sense of discomfort, a discomfort that is not entirely due to material factors. There is something distinctly disconcerting about Aymé's matter-of-fact and highly realistic adaptation of wartime rationing to a law rationing the monthly existence of the population in proportion to their social utility. We laugh, but less unreservedly than in *La Jument verte.* A number of stories in *Le Vin de Paris* are frankly shocking. One is the story of a professional blackmailer who derives a comfortable existence during the post-Liberation months by threatening to denounce erstwhile collaborationists, real or suspected, to the police, and appeases his delicate middle-class conscience by afterwards assassinating his victims. The shocker, in this case, is our realization that Aymé is not telling a fairy tale or a fantasy. He is of course exaggerating, but he is exaggerating a present-day fact of life—the widespread substitution of oversimplified political emotions for minimal human decencies.

This particular story is nearer to Aymé's later novels than many others; and it shows us why these novels are now bare of supernatural or fantastic suppositions. The very quality of social existence, in wartime and postwar France, is sufficient unto itself. Aymé has here written what amounts to a case history of social decay. This includes the period of the Popular Front, *Travelingue* (*The Miraculous Barber*), 1941; the Occupation years, *Le Chemin des écoliers* (*The Transient Hour*), 1946; and the immediate postwar era, *Uranus* (*The Barkeep of Blémont*), 1948. Each novel emphasizes a different phase or aspect of decay, but a number of themes are common to all three: the disruption of both political and parental authority; the hypocritical assertion of meaningless ideals or half-baked intellectual snobberies; the incapacity to look reality in the face.

These themes have excellent satirical possibilities that Aymé has successfully exploited. They also indicate that Aymé's social criticism is based on the purely functional criteria of social survival. And this is largely the case with the first two novels of his trilogy. *Travelingue* is a scathing judgment of the febrile middle-class reaction to the social disorders of 1936; Aymé seems to wish to indicate that the bourgeois classes of this period, although no less grasping at heart than their predecessors, no longer have the courage, competence or practical realism for group survival. In *Le Chemin des écoliers,* which deals with the social and economic corruption of the Occupation years, Aymé seems almost to prefer the unscrupulous realism of the shadier characters to the pathetic bungling of the well-intentioned Michaud family. With *Uranus,* however, the very scale of events forces Aymé to take a somewhat broader view of things and find a standard of judgment other than that of mere social survival.

Uranus is situated not in Paris but in a small provincial town, a setting that gives greater scope for the political exploitation of petty personal antagonisms and ambitions; here this amounts to a virtual reign of terror, which in certain small towns of France was typical of the months immediately following the Liberation. Its general atmosphere is one of servile hypocrisy arising out of the fact that the great majority of the population are erstwhile Vichyites who are forced to dissemble their involvement with the Vichy cause. The greater their involvement with Vichy, the greater their need for uncritical subservience to the Resistance, Communist and Gaullist groups who form the new ruling clique.

Against this uncomfortable background, Aymé coldly sets forth certain of the well-known but little-publicized incidents of the era of "political purification": the unfounded denunciations and arrests; the savage public chastisements; the sordid deals between black-market millionaires and local political bosses. At the conclusion of the novel a pleasant, somewhat alcoholic café proprietor is ruthlessly shot down by the police, and an immature but fairly likeable young Vichyite is arrested and sentenced to be executed for treason.

Insofar as this novel is to be interpreted as a social document, *Uranus* follows the line of Aymé's previous works. Aymé is again condemning what he believes to be the cancerous growth of a corrupt society: an irresponsible middle class, at odds with life, whose natural drives are corrupted by hypocritical pretensions and theorems. Aymé has since developed this thesis in an essay called *Le Confort intellectuel* (Intellectual Comfort), 1950, in which he expresses a belief that the exaggeratedly literary approach to life of the French middle classes has incapacitated them for dealing with the practical necessities. There is an element of truth in Aymé's judgment. At the same time, his mouthpiece, Lepage, grossly underestimates the problem that he has posed. This rather unimaginative character, an undisguised "bourgeois" and proud to be one, seems to believe that the whole problem of social decay can be solved by an old-fashioned common sense that ignores the complexities of contemporary life. Lepage has no trouble in knocking down the straw men, or more often women, deliberately set up for this purpose—his ridiculous spinster sister, for one. But he is no match for the perverted sadism of a Jourdan, a young professor of middle-class extraction and Communist sympathies who is one of the more repellent characters in *Uranus*.

Despite its apparent anti-Communist slant, *Uranus* is more a human than a political judgment. The contrast between the honest, even if mistaken, convictions of a Communist worker, Gaigneux, and the intellectual refinements of Jourdan is emphasized in a dialogue in which the two men are discussing whether or not to expel a particularly contemptible member, Rochard. Rochard has personally tortured a number of collaborationists and originally, for entirely personal reasons, denounced the café proprietor. Gaigneux, who is in favor of expulsion, argues that the brutal and irresponsible conduct of Rochard discredits the party. Jourdan, a man intellectually and physically incapable of violence himself, defends

Rochard's brutality as a magnificent "revolt" against his condition as a worker.

This uncritical exaltation of violent action, without regard for its practical consequences, is typical of a certain type of middle-class intellectual from Sorel to the early Malraux; and Aymé's implied assertion that intellectuals of this type are less concerned with the actual fate of the working classes than with the intellectual, esthetic or metaphysical satisfaction that they themselves derive from the spectacle of working-class revolt is fairly just. Indeed, making allowance for the obvious difference in stature of the two men, there is a hint of Malraux's apparent admiration of the terrorists depicted in his early novels in Jourdan's admiration of Rochard.

The person of Jourdan raises not only the problem of social maladjustment discussed in Aymé's earlier novels; it also raises the problem of evil. The emergence of this problem requires Aymé to adopt a different point of view, and this he expounds through a saintly character, Professor Watrin. Watrin's cheerful and tolerant approach to life, his "conversion" if you like, is the consequence of a nightmare that first visited him after the bombardment that demolished his house and now returns to him every night. He had been reading a description of the dead planet, Uranus, just before the explosion. After the dizzy sensation of this lifeless, sunless, planetary existence which, from that night on, haunts his sleeping hours, he wakes each morning to all the splendor of life on earth—the plants, the insects, the animals, and even man himself, a species for which Watrin feels the same magnanimous and truly Christian love that St. Francis must have felt for wolves and jackals.

This Franciscan reverence for life is implied in Aymé's other writings. The most vicious character in *Le Chemin des écoliers* is a degenerate boy who tortures small animals. In *Clérembard*, 1950, a play, the hero's vision of St. Francis and subsequent conversion follows the heartless shooting of a little dog. In some respects Watrin may be seen as an earlier version of Clérembard himself. Unlike Clérembard, however, Watrin judges the human species, not as the friends or enemies of animals, but as members of the animal kingdom themselves. "You are behaving," Watrin tells one of the characters in the novel, "like a healthy cell whose proportion of phosphorus or of calcium modifies itself according to the organism to which it belongs. Do not be distressed, but admire the imperious sense of harmony that forces you to howl with the wolves." His words are hardly different from those used by Aymé's St. Francis to reassure the hungry wolves that they are conforming to the divine harmony of nature.

A man who views society as little more than a biological organism and demands no more of men than he demands of wolves carries tolerance to almost cynical extremes. From Aymé's own indignant appraisal of certain forms of human bestiality, we may judge that this is not his personal point of view. Watrin's "conversion" seems rather to represent something that Aymé would like to attain: an act of reconciliation with the human race; as with La Fontaine, a way of seeing men as they are and yet forgiving them.

This act of reconciliation, based on a pantheistic respect for life in all its forms, is perhaps the only antidote for Aymé's deep-set hostility to modern, socially conditioned man. And Watrin, even though he may appear as something of a cynic, is far more impressive a character than the narrow-minded, grumbling exponent of a vanished order in Aymé's essay on "intellectual comfort."

PRIVATE WORLDS

To the large-scale novel of historical elucidation one can oppose the circumscribed novel of individual destiny that is only indirectly affected by contemporary events. The novelists of private worlds shun the impersonal aspects of public issues even when they are moved—as are François Mauriac, Georges Bernanos and even Jean Giono—to comment upon such issues passionately, not to say fiercely, in newspaper articles or pamphlets. In their novels, obsessive patterns, human relationships, plot and atmosphere reveal a private emotional and intellectual landscape, though often this private landscape indirectly reflects the pressures of our time.

These novelists, and there are many of them, use the traditional medium of the straightforward novel. They do not need the broad canvases, the elaborate plots and substructures, the shifting scenes and numerous characters that were necessary to the great historical syntheses of the 1930's. Unlike many of their contemporaries, they do not, apparently at least, recast the form of the novel. The significance of their novels lies in the inner momentum of the tale told and the author's ability to involve the reader in his favorite realm.

Many of the best of these novelists are Roman Catholics; but, granting that the novel of a Catholic writer is conditioned to varying degrees by his faith, this is not a sufficient criterion for purposes of literary classification. It is true that a religious vision of life gives a novelist the power to evoke the spiritual repercussions of otherwise insignificant events and greatly enhances the evocative power and the dimensions of his story. For a Catholic novelist, the drama of human salvation is being played out in every human situation. Be-

neath the apparent chaos of daily living he discovers a hidden pattern. This pattern is not disrupted by the violent outer conflicts
which arise in a time of change. The conflict represented is an inner
one, at the very core of the Christian view of life. The time-space
dimensions of his novel are unrelated to those of outward history.
The story is told in terms of the spiritual and of the eternal. The
temporal setting, the material aspects of the world, are only passing
manifestations of the unchanging drama of man's separation from
and aspiration toward God. The salvation of a human being who
blindly makes his way toward God, the salvation of a whole world
symbolized in a group or a village, are the themes of Mauriac and of
Bernanos. These are important themes whose gravity stirs the imagination.

Although a Christian view of life brings with it a sense of drama
that may be propitious to the writing of a novel, the novelist, if he
is to succeed as such, must still graft this onto a personal vision of
life—thus necessarily revealing his own imaginative powers and
limitations. As good a novelist as Mauriac is haunted by this problem. There is no doubt that his work suffered at times from his
ambiguous attitude toward his own creations. A humorless pathos
pervades his tone when he bids us look upon the—to him fearful—
creatures of his own imagination. Why should an author have so
much trouble accepting the stories he invents? Mauriac's bad conscience occasionally makes us uncomfortable, and whenever it pro-
trudes, it tends to destroy the integrity of his fictional world.

In the novels of Bernanos as well, we sometimes stumble on direct
admonition leveled at us in a tone of righteous indignation. The
truth about ourselves and our world is laid bare by a priest who,
forgetting that he is committed to a novel, speaks right out at us
with the voice and the convictions of Bernanos. Whereupon, some
readers may be tempted to disengage themselves quietly from the
meshes of the story, disclaiming any further involvement in a situation that they are unwilling to accept as theirs. Like Mauriac,
Bernanos tends at such moments to destroy the autonomy of his
fictions.

The weak points and the strong points of both these novelists lie in inner dissensions that they have been unable to master. They are unwilling to step aside and let their private worlds *be*. This characteristic is not restricted to these two Catholic novelists. Jean Giono, a determinedly pagan writer, shows somewhat the same tendency in a different form. He will not let the reader be. He must continually point out how right his characters are, how beautifully attuned they are to the universe—that is to say, Giono's universe, so basically different from ours. Unlike Balzac, who lived in the very center of his great fictional universe, untroubled by the world of fact, Bernanos, Mauriac and Giono in some way seem suspicious of the world of fact—and of the reader too—for not quite conforming to their standards. Their uneasiness may come from their awareness that large realms of experience remain outside the domain they have staked out. This limitation is not necessarily a defect in a novel, whose postulates the reader is nearly always willing to accept; but either because of their personal convictions or because they wrote in a time of intellectual anxiety, these three novelists seek to extract from their novels universal values giving metaphysical or exemplary significance to what is actually a limited, essentially imaginative, private world. And yet it is clear that all three are primarily novelists, creators of character, plot and atmosphere, tellers of tales that draw upon a powerful imaginative grasp of life.

To these three major figures one can add two minor but distinctive novelists, Julien Green and Henri Bosco. There are others to whom a slight eminence over their contemporaries gives a passing luster, but, in retrospect, their work appears mannered, dated and flimsy. Henri de Montherlant's problematic literary survival will depend on his plays, not on his novels, though these enjoyed a certain vogue in the late twenties and thirties. Marcel Jouhandeau reached a small audience in the early fifties; however, his books are little more than a series of sketches too closely connected with the idiosyncrasies of his complicated personality to rank as real fictional works.

It is significant that the five major novelists of private worlds chose the French provinces as the setting of their novels. The prov-

inces live according to past rhythms, their standards as yet uninflu-
enced—or so the novelist likes to think—by the uniform standards
of modern life. Thus insulated from the outside world, they are the
geographic equivalents of the private domains with which these
novelists are concerned. The novelist's choice of the provincial setting
allows him to ignore the collective pressures and facilities of modern
existence and explore freely certain aspects of life that are familiar
but already removed from us, survivals of a past epoch. This distance
and familiarity are not of any particular interest in themselves but
are ready-made elements for the building of a highly fictional universe, the solid ground for a take-off into the imaginary.

The first novels of Julien Green, written between 1926 and 1936,
make the most traditional use of the provincial setting. It descends
directly from the conventions of the "Gothic" novels of the nineteenth century, in particular the Anglo-Saxon brand. No doubt
Green's American origin put the full range of English and American
literature within his easy grasp. The sinister, lonely country house
or castle plunged in darkness, haunted by mysterious characters
whose secrets the hero or victim must sooner or later discover in
an atmosphere of terror, is a recurring décor in Julien Green's early
novels. So is the small provincial French town, which at first is
minutely and realistically described, but which becomes more and
more fantastic as the story develops. Châteaux, houses and towns
are closed worlds, and the people in them are trapped, doubly, triply
trapped.

The heroine of the first of these provincial novels, *Adrienne
Mesurat* (*The Closed Garden*), 1927, is trapped in the family house
and garden, trapped in the small world of the village. In *Léviathan*
(1929), Guéret is trapped in the provincial restaurant of Mme Londe,
trapped later in the big house of the wealthy Grosgeorges. Elisabeth,
the heroine of *Minuit* (*Midnight*), 1936, is first trapped in a small
closet-like room in her aunt's house and later in the nightmarish
château of Fontfroide. . . . And the only possibility of escape lies
in death or madness.

The sequestration of the hero or heroine, helplessly abandoned to sadistic torments—a prevalent source of dramatic emotion in the "gothic" novel—is a recurrent situation which Green exploits with all its accompanying themes. The closed world in which the characters live is fraught with horror, peopled by villainous figures, its heroes haunted by veiled or direct threats, plunged in darkness and promised to disaster. The plots are violent and simple. Adrienne Mesurat kills her father by pushing him down the stairs; then she plunges into madness. Guéret of *Léviathan* is obsessed by a desire for a young prostitute called Angèle; he savagely attacks and then disfigures her, kills a man and is finally tracked down in the house of the Grosgeorges. Green's novels all follow such patterns of violence.

But the plots matter little in themselves, and after his first experiments in novel-writing, Green makes no effort to give his story any appearance of verisimilitude. He uses the melodramatic elements in his tale to build a nightmare of increasing tension and terror—a nightmare for the reader, but for the characters who are part of this nightmare, a terrible reality. From the minutely described and realistic décor of *Adrienne Mesurat,* Green takes us into the increasingly fantastic atmosphere of *Léviathan* and then on to the deliberately unreal world of *Minuit.* The secondary characters of the novel meanwhile become more and more clearly mere embodiments of terrors latent in the victims themselves.

Green uses the techniques of the thriller and, as he freely admits, plays on the ambiguous psychology of a childish fascination with terror—his own terror and ours. His heroes exhibit the helplessness of victims moving voluntarily to a violent end, as children move through horror stories. Held in someone else's power, they struggle hardly at all, so exciting is the apprehension of disaster; the giant or dragon is hidden in the shadows, and they are his promised victims. Their fearful excitement, which the reader shares, pervades the whole drama as they are carried toward their destruction. The atmosphere Green creates is somewhat akin to that of Henry James's *The Turn of the Screw.* It is moral rather than merely physical terror. But Green's world is duller in color and less consistent than James's.

With the possible exception of *Adrienne Mesurat,* the atmosphere of these novels is from the outset so overcharged with abnormal pressures that the hallucinatory scenes seem preposterous rather than convincing. The obsessive themes are not sufficiently sustained either by the creation of character or by some suggestion of significance. *Minuit,* in this respect, is characteristic.

After her mother's suicide, the little girl, Elisabeth, experiences a night of horror, from which she escapes, screaming, into the deserted streets of the village. By chance she meets a kind-hearted man who takes her home and adopts her. Green jumps over the ensuing years of supposedly normal life. Then the nightmare catches up with Elisabeth again. Her protector dies, and Elisabeth is led away, passively, to a strange château, Fontfroide. This castle is haunted by innumerable bizarre characters, all dominated by a small visionary autocrat who wants to make night the rival of day and death the reality of life. Elisabeth lives on in this sinister castle until she feels a sensual attraction to a beautiful young man, Serge. Together they attempt to escape, but Elisabeth, after Serge, finally plunges dizzily into the outer darkness, falling at last into the void of death to which she belonged from the very start.

The book seems to be essentially the fictional elaboration of an obsessive death dream—perhaps a death wish. But, as is characteristic of Green, it is linked to an erotic motif. Elisabeth's mother committed suicide because of an unhappy love affair with the strange owner of the château, and it is hinted that she could not control her sexual impulses. Elisabeth's benign protector dies on the day that Elisabeth experiences an uncontrollable sexual attraction. And Elisabeth dies after she has yielded to Serge's brutal embrace.

Green's characters have often been interpreted in terms of an aspiration toward purity; but they seem rather to be motivated by the fascination, terror and guilt aroused in them by sensual relations and, in particular, the violence of sexual attraction. Love and death are old partners in literature, but in *Minuit,* as in all Green's tales, the linking of the two themes is shallow.

The human relationships Green depicted in an atmosphere so densely charged with suspense long remained disappointingly schematic; and consequently the events leading to death or murder lack the rigor of tragic necessity. What these early novels bring is the emotional excitement of melodrama. Green has the imaginative power to dislocate the normal atmosphere of life by releasing in his characters a basic uneasiness, a latent erotic anguish. This anguish grows immeasurably until it eventually destroys both the characters themselves and the nightmarish world it had evoked. But this double destruction has little significance; it is no more than the exorcism of an array of phantoms. The careful, almost stiff writing that is Green's instrument par excellence gives his novels the semblance of a strong framework. It is actually more of a shell, forcibly holding together a world that is falling apart.

As his *Journal* shows, in the years following *Minuit* Green went through a spiritual crisis that ended with his return to the Roman Catholic church. This spiritual change, which was perhaps due to the impact of the Second World War, affected his novels, to which he attempted to give the scope and fullness of experience which they lacked. Of these later novels—*Varouna (Then Shall the Dust Return)*, 1940, *Si j'étais vous (If I Were You)*, 1946, and *Moïra,* 1950 —the best no doubt is *Moïra.*

Moïra is set in America. It tells the story of Joseph Day, an intransigeant and vigorous young puritan, who at eighteen enters the University of Virginia. Joseph believes in good and evil and considers sin as residing first and foremost in carnal impurity. He draws around him a group of friends and unconsciously, but uneasily, succumbs to the sensuous attractions he abhors. A facile young woman, Moïra, will be the instrument of his tragic downfall. He murders her after a night that, in his mind, is a night of damnation. In this novel, better than in any other, Green has succeeded in creating a coherent world and a tragic story. Yet, Green's particular interpretation of the hidden motivations that lie behind his character's tragedy limits the meaning of the novel. What Joseph is actually attempting to kill, Green suggests, is the figure of a fellow student, Praileau, to whom he is unconsciously attracted. Joseph's disgust for carnal impurity is thus apparently due to his hidden homosexual drives rather than to his religious convictions. What the book gains in the limited field of individual torment it loses in general significance.

Nothing could be further removed from Green's dark world of torment than Henri Bosco's calm and luminously peaceful world. His novels seem to grow out of the very soil of Provence, bathed in sunlight, secure in the possession of age-old rhythms of living. The mystery at the heart of Bosco's stories is never concerned with individual passions or desires but with man's relation with the earth around him, its hills and rivers, its plants and animals, its seasons, the slow pulsation of its life. Immersed in classical literature, familiar with the Bible, Bosco draws on the more esoteric of the cults: the mysteries of Eleusis, the Rosicrucian beliefs and rites, the old Egyptian lore still extant in the beliefs of the gypsies. Bosco's work as a whole is rather inhuman, rather static, circumscribed by its very detachment and by the intensely poetic but unvaried elements that go into its making.

His novels are set in villages and farms in a world abstracted from ours—a world wherein the daily routines and occupations of living disappear to make way for the magic adventures told. Carefully prepared, slowly developed, these adventures are willingly entered into by the characters in the novel. Each quietly plays out his role and then returns to his initial tranquillity, but carrying the poetic aura of the strange events in which he has participated. Their common participation in the adventure binds the different characters together and creates the basic unity of the novel.

Several of Bosco's best stories, such as *L'Ane Culotte* (The Donkey Culotte), 1937, and its complement, *Le Jardin d'Hyacinthe* (The Garden of Hyacinth), 1946, center on children; and the general spirit of these stories is well suited to the fresh visions of childhood, uncorrupted by any form of modern living.

Other tales—*Le Mas Théotime* (The Theotime Farm), 1945, and *Malicroix,* 1948, among the best—are concerned with powerful, occult happenings that disrupt the quiet, dignified routines of life in the isolated farms of Provence. Routine in Bosco's novels is not, as it might be in a Flaubert novel, a form of sclerosis. It is an equilibrium, a state of plenitude, an order of living. Human beings living in contact with the Dionysian forces of nature have learned how to hold them under control. They have entered into a pact with these forces, a pact that some mistaken act or gesture may endanger. Mysterious disturbances then appear bringing anxiety, apprehension and violence. Without clearly knowing what is at stake, the human beings become involved in hidden struggles, along with other benign or malignant forces. And the peaceful order of life is threatened.

Bosco, like the characters that he depicts, is at home in the fantastic; and the fantastic, the occult, the mysterious, are at the heart of life as he knows it. *L'Ane Culotte* tells of the adventures of two young children, a girl, Hyacinth, and a boy, Constantin, brought up together in a peaceful village house. The fantastic appears in their lives in the form of a gentle, patient donkey, who comes down alone to the village and stops at the small stores where provisions are loaded onto his back. Culotte also occasionally brings flowers for the church festivities. The donkey, as sometimes happens in the south of France, wears pants on his hind legs; hence his name.

It is natural that the children should venture out after the donkey to discover the region from which he comes. What is peculiar to Bosco is the secrecy that shrouds their ventures and the rapt wonder in which they live. Separately, they reach the realm of Cyprien, master of the donkey. Cyprien is a lonely and powerful figure in possession of the secret power that Adam lost, the power of full lordship over the earth. In the arid hills he has created the Garden of Eden, a garden of perpetual spring where no evil exists: Death and suffering and strife are vanquished. In this Eden, however, a dark and fearful being exists, an immense black snake, as old as the old earth itself. How, in a moment of anger, Cyprien destroys his Eden, lets loose the snake and carries Hyacinth off to roam the earth with the gypsies make a strange and haunting tale. Hyacinth's return to humanity in the *Le Jardin d'Hyacinthe* is just as mysterious and magically appealing.

Bosco's novels have intense evocative power; they suggest, indirectly, a poetic and essentially spiritual vision of life, devoid of any superficial agitation, unrelated to any one period of time. Their slow tempo, the beauty of the earth described and the mysterious yet apparently inevitable ordering of events gives these stories an appeal all their own. His symbols are clear: the snake, the Garden of Eden, the animals of the zodiac, the wild boar, the fox. But the reader never quite knows what forces are really in conflict, nor how far or in what way the characters are involved. Bosco never comments or explains, either directly or through the main characters who generally serve both as narrators and participants. Both plot and character are overshadowed by the personal vision which sustains them. At the close of the novel we are left to meditate upon a mysterious allegory, uncertain as to what it really conveys. Is it shaped by a personal and clearly defined view of human contact with the natural universe? Does it embody Bosco's peculiar sense of man's participation in the beauty and mystery of this universe? The uncertainty in itself is pleasing, as is the peace that lies at the heart of these stories.

Jean Giono's native province is not far distant from Bosco's, a little more to the north, a little further to the east; yet nothing could be more different than the use these two writers make of their setting. Giono's universe is animated to the point of agitation. Everything in his novels is in motion, and everyone is engaged in some precise action. Born in the Alpes Maritimes, Giono likes to situate his tales, not in his native village of Manosque, but in the distant hills, sparsely populated plateaux and isolated villages beyond his immediate reach. There he can more easily set up a world untouched as yet by any modern conveniences, even a post office. His universe, like that of Bosco, is self-sufficient; he peoples it with a race of men that only by error can be looked upon as existing outside his books.

These people are not peasants; they exist apart from the rest of humanity, one and all varieties of a single species. They are Giono's noble race of man. Engaged in their own forms of living, they are free, free to start out at a moment's notice on the adventures suggested to them by their creator—a great quality in the eyes of a novel reader. It is quite clear from the outset that they are entirely conventional, just as conventional as the Shepherds of Arcadia and, in their own way, just as appealing.

Giono's fictional output is enormous and it shows no signs of flagging. His development as a storyteller has been continuous, but the basic conventions he uses have not changed. The Provençal landscape furnishes him with the materials of his world. But he molds it, enlarges it, detaches it from reality, empties it of its essentially civilized character, and fills it to overflowing with elements taken from his own imagination. The hills of Provence become mountains, the streamlets become rivers, the bouquets of trees turn to forests. And the wind blows, the stars shine, on the immense space of a new, unrecognizable planet made for Giono's race of men as never at any time our earth was made for us.

The visionary quality of this décor is almost lost because of Giono's almost childish delight in anthropomorphic description. No tree in Giono—and they are there by the hundred—no stream of water, no small seed, no large glacier, fails to vibrate with human feeling. The transfer is solemnly made. Everyone in Giono's novels must approach every phenomenon of nature as if it were humanly animated; so persistent is this trait that the grandeur of Giono's natural world often gives way to a sort of crowded fussiness. We lack air, so concretely busy is the wind, so intent on its affairs. A strong sense of the great cosmic flow of life presides over the genesis of Giono's tales, but all too often he is content to express it by way of a monotonous, pervasive and all too simple animism.

The human beings and the human communities that live on Giono's planet have unusual powers of communication with all the natural phenomena around them. They are really one with their environment, and, like Giono himself, they merely say in words what the universe says in a variety of ways. Their language, like their earth, like themselves, is highly conventionalized. The conventions are perfectly acceptable as such. Giono's men and women live a life that is neither essentially rural, nor subject to any of the hardships of peasant existence. Giono has settled them in small self-sufficient communities, or so-called farms, but they are really adventurers— adventurers who live rather like a confident crew on a ship on the high seas, attentive to the atmosphere, to the wind, to the water. They have no use for instruments such as the thermometer or the barometer because they *know* with an awesome immediacy exactly what nature is doing around them. They are simple, strong men and women who live naturally off the earth. Giono concedes that they occasionally must plow, but even then they are more likely to be seen plowing at night because the beauty of the stars has moved them.

Giono's men, in short, are poets, and their great adventures are quite simply and romantically love adventures, newly and sumptuously orchestrated from without by all the beauty of an unpolluted "natural" universe. Man, in his innocence, his oneness with nature, first stands alone with his fellow men. When he has found the woman who must by some mysterious necessity be his companion, he attains his full stature. He builds a house, sows grain, and lives with Biblical simplicity, a free man in full possession of the "true riches" of life, an enviable man indeed if we compare his realm to our world of social interdependence, military conscription, radio and television, international tensions and bureaucratic complications.

When Giono's first novel *Colline* (*Hill of Destiny*) appeared in 1929, it struck a fresh, new note. The very conventions within which Giono works were a welcome relief to a reading public weary of the sophistication and complexities of the all too prolific novel of the 1920's. After Proust and Gide, Duhamel and Romains, Cocteau and Giraudoux, what could be more restful than a world of wind and sun and simple men who apparently had never heard of psychological analysis, never confronted any social problems, never read any books. Giono had been preceded in this vein by the Swiss novelist

Ramuz. But Ramuz was more somber, less optimistic than was Giono.

For Giono the world of his imagination was undoubtedly a refuge, as it was for many of his contemporaries. Brought up by his father, a shoemaker, in the small town of Manosque, Giono, except for one brief interval, had never left home before 1914. From his father, whom he loved, he learned to respect the solid virtues of the poor but independent artisan. He read the Bible with his father and later, in the free hours left him by his job as a bank clerk, discovered the classics, in translation. He read Sophocles and Homer, whose tales, as he says, he could find "unchanged" in his own province. Later on Melville—at least Melville's *Moby Dick*—also stirred his imagination, and Whitman moved him deeply. These combined influences could not fail to develop his epic imagination. Perhaps it is because Giono discovered these books for himself that they brought him only what he could best grasp, their visual qualities, beyond which he does not seem to have penetrated. It is to Homer, rather than to Sophocles, that he turns and, in Homer, to the *Odyssey* rather than the *Iliad*.

When in 1914, Giono, a boy of nineteen, was sent to the front with the infantry, he was totally unprepared. Four years later, when release came, his revolt was complete; he fled from the modern world and banished it from his novels. In a sense they are the antithesis of the reality he had experienced. Giono was soon to confuse fiction with fact and to build his imaginative constructions into an ethics wherein pain and suffering were cut down to his own scale. He accepted the role of prophet, a prophet who, like many others of his kind, had not been able to come to terms with reality. That happiness lies in a simple life and complete communication with nature is a common illusion, a dream to which we cling in our desire to re-create, like Bosco's characters, the Garden of Eden on this earth. As a serious intellectual and ethical message, the belief falls a little short. Giono was particularly well fitted to make literary capital out of it, however: so real is his love of his native province, so vivid his sensuous perceptions, so strong his imaginative powers. And he knows how to tell a story.

His first trilogy, *Colline, Un de Baumugnes* (*Lovers Are Never Losers*), 1929, and *Regain* (*Harvest*), 1930, is made up of three short novels. *Colline* is an account of the death of an old peasant, Janet. Janet, by evoking the hidden forces of the earth, succeeds in creating a real panic in the small village of which he is the center. An atmosphere of terror descends upon the villagers and passes away only with Janet himself. Free of any moral, the little tale is admirably composed.

In *Un de Baumugnes,* Giono tells the tale of Albin's love for Angèle and of his victory over the obstacles to their happiness: Angèle's seduction, her eventual prostitution, her return with her fatherless child, her imprisonment by her father in a dark cellar. The redemption of Angèle by Albin's love and her subsequent happiness are told quite simply. The story is unpretentious and moving.

Regain is a somewhat more ambitious version of this theme. Panturle, living alone in an abandoned village where only he and a strange old woman remain, is slowly reverting to animal brutishness when a young woman, Arsule, appears by chance in the village. The double salvation, through love, of Arsule and Panturle, as together they create a home, plow the earth, grow wheat, make bread, and thus create what Giono points to as a real and satisfying community, is quite simple and a little over-solemnly told. *Regain* is a good story that Giono tries to turn into a parable.

With *Le Chant du monde* (*The Song of the World*), 1934, Giono enlarges his canvas. The story here is less simple and appears to carry some symbolic significance. Each character seems to embody a theme, and the subject is less man himself than a full orchestration of various conflicting elements, their blending into a harmonious whole. Matelot, a former sailor who has become a man of the forest, and Antonio, the man of the river, leave in search of Matelot's son, the red-headed twin who has inherited the force of his dead brother. The red-headed twin, always connected with the sun or the fire element, has disappeared into the upper reaches of the country, into the realm of Maudru, a powerful figure who reigns over hundreds of bulls.

The two men journey up the river to the land of the Maudrus and eventually arrive in the house of a wise, hunchbacked healer, Toussaint. They find that the red-headed twin had eloped with Maudru's niece, Gina, and in his flight from the wild clan of the Maudrus, had carried her off into hiding in Toussaint's house, where she now frets and fumes. All the characters are obliged to pass the winter in Toussaint's house, waiting for the coming of spring when the red-headed twin will be able to face his antagonist, Maudru.

The first part of the story develops with epic proportions, suggesting all the while that Giono is creating a myth—a myth analogous to that of the adolescent sun god who disappears with winter to be resurrected with the coming of spring. But Giono fails to give dramatic power and symbolic significance to the long period of waiting imposed by the winter months, and from this point on the plot becomes banal. The red-headed twin and Maudru, these two antagonists whose appearances have been so well prepared, are weak and insignificant. When spring brings liberation, the twin burns Maudru's house, and he and Gina, with Antonio and a blind woman Antonio met during the course of his adventures, return, carried back to safety on a raft.

The themes of death and love are woven into the tale and connected with the wildness of the Maudru country, where Matelot dies at the end of winter. With the victory of the flame-like twin over the brute strength of the bull, order is re-established and harmony reigns. The story has somehow lost its power, and the artificially simple pronouncements of Toussaint and Antonio on love, death and evil are inadequate. Neither love nor death is so simple as Giono would have them be.

Giono's next two novels, written before 1940, *Que ma joie demeure* (*Joy of Man's Desiring*), 1935, and *Batailles dans la montagne* (Battles in the Mountain), 1937, show more clearly than *Le Chant du monde* where Giono's weakness lies. The intellectual armature of his work is too elementary to sustain his tremendous mythical structures. His portrayal of human feelings is rudimentary, perhaps voluntarily so, overly sentimental and slightly vulgar. A righteous naïveté informs his moral judgments and his stories. Dynamic in their outer movement, they are inwardly static.

Only after the shock of World War II did Giono seem to gain the stature to face these limitations. His abundant creative energy has not waned, but his new works are "chronicles" of varying value, unalloyed in their fictitious texture. One of the best of these, one of the best too of Giono's novels, is the strange, terrible and beautiful *Le Hussard sur le toit* (*Horseman on the Roof*), 1952. Angelo, the Italian hero of this tale, a young cavalry officer, sets out from Italy and travels up through France during the great cholera epidemic of 1838. His incredible odyssey, his sojourn in the attics of a small town, the fantastic scenes he witnesses, his final return, are skillfully and unpretentiously told. The plague itself, as in Camus's novel, and the mysterious "horseman on the roof," who is the only character to escape the plague, have their own metaphysical overtones, but Giono does not press them very far. He is content merely to paint with tranquil objectivity the fantastic transformations of the world as the plague marks off and decimates the human inhabitants.

Giono's vast frescoes reflect his fundamental optimism and love of life, his deliberate refusal to deal with the complications of human psychology. The visionary, quasi-divine quality of this "natural" world stands in striking contrast to Mauriac's narrow, introspective world of tormented and solitary human beings, a world where no man or woman can ever satisfy his deepest aspirations.

"You are free to drag into the world a heart that I did not create for the world; free on this earth to hunt for a food that is not destined for you; free to try to satisfy a hunger that will find nothing equal to it: All the creatures in the world will not appease it, and you shall run from one to the other."

Such is the fate announced to Yves Frontenac, the hero of Mauriac's *Le Mystère Frontenac* (The Frontenac Mystery) and a character very close to the novelist himself, for the novel is semi-autobiographical. Such, according to Mauriac, is the fate of man, condemned to wander unsatisfied on this earth, exiled from the love of God that alone gives meaning to man's relationship with the Creation. Human beings therefore attempt to satisfy their inner void—a void that can be filled only by God—through the spiritual and physical possession of their fellow beings.

As a novelist, François Mauriac himself, as he has admitted, is haunted by the secret that lies at the heart of all human beings. In one of his last novels, *L'Agneau* (*The Lamb*), 1954, he analyzes the satanic nature of the fascination we exercise over each other, preying one on the other to satisfy our emotional needs. The spiritual crisis he went through in mid-career was in part due to his own uncertainty on that score. As Mauriac sees it, the novelist, like the priest, is deeply concerned with the fate of human beings; but unlike the priest, he uses them for his own ends, like a Mephistopheles in disguise.

This somber drama, which lies at the heart of the Mauriac novel, is played out, almost exclusively, in Mauriac's native Guyenne, a region where he still often lives in his estate of Malagar and to which he makes constant imaginative reference. The Bordeaux countryside, with its vineyards and farms and beyond them the flat stretches of pine forests that reach down to the sea, provides the physical setting for the novel. The characters, taken from the rich Bordeaux estates, betray an obsessive lust for possession which is symbolized in the autocracy of the country house set in its own lands, the power exercised over the individual by the family, the binding strength of provincial rituals and traditions, and the continuity assured by the patient accumulation of wealth. Wealth in the family is not considered a source of pleasure. It is the tangible form of a passion to possess materially and completely, that passion which, according to Mauriac, can never be assuaged. But the particular atmosphere of the novel comes rather from an imaginary inner landscape that Mauriac seems to carry in his mind both as a memory and as an image of remorse.

"Do not hope that I shall allow you to forget me," it whispers in Mauriac's *Bordeaux*. "The more the life you lead differs from the life I gave you, the more distinct I shall become inside you. And do not hope that the human beings which preoccupy you now will ever penetrate your books without passing through me. I must first draw them toward me, absorb them, so that eventually they will be reborn in my atmosphere, the only atmosphere in which your miserable creatures come to life."

This inner landscape pervades Mauriac's novels, imposing a strong and simple pattern and carrying its own recognizable atmosphere. The light pouring like "liquid metal" through the shutters of the houses, the "outer furnace," the "torrid" summer days, the tight circle of the pine trees, the strident cicadas, the forest trees always ready to blaze, are characteristic of Mauriac's tales. His imaginary land can also seize one in a glacial grip, but never can it give relaxation or temporary comfort. There is a terrible beauty in it, an alien, disquieting beauty, that generates disaster. It is the purgatory of Mauriac's world, from which the sole escape is to the indifferent "asphalt" of Paris's nonchalant hell. An inner rhythm carries Mauriac's novels, and his characters with them, from Bordeaux to Paris. But this movement is illusory, for Guyenne holds Mauriac's characters as surely as it holds their creator. They must always in the end return.

Mauriac's novels are further circumscribed by his obsession with a single aspect of the human personality, an aspect which to him is the very fabric of human existence. He is a creator of characters, and these figures loom before us, larger than life, but outlined rather than presented in careful completeness; three dimensional certainly, but impenetrable. Mauriac has stripped them of the wealth of activities that usually go into the making of a human life. Such activities are there no doubt, vaguely sketched out in the background on a very small scale, as are the secondary characters.

In the foreground are one or two main characters, embodiments of that part of the individual which cannot be communicated, cannot reveal itself. No relation with any human being can therefore bring them satisfaction. Love, whether in or out of marriage, is a makeshift, a passing illusion that in the last analysis is nothing but a shameful and senseless "struggle of two bodies in the dark." In marriage man and woman are locked in a deadly duel. Friendship is unknown, and family ties are hated bonds, a "vipers' tangle."

The story that Mauriac tells is the story of individual solitude and hunger, a spiritual hunger that springs from the deep realms of the subconscious where our hidden aspirations, lusts and frustrations lurk. The plot is less a succession of events than the welling up of this secret inner life; this life breaks through to the surface and then subsides, sometimes becoming perceptible in an action, more often simply in the modifications it imposes on the relations of the central character to those around him. There may be no external evidence of a life thus led in secrecy, merely a dramatic heightening of the atmosphere.

This rejection of the many superficial facets of life has saved Mauriac's work from any hint of triviality, but it has also limited his scope. Compact, economical, poetic, in their concentrated unity of atmosphere or time, his novels lack range, movement and variety.

From the outset of his career in 1910, Mauriac regularly published novel after novel, almost year after year. Yet one cannot truthfully speak of a development or a renewal either of pattern or of technique. *Le Baiser au Lépreux* (*A Kiss to the Leper*), 1922, a short story rather than a novel, successfully struck the vein that Mauriac has since continued to exploit in slightly more ample works or with minor shifts in emphasis. It is a beautifully written tale, one of Mauriac's best.

The hero, Jean Péloueyre, the heir to the Péloueyre estates and wealth, is a poor, physically degenerate young man of twenty-three, too intelligent not to see himself for the poor creature that he is. Unoccupied, he lives with his old father, M. Jérôme, and leads an aimless existence under the avid supervision of his cousins, the Cazenaves, who are lying in wait to snatch up the inheritance. To foil these expectations, M. Jérôme arranges a marriage between Jean and a beautiful seventeen-year-old girl, Noémi d'Artailh, whom Jean secretly and shamefully desires without daring to hope that she might ever look at him. And so the "frightened little black male" and the "marvelous female" are married. "One does not say no" to the young Péloueyre. "One does not say no to farms and flocks of sheep, to silver, to linen inherited from ten generations and piled deep in high cupboards—to ties with all the best families in the region." And Noémi is sacrificed, with Jean.

This "kiss to the leper" involves both in a mute tragedy caused by the physical barrier between them; the horror Jean inspires in his wife is felt and not expressed and is accompanied by the growth of the spiritual charity that binds Noémi to Jean even beyond life. After Jean's death the beautiful, sensuous young woman will refuse the fulfillment offered by another man. In that act of renunciation she appears, as do few other Mauriac characters, greater than her fate. The story is well told, free of all analysis, convincing. Mauriac deals with unexpressed and baffling feelings that engender suffering; the suffering is mutually shared, never quite understood, undeserved yet borne with dignity.

Less moving but more powerful is *Genitrix*, 1923, a novel that deals with the Cazenaves. At the Cazenave farm of Langon young Mathilde Cazenave lies dying, dimly conscious of the monstrous shadows cast on the wall by her husband, Fernand, and his mother, Félicité, a grotesque inseparable couple against whom Mathilde is powerless. "She heard the porch door creak. This was the hour when Mme Cazenave and her son, carrying a lantern, crossed the garden to go to the private outhouse built next to the peasant house and whose key they kept. Mathilde could see the daily event: one waiting for the other and the ceaseless conversation through the door, on which a heart was drawn. Once again she felt cold. Her teeth chattered. . . ." But then she is left to die alone. For her husband Fernand she had been nothing more than a weapon, rather casually picked up, to help him in his fight against his mother, who holds this fifty-year-old boy in a state of infantile dependency.

Mathilde's death proves to be a far more potent defense than her presence. Obsessed by the love that has escaped him, Fernand abandons his room next to his mother's and turns Mathilde's room into a sanctuary. For a short while his eyes are open to the sterility of his own life, and he escapes from the tyrannical hold of Félicité. For a short while, too, the Genitrix renounces her power, only to take possession of her son more surely after her death. In his empty, lonely house Fernand becomes an incarnation of his mother. The passion of the Genitrix has given her cherished son, not the fullness of life, but the barrenness of death.

Genitrix is a powerful novel. Its effect is somewhat weakened, however, by Mauriac's reluctance to let his magnificent characters be. Instead of stepping aside and allowing the reader to draw his own conclusions, Mauriac suggests that Fernand's mute longing for the love of the dead Mathilde is a longing for something no human being can give; that Félicité's jealous and sterile love is simply misplaced and that her suffering, her bafflement, open before her vistas of human charity; that although Mathilde, Fernand and Félicité can draw nothing from each other except suffering, suffering is the road to salvation. In spite of this interference, Félicité and Fernand generate their own reality; they are tragic figures helplessly tied to each other and yet walled in their own solitude. Félicité Cazenave moves through the volume with slow, irresistible force. Her darkness of mind, her cold cunning and her undivided energy give her a kind of greatness. What also appeals to the reader is the clarity of color and outline, the simplicity of the gestures. No side issues or extraneous details cloud the central situation. But it remains a mere situation, essentially static.

This is also true of *Thérèse Desqueyroux,* 1927. Thérèse is a character so close to Mauriac's heart that he was never quite able to move away from her. To the first and best story about Thérèse he added three short sequences. The last and most important is *La Fin de la nuit* (*The End of the Night*), 1935—a somewhat misleading title since this novel does not really bring Thérèse's story to any definite conclusion.

When the novel begins, Thérèse, a young and handsome woman, is riding home at night from a trial. She has just been acquitted of the charge of attempted murder. As she journeys home, she recalls in a series of flashbacks the events that led her to try to murder her husband, Bernard. Bernard knows that the accusation was well founded. But the family has stepped in to clear her name of the charge, not out of affection, but because Thérèse belongs to the family; oppressive, stiff with proprieties, they are concerned only because their honor is at stake. As she approaches the Desqueyroux estate, the hope that Bernard may understand touches her for one instant, but the hope is instantly shattered. Bernard will save the honor of the family but not Thérèse, and he banishes her to her isolated property of Argelouse.

When, after several months, Bernard sees the ravaged face of Thérèse, his vengeance—an attempt to destroy her as she had attempted to destroy him—seems impossible to him. Thérèse is free to go to Paris, and Bernard accompanies her. For a few minutes as they sit on a café terrace, Bernard and Thérèse come close to an understanding. The moment passes, and they separate. Thérèse's later adventures in Paris, her encounter with a psychiatrist, her return to Argelouse and Bernard, add little—one might almost say nothing—to the figure of Thérèse.

Blind to what moves her, as are all Mauriac's characters, Thérèse, in her journey back to Argelouse, saw rather than understood the events that led her to put into Bernard's glass the drops of medicine that could have killed him. Brought up as an only child in the comfortable middle-class society of the landed peasantry, Thérèse was a victim of the emotional sclerosis around her. Blindly, she sought the warmth of love through human relationships; blindly, she destroyed them when they failed her. Bernard, grossly material, untormented, easily satisfied physically, becomes the enemy. And one day, as fire blazes through the close ranks of his pine trees in the Landes, she pours the extra drops of medicine into his glass. She is like a sleepwalker who moves toward the act as though it were predestined. Her exile from the fullness of a life she vaguely apprehends is the source of her disturbing compulsion to destroy. She is governed not by the mind but by some dark, mysterious force within her.

Mauriac has said that he could not find a way—a Christian way—to save Thérèse because he could not imagine the priest who could hear her confession. Here again we sense the element of interference that somewhat weakens the effect of Mauriac's novels. Why must Thérèse be saved? Why, the reader feels, not let her carry her own burden, her own mystery, till the end? Why should Mauriac have over Thérèse the advantage of lucidity, a lucidity of which he strips her entirely? When a novelist gains so complete a control over his characters he necessarily deprives them of an important dimension of existence. And Thérèse, seen in the light of Mauriac's judgment of Thérèse, loses something of her passionate and closed existence.

What Mauriac hesitated to do for Thérèse he found the courage to do for Louis, the crotchety old hero of *Le Noeud de Vipères* (*The Vipers' Tangle*), 1932; for he brings Louis to the brink of salvation. The hunger and thirst for love, which in Mauriac's world can never be satisfied by human beings, here find the divine source that satisfies and quenches. The road to this salvation, which becomes clear with Louis's death and the end of the story, is traced by the old man himself, although he is supposedly unconscious of the direction of his narrative.

In his estate of Calèse, Louis, a successful lawyer and multimillionaire, lives surrounded by his wife, children and grandchildren—all of whom hate and fear him. This is the typical "vipers' tangle" that symbolizes almost all family life in Mauriac's novels. To his wife, Isa, he addresses the diary she is to read after his death. The diary records both Louis's past and present solitude. It is a self-portrait and a self-justification that prepare the way for his ultimate redemption. More ample than most of Mauriac's novels, *Le Noeud de Vipères* is a story in which the development of a character and the slow creation of a baffling human situation are convincingly treated. The sobriety and pathos of Louis's writing, borrowed from Mauriac, lend their aura to the tale, although many a reader is no doubt alienated by what appears to be Louis's extraordinary lack of sympathy for those around him, in particular his wife Isa.

Louis recalls his lonely childhood as the only son of a mute, tenacious, well-to-do peasant woman. No ray of joy or beauty touches this physically awkward, sensuously underdeveloped young man until, through his mother's negotiations, he marries Isa Fondaudage, a charming young aristocrat whose family need money. Louis's shy love and happiness are blighted when he discovers that Isa has previously loved another man. In what appears to be an act of wanton, arbitrary harshness that reveals a total lack of human understanding, Louis closes his heart to Isa's love—a real love as we shall later discover. We then follow the old man's retreat into a domestic tyranny based on his possession of great wealth that he withholds or gives, destroying the children he despises like a petty Cronus.

In his lonely voyage through life, so much of which is given over to the emotion of hate, Louis hides a vast but frustrated capacity for love. This he offers to a few privileged beings—a little daughter and a nephew—whose purity attracts him. When these two die, no one remains within his immediate family circle to test the endurance of his love—a love that Isa, his wife, so well deserved. Yet Louis, the domestic monster, is ultimately saved.

Le Noeud de Vipères carries the spiritual drama portrayed in all of Mauriac's novels to almost paradoxical extremes: to a point where human understanding and human charity appear not only irrelevant to but antagonistic to the love of God. It is difficult to accept a point of view that so totally rejects all human loyalties on the premise that they are obstacles to divine salvation, but this narrowing of his sympathies sharpens and intensifies Mauriac's focus on his principal subject, the individual's relation to God.

A more valid criticism may be raised, not against the Mauriac point of view itself, but against Mauriac's tendency to impose his point of view upon his readers; against his habit of appearing on the scene of his own novels, of commenting upon the actions of his characters and surreptitiously directing them to his own ends. This tendency, which has been criticized by Sartre in his well-known article on Mauriac, is perhaps due to a conflict in Mauriac between the novelist and the Catholic. We know, from a lengthy passage in

Mauriac's *Journal*, that at the time he was writing *Le Noeud de Vipères*, he was in the throes of self-questioning: Was the novelist betraying the Catholic in him? The novelist in Mauriac is obviously fascinated by the power of attraction of his "dark angels," obliterating all the more moderate ways of living in this world. The Catholic is disturbed by this magnetic power and hence must point a moral, at once labeling these characters as "sinners," underlining the gravity and horror of their sins, and finally warning the reader that these "sinners," *because* of their insatiable passions, are nearer to possible redemption than those who in the dullness of their souls are content with the existing order of the world—the reader himself, for example.

The ambiguous mixture of fascination and terror with which Mauriac regards his own characters is no doubt a part of his spell as a novelist. It apparently goes back to early childhood memories. He describes himself as a child in the dark house in Bordeaux, listening in fascinated terror to the horrible tales of the neighbors' sinful deeds to which his mother's pious friends alluded cautiously. And the four or five best of Mauriac's novels are those in which he seems to give shape to these childhood phantoms. At the same time, one feels that Mauriac's stature as a novelist would have been greater had he been able, in later life, to see these phantoms of adolescence with greater objectivity.

Better ordered, more satisfying esthetically than the novels of Julien Green, closer to the source of human living than those of Bosco, Mauriac's novels are sustained by the brilliance of their tense atmosphere. But they can stand no dilution, and dilution for moral purposes is the pitfall that Mauriac finds difficult to avoid.

Bernanos was not a prolific writer, nor by any means a professional "man of letters" in the manner of Gide or Mauriac. He did not begin his career as a novelist until his late thirties. In 1926, when he published his first important work, *Sous le Soleil de Satan* (*The Star of Satan*), Mauriac, only three years his senior, had already brought out more than half a dozen novels.

A rebel at odds with his own time, and a militant Catholic,

Bernanos started out as a journalist and pamphleteer engaged in right-wing Catholic and royalist movements. From the team of journalists with whom he worked, from Léon Daudet, in particular, and from such a hater of the modern world as Léon Bloy, he acquired a gift for virulent invective, which he used in many a diatribe —against the hypocritical conformism of the churchgoers, against the cynical brutality of the Franco regime in Spain and against the collaboration of the Vichyites.

The blows he struck may seem pitifully inadequate and rhetorical, but Bernanos spent his life battling with the real moral horrors of his day, as well as with the monsters lurking in the depths of his own soul. And this is the very stuff of his novels.

Deeply involved in the conflicts of our time, marked by his four years of war in the trenches, Bernanos was a man of violent passions, angers and neuroses. From the moment, after the success of *Sous le Soleil de Satan,* he left his insurance company to live by writing, his life was a sort of epic, an increasingly anguished, dramatic and agitated epic. Poverty-stricken, in continuous physical pain during the last fifteen years of his life as the result of a motor accident, perpetually moving from place to place with his wife and six children, Bernanos lived a life of risk and adventure, of scandal, in the Biblical sense, and of violence. Paris, the South of France, Mallorca, Paraguay and Brazil during the war years, then Paris and Tunisia, received the tempestuous writer and his family and the strange friends who attached themselves to him. This was the very antithesis of Mauriac's carefully protected existence in his rich Bordeaux estate of Malagar.

In contrast with the stylized, clearly constructed and brilliant world of Mauriac, the world of Bernanos is a dark and almost shapeless mass, forever looming up out of chaos. Evil, for Bernanos, is not that residual evil Mauriac detects in the covetous yearnings of the flesh. Evil is Satan, who walks in triumph among us, flourishes in our institutions and turns our lives to dust. Each one of Bernanos's novels is a struggle with Satan as Bernanos perceived him at work in his environment. Bernanos's personality reflected the tumult around and inside him; created it, too.

Before the scenes taken from the outside world became material for his novels, they went through a process of violent inner transformation. No casual reader would connect the strange adventure of the heroine of the *Nouvelle Histoire de Mouchette* (New Story of Mouchette) with the scene that inspired it. He began to write this novel in Mallorca at the time of the Spanish Civil War, "when," he says, "I saw trucks passing by, and in the trucks between armed guards, miserable human beings, their hands on their knees, their faces covered with dust, but sitting up straight, very straight, holding their heads high with the dignity Spaniards have in the most atrocious situations. . . . Naturally, I did not deliberately decide to make a novel out of this. I did not say: I am going to transpose what I saw into the story of a little girl tracked down by misfortune and injustice. But what is true is that if I had not seen these things, I should not have written the *Nouvelle Histoire de Mouchette*."

But without this information, who would connect the wretchedness of this fictional heroine with the immense wave of pity and anger he felt at the sight of the passing trucks. The world of Bernanos mirrors the age in which he lived and for which he felt an immediate concern, but it is so strangely distorted as to seem a fantastic and purely arbitrary invention. It is created out of what Bernanos felt, felt almost organically; for these feelings determined what he saw morally and imaginatively. His inner visions are as abrupt as were his outer lapses into unbridled fury. And his novels are a series of discontinuous, juxtaposed scenes. Their atmosphere is increasingly obsessive and is propitious to the creation of monstrous beings and situations which arise out of an inner darkness.

Each one of Bernanos's books is a battle against these visions. That he should call them "evil" or "satanic" is not surprising. Each novel is a means of casting out the vision, as Christ cast out devils from the possessed. So tormented is the course of the story, it is impossible to tell or to summarize its "plot." Bernanos's novels, as he himself has said, are his "furious dream."

It has been said that Bernanos's world is a Manichaean world in which the priest, the representative of God, fights a terrible battle against Satan, who, in the eyes of Bernanos, now almost totally possesses our earth. This Manichaean world is more concretely a medieval world of monsters and gargoyles, of moral weaknesses or vices incarnate, against which the writer-priest, Bernanos, wages *his* desperate battle. It is a world doomed, were it not for that courageous figure in black, the priest. And this image is surely symbolic of the faith that sustained Bernanos against all odds and kept him sane through many a personal descent into Hell. "For your peace of mind," he wrote a young novelist, "give, give names and faces and adventures to your demons . . . your beasts."

Bernanos's vision of our time coincided with his own inner struggle: He could not come to terms with an age of spiritual and physical breakup in which men butcher each other anonymously and smother in the oozing mud of trenches. This latter aspect of World War I haunts Bernanos's fictional world. Hell, for Bernanos, is often mud, a mud in which the human being slithers and slides until he is swallowed up.

The moral atmosphere and the inner coherence of Bernanos's world go back to his childhood, a childhood he defends against the aggressions of an adult world; he is as much a victim of the adult world as the Spaniards in the truck. The sin without remission is, for Bernanos, the sin against childhood. Humiliated children, betrayed, unloved, brutalized, raped, murdered, driven to despair and suicide, are present in all his novels. The ever-repeated crime we encounter is the murder of a child, or, as in *Journal d'un curé de campagne* (*The Diary of a Country Priest*), the indirect murder by universal conspiracy of a young priest, little more than a child. Each novel is an indictment, a cry of horror for the world that kills childhood, the spirit of childhood in mankind. And here again the inner world of Bernanos's obsessions and his personal view of the tragedy of our time coincide: The good priest is the knight-errant, the defender of divine innocence; the same is true of Bernanos, who is defending his child's world against the inroads of bitter experience, like that of war. "As soon as I take up my pen, what comes back to me immediately is my childhood, my quite commonplace childhood so like everybody else's and from which I draw all that I write as from an inexhaustible source of dreams. The faces and landscapes of my childhood, intermingled, stirred into a confused mass by that sort of subconscious memory that makes a novelist of me. . . ."

The scenes of the novels are taken from Bernanos's childhood environment, but this flat, northern countryside is transformed according to the spiritual significance it has in the different novels. Ambricourt, the village of the country priest, lies in wait for him avidly under its layer of dust, the dust of accumulated boredom. The "dead parish" of M. Ouine is soaked in water; it is a marshy land in which all the characters flounder; water oozes everywhere; a sort of wet Dantesque hell. In the *Nouvelle Histoire de Mouchette* a violent, hallucinating deluge beats down on the forest.

Nowhere in any of the novels do we find a trace of what might be the France of our time. Bernanos no doubt intended to portray the various layers of French society. His novels are actually concerned with a few very limited elements of this society: the village, the château, the church with its priest, the mayor sometimes, and the village artisans. The priest is at the heart of this world and in his relation to the parish gives meaning and poetry to the apparently chaotic, formless events. His fate and that of the human beings he encounters are inextricably linked; for the priest must enter into communion with the evil in his parishioners before he can snatch them from the living death in which Satan has plunged them. All Bernanos's novels have in common this recurring theme. But they show a marked transformation in the novelist's art and in his use of his fundamental novelistic elements. *Sous le Soleil de Satan, L'Imposture,* 1927, and *La Joie (Joy),* 1929, form a first group; *Un Crime (A Crime),* 1935, *Journal d'un curé de campagne,* 1936, *Nouvelle Histoire de Mouchette,* 1937, and *Monsieur Ouine,* 1946, form a second group which is closely integrated and clearly differentiated from the first.

Sous le Soleil de Satan interweaves two stories. The first is the story of Mouchette, a rejected and unloved girl who, sinking into despair and suicide, is finally possessed by Satan. Satan also plays a part in the second story, the story of l'Abbé Donissan. Satan tempts Donissan, as he tempted Christ on the Mountain, but with the worst of all temptations in the view of Bernanos: despair. The encounter with Satan is physical. Donissan meets Satan himself, then recognizes his presence in the pale hard face of Mouchette, whose path he crosses by chance. Donissan triumphs over Satan, and his victory is linked to the gift of seeing the state of a soul. This gift makes a saint of Donissan, and saves Mouchette by breaking through the wall of her despair before she dies. Before his own death, Donissan, as the Saint of Lumbres, will have to go through a moment of despair and solitude as terrible as Mouchette's, whose destitution is a prefiguration of his own. Donissan's life as a saint, his trials and his death, are closely connected with those of a real priest, the Curé of Ars. The novel as a whole shows the inexperience of the writer, but, fairly traditional in technique if not in content, it is a good introduction to the peculiar world of Bernanos.

L'Imposture and *La Joie* form a sort of diptych: the story of a damnation and the story of a redemption through a child saint, Chantal de Clergerie. L'Abbé Cénabre is the impostor, the false priest who, though he has lost his faith, continues to perform the empty rituals of his sacred office and lives in daily inner betrayal of his God. Cénabre is a living lie, and all that is around him turns into an empty shell. Evil for Bernanos is precisely the empty imitation of what is real, and Satan is the mock appearance of God. Chantal, the heroine of *La Joie,* lives in the radiance of her total surrender to God. Her clear-sighted charity sheds its light on her mediocre entourage. But the forces of evil combine to destroy her, and she is murdered by Fiodor, the sinister valet who haunts her footsteps. At her death bed Cénabre loses his mind; but he regains his faith, becoming as childlike as Chantal's former confessor, the innocent, almost imbecile saint, Chevance.

The outline of these stories gives only a poor idea of their significance. For Bernanos each was a spiritual adventure, and, as he said, "all spiritual adventures are calvaries." For the eventual victory of light over darkness, the price paid is the price Christ paid upon the Cross, and Donissan, like Chevance or Chantal, must go through the anguish of the Passion and cry out, as Christ cried out to his Father: "Why hast Thou forsaken me?"

In Bernanos's first books the spiritual and physical adventures do not quite coincide, and the satanic element is too apparent, too individualized to be altogether convincing. With the *Journal d'un curé de campagne* and, still more, with *Monsieur Ouine,* Bernanos moves toward a mastery of the novel and a real innovation of technique. These two novels, written in most part at the same time, are also companion pieces. The first tells the story of a young, sick, poor and awkward priest's day-by-day encounter with his parish. Indolent, somnolent and bored, in a sort of collective indifference to life, the parish is gradually being destroyed by the cancer of evil. It is spiritually empty, and each individual in it must carry his own burden of inner deficiency for himself. In the château, the Countess is slowly being destroyed by her refusal to accept the death of a beloved child; left to herself, her living daughter Chantal is moving toward despair and suicide for lack of love. In the village the children are already spiritually contaminated. It is the task of the poor country priest to fight for their spiritual survival, to reach the walled-up sources of their souls and save them from the annihilation threatening them.

The humble Curé of Ambricourt would not of course couch his mission in those terms. Bernanos has given him no insight into his own case, not even the knowledge that he has a cancer that will destroy him physically. The Curé of Ambricourt, Bernanos's favorite character, is humble, awkward, innocent and inept in all the material aspects of life. But he has one gift, the same as Donissan's. He sees not the body but the soul, and as he undergoes his humble calvary, he accomplishes his mission. "All is grace" are his last words. His story is that of a parish saved. The priest has day by day assumed the burden of the evil he eradicates from others. Grace in the world of Bernanos does not mean peace but the courage to bear the cross of human suffering.

In the *Journal d'un curé de campagne* the inner and external events adhere closely one to the other. The humble external event suggests a spiritual reality but never exactly delineates what is taking place as the figure of the priest, by its very existence, dislocates the superficial order of the parish.

This technique is still more apparent in the strange and unique *Monsieur Ouine,* a novel in which Bernanos abandons his passionate use of rhetoric and ceases to fight for his ideas under the cover of his creatures. The whole story revolves around the murder of a little cowherd. Neither the circumstances of his death nor the identity of his murderer is ever known. The murder is nevertheless at the core of the organic dislocation of a world, a "dead parish." The whole parish slides into hallucination, madness and death, under the eyes of an adolescent, Philippe, who watches this disintegration with cold detachment.

The book is dominated by the figure of M. Ouine, a professor living in retirement in a château where everything is rotting away, including the invisible owner, who is dying somewhere in a locked room. For a short while, before he too dies, M. Ouine will be the master Philippe chooses after escaping from the close, overly feminine atmosphere of his mother's home. M. Ouine is vision without charity, curiosity without knowledge, an empty flask, the last seemingly coherent force in a fast-decaying world. With his death, it too disappears—for Philippe, at least. He is left with little hope other than that of taking the open road alone. Toward what?

Monsieur Ouine has been considered chaotic, and rightly so, for it deals with a nightmarish and seemingly unrelated series of experiences. Yet Bernanos worked on it for several years and composed it with apparent care according to a formula of his own. What we read is not a story in the simple sense of the word. We are caught, like Philippe, in the collective metamorphosis of a parish that is turning into a subhuman, incoherent, fast-dissolving animal world. This metamorphosis, unlike Kafka's, has many different parts, each one an aspect of the whole terrible transfiguration of the world with which Bernanos started. The characters do not know what is happening to them or to others around them. Each is plunged in his own obscure adventure, and zones of darkness separate the episodes in which they encounter each other. This is the reason for the imprecise contours, the strange lighting of the scene, the mysterious, irrational quality of events and, more particularly, of relationships. In this instance, at least, Bernanos may well be the precursor of a new approach to the novel, an innovation produced by the sheer intensity of vision on which his world rests.

To some, Bernanos is the great French novelist of our time. To others, his world is closed, even distasteful. Many a reader has perhaps been discouraged by the doctrinaire approach to his novels adopted by certain critics. Bernanos is actually no more a theologian than he is a politician or an economist. He is in all his writings a creator of myths. Two myths possess his mind and tear his world apart. One is the myth of the immediate and quasi-universal destruction of our human heritage; the other, which is continually threatened by the first, is his faith in salvation through Christianity. The fictions Bernanos wrote are attempts to synthesize the two.

Perhaps Bernanos's vision of reality and the astonishing gallery of demons that torment him are too highly individual, too violently imposed upon his fictional world to take on universal significance. What remains is the powerful, exasperated and exasperating individual whose own daily life took place on just such a heroic and tempestuous plane. Through the few characters who really live in our imagination, through the tormented atmosphere of the novels themselves, we can make our way toward so genuinely individual a vision of our world, so sincere a cry of distress on its behalf, that we feel we have touched something essential, something that is of greater significance than anything encountered in the polished and more traditional novels of Green, Bosco, Giono or Mauriac.

It is not surprising that these builders of private fictional worlds should on the whole reveal a somewhat narrow range of human experience. Nor, in view of their personal conception of the novel, should we expect them to do otherwise. If these novelists fall short of greatness, it is because they seem to have used their medium to conceal a personal limitation of some sort. All five of them are directly or indirectly concerned with evil. This, surely, is what makes them significant in a time so vitally reawakened to the "tragic sense of life." Yet not one of them is able to face the literal fact of evil, or that ambiguous mixture of good and evil of which reality is made. While Bosco and Giono tend to minimize the powers of evil, Mauriac and Green seem intent on fabricating a fantastic hell where evil becomes so dense, so pure and so overpowering as to take on the proportions of a supernatural force. In either case we seem to be witnessing not a direct and open confrontation but a last-minute exorcism of an all too fascinating antagonist.

All this no doubt is true of Bernanos as well. And yet we sense here, not quite the stark reality of evil itself, but the reality of a personal encounter with evil. This painful and often violent emotional integrity sometimes pushes his novels near the brink of total chaos. And the paradox remains: The richest of these private worlds, the one destined perhaps to have the most decisive influence on the younger writers, is the one that is the easiest to pull apart esthetically —the world of Bernanos.

ESCAPES AND ESCAPADES

There are scandalous moments in the course of literary history when the younger generation is suddenly impelled to break the furniture and scratch obscene inscriptions on the walls. The very idea of "literature" becomes suspect. "Literature" is something one has learned in school and which has failed to meet the test of life: a vast and dismal hoax. But in order to expose the mockery one keeps on writing books—books which defy all accepted standards of what a book should be but which, in retrospect, are part of literature. This, briefly, is the history of many French novelists who reached maturity during the period of World War I: the generation that had been brought up on the novels of Bourget, Barrès and Anatole France and whose first taste of life coincided with this unprecedented holocaust.

Their first impulse was a destructive impulse, to demolish the ideas, the values, the meanings and the very language on which existing literature was founded. Their primary weapon was the age-old weapon of the literary scandal. At one end of the scale we have the automatic writing of the surrealists; at the other, Céline's use of contemporary Parisian slang—four-letter words and all. Literature, however, is a fairly rugged institution. These would-be demolishers, by smashing in a window here, tearing down a partition there, actually turned out to be her saviors. They cleared the air of stuffy bookish smells, made room for a considerable amount of personal experimentation and opened a series of fresh perspectives on the world.

Unlike their predecessors, such men as Duhamel and Romains,

the postwar novelists were not inclined to view this world as a very serious enterprise. Poe wrote a story about a man who visits an insane asylum and is astonished to discover that it is the lunatics who are running the asylum. There is something of his astonishment in the "anti-novels" of the surrealists and in the novels of Cocteau, Giraudoux, Céline and Queneau. This astonishment takes many different forms. The surrealists were delighted to discover a topsy-turvy world that offered so little resistance to their extraordinary flights of fancy. There is a similar sense of the fantastic in Cocteau and Giraudoux and Queneau, but it is tinged with irony and sadness. Their world no longer is that flimsy décor, manipulated so easily by the surrealists. It has recovered its weight, its gravity, its store of disenchantments. Fantasy is no longer a way of playing with this world. It has become an avenue of escape. With Céline the irony hardens into misanthropy, the humor into angry, ribald laughter. Astonishment now takes the form of outright physical revulsion.

We are close here to the "nausea" of a Sartre. And, in one sense, the world described by Céline is more similar to that of Sartre than to that of Giraudoux. But Céline, unlike Sartre, does not really adhere to the reality that he perceives. He is an inveterate, if unsuccessful, fugitive from life. "You have to hurry to cram yourself with dreams in order to be able to get through the life that's waiting for you outside, when you've left the movies; to last out a few days longer in the midst of that atrocity of things and people." The puritan, the realist, the relentlessly self-conscious intellectual in Sartre will not permit this type of self-delusion. He belongs to the age that made "lucidity" the first of its commandments.

There is undoubtedly a certain measure of self-deception in a deliberate abdication from humanity. Men, meanwhile, are killing and torturing each other in China; Hitler is organizing his revolution in Germany; Franco has "liberated" Spain. Our irresponsible dreamers are soon to be tripped up by the historical realities they so despise. Giraudoux will not appear to advantage as Minister of Information in 1939. Still less Céline as a willing mouthpiece for official Nazi propaganda. But historical reality is not the whole of life. Between the political optimism of the 1900's and the political desperation of the 1940's we can make room for the amoral innocence of Eden.

The Surrealist Anti-Novel

During the year 1923-24 three writers who, to a large extent, had created the prewar novel—Pierre Loti, Maurice Barrès and Anatole France—happened to die. And during the same year André Breton, leader of the nascent surrealist movement, published his first manifesto. It was to be expected that the collision of these two events, the last rites of three respected literary veterans and the organization of the surrealist revolution, would produce sparks, but Breton's obituary of Anatole France surpassed all expectations:

"Loti, Barrès, France, let us at least put a beautiful festive banner on the year that did away with these three sinister simpletons: the idiot, the traitor and the policeman. With France, a bit of human servility has passed away. Let us celebrate the burial day of ruse, of traditionalism, of patriotism, of skepticism, and of heartlessness. . . . To incase his body let them empty, if they wish, a bookstall, such as is found along the *quais,* of those old books 'that he loved so well,' and let them throw the whole thing into the Seine. Now that he is dead, this man must not be allowed to make any more dust."

Today, when we look back on this benevolent old man, guilty of little more than an inflated literary reputation, we are surprised that he should have aroused such violent passions. Undoubtedly Breton was aiming for a scandal, a double scandal in the sense that he was deliberately offending both the literary standards of the day and a more general human respect for death. It is also true that to Breton, the benign and bearded figure of Anatole France, whose "delicate irony," "smiling skepticism" and "hellenic graces" had so delighted his contemporaries, was guilty of a monstrous crime, that of calmly accepting the existing order of things. To a generation thirsting for fiery alcohols he had politely offered a dish of lukewarm camomile tea.

This camomile tea approach to life is strangely enough a powerful literary force. The reading public seldom refuses a pleasant sedative. Perhaps the only effective antidote to Anatole France was the irritant exploited so successfully by Breton and his disciples: an explosive and infuriating "so what?" The surrealist "so what?" is apparent in the scandal-mongering literary productions, lectures and art exhibits of the twenties. It helps explain the peculiar prestige of certain legendary figures of surrealism. It does not, however, account for the whole of surrealism. Indeed, had surrealism consisted entirely in the purely negative action of public scandals and private suicides, it would have been as short-lived as its predecessor, dadaism. The destructive "so what?" with which the surrealists battered the walls of practical necessity was backed by a positive faith in the deeper and more significant experience of life vaguely apprehended in childhood, in dreams, in occasional moments of heightened sensibility. And the surrealists themselves, these outwardly irresponsible *enfants terribles,* were aiming in deadly earnest at a total, if somewhat perverse, regeneration of the human race.

It was natural, given their literary aims and techniques, that they should have been attracted to the field of poetry rather than that of fiction. Indeed, for Breton, fiction was so irrevocably allied with the names of Bourget, Barrès and Anatole France that he considered the novel itself a hopeless product of "the realist attitude, born of positivism from St. Thomas to Anatole France"—an attitude that he defied with his habitual but in this case particularly pertinent "so what?": "What I really cannot stand are these feeble discussions about this or that move when there is nothing to win or lose. When the game is not worth the candle." And yet to the very extent that they subordinated literature to life, that they earnestly attempted to understand and bring to light the hidden potentialities of the human imagination, these would-be poets were really unconscious novelists. They were not of course novelists in the traditional sense of the word, nor could the problems they investigated be handled with traditional instruments. They were innovators, and the special surrealist innovation lay in an adaptation of poetic techniques, in particular the technique of metaphor, to novelistic ends.

This development would no doubt have taken place even if the surrealists had never existed. Poetry, after Baudelaire, Rimbaud and Mallarmé, had become so rich in possibilities that the more gifted novelists naturally turned to it rather than to the exhausted novel for inspiration. Gide's novels are strongly influenced by the symbolist theories of late nineteenth century poetry. Proust, whom Breton unperceptively dismisses as another "analyst," had conceived his novel in terms of poetic analogy long before the surrealist manifesto ever saw the light of day. Yes—but no one, not even the surrealists themselves, had realized what was happening. Poetry, during the early years of this century, had been conceived as something utterly distinct from prose. It was consequently the minor, partial aspects of both Gide and Proust that struck, and influenced, the secondary writers of the day. The surrealists, however inferior to Gide and Proust in literary talent, had thoroughly mastered the art of attracting public notice. By their writings, their manifestoes and the very violence of their methods, they succeeded in giving wide publicity to a literary tendency that in France, as elsewhere, has become an important aspect of contemporary fiction: the destruction of the barrier hitherto dividing poetry and prose into two watertight compartments.

The surrealists themselves, given their antipathy to the existing novel, never admitted that they were using the novel form. But how else can we describe Breton's *Nadja,* 1928, or Aragon's *Le Paysan de Paris* (The Paris Peasant), 1926? Neither one reveals that uncontrolled flow of the subconscious mind apparent in certain surrealist poems. Breton uses the tight and highly controlled prose style of his manifestoes. Aragon is intent on communicating an intelligible meaning. In each case we are offered, not simply the immediate expression of the poetic imagination, but a methodical investigation of the poetic imagination at work. The result is neither poetry nor criticism. The negative influence of the conventional novel form is frequently apparent, however, and this negative influence is a connecting link—of sorts. *Nadja* and *Le Paysan de Paris* are perhaps best defined as "anti-novels": a deliberate transgression of the established rules of the game.

The novel, by its very nature, is a fiction, an artificial reorganization of the raw materials of life. Much as the surrealists despised the "realist attitude," they were even more strongly opposed to "artifice." Speaking of Huysmans, Breton exclaimed: "How far I separate him from all the empiricists of the novel who attempt to bring forth characters distinct from themselves and situate them physically, morally, as they may desire, for the sake of one prefers not to know what cause!" The surrealist anti-novel is a direct transcription, not of the irrelevant routines, but of the surprising and unexpected shocks of life. Like Salvation Army converts, Breton and Aragon are giving personal evidence in favor of their creed, "le merveilleux du quotidien"—the miraculous quality of daily life.

This naked realism, unexpected, amusing, even slightly fantastic when kept in its place, becomes a serious bore when it degenerates into a childish insistence on "this is the way it really happened." Breton, in particular, often resembles the naïve storyteller who imagines that his story—whether this be of an unusual coincidence or a supernatural event—gains in interest and credibility by frequent and solemn guarantees as to its authenticity. But perhaps this is all part of the scheme. The surrealists believed that certain privileged people, objects and places have inexplicable psychic powers. For the individual imagination this certainly is true. We all have our personal fetishes. The collective fetish is possible only in hermetic and highly unified communities. And this exactly describes the surrealist group at its inception. Like the Brontë sisters living on their moors, Breton and his disciples invented a mythological kingdom in the heart of postwar Paris. Its headquarters was the Passage de l'Opéra of Aragon's *Le Paysan de Paris,* a covered arcade since destroyed to make room for the further expansion of the Boulevard Haussman. Its divinities were peculiar, marginal figures like Breton's Nadja, a mysterious "seeress" who ended up in an insane asylum. Both *Nadja* and *Le Paysan de Paris,* however personal in feeling, are thus supported by the wider framework of surrealist mythology. And Breton's insistent "this is the way it really happened" is no doubt intended to emphasize this aspect of his book.

Although many members of the surrealist clique knew Nadja, Breton was the only one who established any degree of personal intimacy with her. His resulting adventure, which shows the supernatural effects of certain emotional affinities, is no doubt a particular example of an over-all phenomenon generally classified as "love." Jules Romains, with his *Psyché,* once attempted something of the kind, but he made the mistake of naming the word, of analyzing the situation, of bringing grossly scientific instruments to bear on an intimate and inexplicable phenomenon. Breton's whole art lies in his refusal to analyze, explain or understand. He knows nothing of Nadja's past or present conditions of life; he meets her, quite by accident, in the street. And the exact nature of their relationship remains vague. This intentional silence on Breton's part liberates his heroine from the practical limitations of time and space, of cause and effect, so that she appears less a woman of flesh and blood than "a free genius, something like one of those spirits of the air which, through certain magical arts, we can momentarily attach to ourselves but which we never can enslave."

More important still, Breton's silence focuses our attention on the fact, not the external conditions and consequences, of his relationship with Nadja and helps to persuade us that this fact is not merely another example of the general phenomenon of love but a unique and miraculous "resonance" that momentarily transcends existing reality. An old theme thus recovers some of its inexplicable attributes, familiar enough in legends and fairy stories but conspicuously absent in any objective analysis of the emotion of love.

Aragon's *Le Paysan de Paris* "remagnetizes," to use surrealist language, another familiar theme, the magical influence of certain remembered scenes. The Passage de l'Opéra, already destroyed when Aragon wrote this book, has the nostalgic glamor of a thing remembered. "I do not make a step toward the past," he tells us, "without rediscovering this sense of strangeness that seized hold of me, when I was still wonder itself, in a scene where for the first time I became conscious of an inexplicable coherence and its radiations in my heart."

This introductory passage is reminiscent of the opening sentence of Barrès's *La Colline inspirée:* "There are certain places where the spirit breathes." But the surrealists, as Aragon proclaims, "no longer worship the gods on high places." Aragon's enchanted scene, in striking antithesis to the traditional concept of a sacred site, is the impermanent, illogical, unheroic and highly metropolitan Passage de l'Opéra. Nor is this scene, like Barrès's mountain top, merely a privileged setting for the unincarnate spirit of Christianity. It is an underground Olympus for the numerous apparitions of a modernized mythology.

A siren appears momentarily in the green, nocturnal light of a shop window. The eternal spirit of Don Juan glitters in the two-toned shoes of a Parisian pimp. An unknown and yet familiar woman steps lightly out of a beauty parlor:

" 'Nana!' I exclaimed, 'but how you are gotten up in the latest fashion of the day!'

" 'I am,' she said, 'the very latest fashion of the day, and it is through me that all things breathe. Do you know the latest songs? They are so full of me one cannot sing them: one whispers them. Everything that lives on reflections, everything that glitters, everything that perishes follows me. I am Nana, the idea of time.' "

It is safer to speak of parallel developments than of influences, but these new gods and goddesses, half-human, half-divine, are familiar personages of the postwar novel. Already in Proust the fashionable ladies of Paris society hover on the edges of the animal and vegetable kingdoms. Giraudoux's young girls inherit the mysterious powers of nymphs and sybils. Cocteau's heartless adolescents are clearly related to the minor pagan deities. And presiding over the whole adventure, the venerable goddess of Time, Death, Change, the Passing of All Things, gravely acknowledges that she too is mortal as she glimpses her reflection in a fashionable dress, a popular song, the latest dance—some glittering facet of the modern world.

The only critical test that can be applied to *Nadja* or *Le Paysan de Paris* is the test that Breton and Aragon themselves apply to literature: Does the poetic reality coalesce? Is the spell sustained? Are we really transported into an enchanted surreality? The answer is both yes and no. Nadja is certainly an enchantress and the Passage de l'Opéra an enchanted scene. But the magical potential is never fully exploited in either case. Or, to put it differently, nothing ever happens. The promised surreality is always bypassed, the expected revelation always eluded. Just as he is standing on the threshold of an enchanted kingdom, Breton discovers that he is unworthy of Nadja. Aragon's excursions in the Passage de l'Opéra conclude, not, as he has led us to expect, with "an accession, beyond all my powers, to a still forbidden domain," but with another dose of theory about the "modern world." Past masters in the art of preparation, Breton and Aragon are continually opening magic casements on a perfectly blank wall. And in this respect the surrealist "anti-novel" might be described as something of an anticlimax.

In point of fact, the anticlimax is to be expected. Neither Breton nor the early Aragon is inclined to satisfy the reader, particularly in a genre for which each had so much contempt. Nor are they willing to accept the necessary artifice, if not of plot, at least of pattern and of composition—a unifying factor of some sort. None of the writers connected with surrealism—Aragon, Cocteau and Queneau, for example—matured as a novelist until he had broken with the movement.

Jean Cocteau: A Modern Daedalus

It would not have been surprising if a man so ostentatiously "modern" as the Cocteau of the 1920's had eventually seemed dated; if so precocious and versatile a talent had eventually worn thin. This erstwhile prodigy of a dozen avant-garde movements, familiar with all the great artists of his time; this high-spirited, unruly "mannerist," so bent on scandalizing, astounding or simply amusing his contemporaries; this improbable new member of the Académie Française, decked out in blue instead of the customary green—one is naturally disinclined to take him very seriously. Yet Cocteau is a serious poet; on occasion, he is one of the best of his time.

The word "poet" applies, whatever the medium he happens to be using. Cocteau himself lists his works under the headings of poetry, poetry of the novel, critical poetry, poetry of the theater and poetry of the films. And whatever the medium, these works are generally based on an identical theme: the drama of the poet, either taken out of traditional mythologies or projected into one of Cocteau's personal mythologies.

This drama is perhaps best adapted to poetry itself or to the theater. The novel, as used by Cocteau, is somewhat experimental, halfway between the traditional nineteenth century novel and a totally new conception of the novel form. It is only with his last major novel, *Les Enfants terribles* (*The Children of the Game*), 1929, that Cocteau is altogether successful. And even here his theme is more restricted than in the case of his two best plays, *Orphée*, 1926, and *La Machine infernale* (*The Infernal Machine*), 1934. But from the point of view of the novel itself, the Cocteau novel is an interesting experiment.

The everyday world of recognizable people and places naturally plays a greater role in Cocteau's novels than in his poetry and theater. But Cocteau, by his choice of scene and atmosphere, sees to it that this world is fragmentized, disrupted, torn apart. Here, for example, is a quotation from *Le Grand Ecart* (*The Grand Ecart*), 1923: "Displaced objects lay around like the dirty laundry, boxes, combs, we find in a hotel room. Jacques did not suffer from this disorder. He no longer saw it." From *Thomas l'Imposteur* (*Thomas the Impostor*), 1923: "The war began in the greatest disorder. This disorder never ceased from the beginning to the end." From *Les Enfants terribles:* "A first glance at this room was startling. Had it not been for the beds, one would have taken it for a storeroom. Boxes, underwear, bath towels, were strewn upon the floor."

These passages, and there are many similar ones, might seem to indicate the continuing influence of Cocteau's surrealist past. But Cocteau's apparent obsession with the forces of disorder, his frequent, and highly effective, manipulation of the symbols of dirty laundry, old combs and unmade beds, is in no way the expression of an esthetic theory. In one of his earliest writings Cocteau had already affirmed: "A rigorous equilibrium is indispensable if one rejects the conventional equilibrium." And in 1926 he was to launch a literary manifesto, *Le Rappel à l'ordre,* calling his contemporaries "back to order."

Disorder, for Cocteau, especially for Cocteau the novelist, is merely the "rejection of the conventional equilibrium" that precedes the poet's ascent to a higher and more intimate equilibrium of his own, an equilibrium found only in death, the symbolic death of the poet to the world. The theme of poetic "ascesis," which Cocteau apparently attempted to act out himself in his experiments with dadaism, opium and Catholicism, recurs in all his works. Even if the theme is not explicit, it is felt in the icy, mineral quality of Cocteau's imagery: his statues and snowballs, his demonic mechanical contrivances, his constant transposition of reality into artifice.

This latter device no doubt explains Cocteau's popular reputation as a literary charlatan. But for Cocteau, artifice is a serious matter. He sees in it that depersonalization, that dehumanization of reality, which to him is an essential attribute of poetry. His "Now I am something altogether mechanical" is a cry of triumph. And when, in a letter to Maritain, he asserts: "You rise like a cork toward the regions that demand you. As for me, I fly in machines. . . ." Cocteau is not really acknowledging a spiritual inferiority; he is explaining the difference between religion and poetry. The ingenious Daedalus, who first conceived the possibility of artificial wings, is generally thought of as an architect; since Cocteau, we can see him as a poet.

In explaining his addiction to opium, Cocteau observes: "Certain organisms are born to be a prey of drugs. They require a corrective without which they are unable to make any connection with the outside world. They vegetate in a twilight zone. The world remains a phantom until a substance gives it form." Jacques Forestier, the hero of *Le Grand Ecart* and the most directly autobiographical of Cocteau's fictional characters, represents the case of a potential drug addict who never finds his drug, a diver in his heavy diver's costume forgotten on the surface of the earth: "To rise again, to take off the helmet and the costume; that is the passage from life to death. But there comes to him through the tube an unreal breath that allows him to live and fills him with nostalgia."

This opening passage suggests interesting possibilities; but Cocteau never succeeds in deriving the substance of a novel out of Jacques's fatal unadaptability to life. What he has done is to graft this introductory theme onto the conventional story of an adolescent in the throes of disenchantment. And Cocteau, who specifically relates his hero to the typical Balzac adolescent arriving in Paris from the provinces, seems to have taken a good part of the story out of Balzac's *Le Père Goriot* (*Old Goriot*). Jacques Forestier, adrift in Paris, bears a fleeting resemblance to Eugène de Rastignac; the squalid pension where he lives, to the Pension Vauquer; his heartless mistress, Germaine, to the Baronne de Nucingen. Indeed, a principal cause of Jacques's final disillusionment is directly transcribed from Balzac's famous novel. Just as Balzac's baroness stubbornly refuses to believe that her father is dying, because she wishes to attend a fashionable ball, Germaine conceals a telegram informing her of her father's death, because she wants to go to the theater.

Cocteau's undisguised debt to Balzac is not in itself a weakness—Proust also has borrowed from Balzac—and Cocteau's treatment of the Balzacian theme of "lost illusions" is skillful. He knows how to turn the knife in the wound. Unfortunately, however, this theme is not really connected with Cocteau's original and more important subject: the poet's death to the world. The original subject recurs, somewhat abruptly, in the final pages of the novel when Jacques poisons himself and experiences a momentary illumination: "Jacques rises. He loses footing. He sees the other side of the cards. He is not aware of the system that he is disrupting, but he has the presentiment of a responsibility." But Jacques's attempted suicide is unsuccessful, and he returns to life, less as an exiled poet than as a disillusioned lover.

The unsuccessful suicide provides a more pathetic ending to this novel than death—the conclusion of Cocteau's two later novels—would have provided. Still, this element of human pathos, which no doubt stems from Cocteau's personal involvement in the story, is incompatible with his conception of the poet. Who *is* Jacques? the reader is left to wonder. A poet astray on the surface of the earth, or a nice, if somewhat spineless, young man who has fallen into bad company? And what *is* disorder? The eternal dissonance of poetry and life or the misplaced sentiments of an untidy heart? The universal and the particular in this novel are badly jointed. Instead of reinforcing one another, they rub and jar; and at these points of friction the fine edge of poetry is worn down to mere sentimentality, none the better for its superficial disguise of modernism, paradox and bravura. Cocteau's concluding sentence is worthy of de Musset at his very worst: "To live in this world one must follow its fashions, and the heart is no longer worn."

Thomas the Impostor, the hero of Cocteau's second novel, is another displaced adolescent, but one who has found an artificial equilibrium in a fictional existence. Guillaume Thomas, taking advantage of the confusion during the early months of the war, has lied about his age (sixteen), borrowed the uniform of a friend, and finally posed as the nephew of a famous general, Fontenoy. Cocteau hastens to inform us, however, that this is not an ordinary imposture, a vulgar means of "getting ahead." Guillaume, floating on the edges of a dream, is more at home, more himself, in a fictional than in a real existence. Aided by a Polish princess and her daughter, Henriette, Guillaume soon finds a place for himself in a hastily improvised ambulance service and is eventually expedited to his predestined environment, the fantastically camouflaged confusion of the northern front.

At the end of the novel the two conflicting personalities, Guillaume Thomas and Thomas de Fontenoy, are finally reconciled: Guillaume, who has volunteered to carry a message to another post under extremely dangerous conditions, is spotted by an enemy patrol and shot down.

" '—A bullet, he said to himself. I am lost if I don't pretend to be dead.' But fiction and reality, in him, were one. Guillaume Thomas was dead."

Thomas l'Imposteur, in contrast with *Le Grand Ecart,* is written with considerable detachment. Its hero is modeled not on Cocteau himself but on a young impostor that Cocteau encountered during the war. Self-pity thus gives way to sparkling irony. At first glance we seem to be confronted with a pure satirical fantasy in the early manner of Evelyn Waugh. We soon realize, however, that Thomas is actually another incarnation of the poet, a poet who succeeds in divesting himself of his human identity and whose "imposture" is ultimately authenticated by death.

The symbol is no doubt valid as a symbol, but is it anything more than an abstract symbol? We are quite willing to believe that artifice, under certain circumstances, can become real; lies, true; disorder, art. But has Cocteau really shown that this has happened? That Guillaume should die at the very moment he is pretending to be dead provides a neat conclusion to the novel. Does this, as Cocteau would apparently have us believe, really give retrospective reality to Guillaume's whole imposture? And the elegant detachment of Guillaume and his Polish patroness, their attempts to exploit the wartime situation in such a way as to enjoy the best possible view of the fireworks, the ambiguous emotional relationship that binds the two of them together—does this whole moral climate of exquisite snobbery really attain the "higher equilibrium" of poetry? It seems rather to be the Cocteau version of an atmosphere that Stendhal used for an entirely different purpose.

Here again Cocteau has taken an existing novel theme, that of Stendhal's *La Chartreuse de Parme* (*The Charterhouse of Parma*) as the vehicle for a totally unconventional novel subject. And here again the experiment, however interesting as such, is not entirely successful. Like one of those pioneering ventures in aviation, *Thomas l'Imposteur* never quite gets off the ground.

Cocteau's latest try, *Les Enfants terribles,* is, within its given limitations, a conspicuous success. His formula is simple: to push to their extreme consequences the fierce passions, strange tribal conventions and innocent perversions of a group of children living in a universe completely insulated from adult interference.

Childhood, Cocteau tells us, is a kingdom unto itself like the animal and vegetable kingdoms. In this novel the kingdom is constituted by the relationship of a young girl, Elizabeth, and her younger brother, Paul. Situated in their wildly disordered bedroom, "the room" as it is called, this private universe has its own language, fetishes and rituals, in particular "the game"—a special technique, perfected by Paul, of "sleeping while still awake a sleep that makes one invulnerable to others and restores to objects their veritable meaning"; it offers a dangerous enchantment, of which Paul is the passive conductor and Elizabeth, the jealous guardian.

As Elizabeth is aware, this enchantment is constantly threatened by shifting relationships and loyalties—or the normal process of growing up. For this, however, she is prepared. Two possible threats, Paul's schoolmate, Gérard, and her own friend, Agathe, are neutralized by adoption and come to live in "the room." When Elizabeth realizes that Gérard has fallen in love with her and Agathe with Paul, she again neutralizes the two intruders by persuading them that each is morally bound to marry the other. Even Elizabeth's marriage to an American millionaire fails to disturb the existing equilibrium, since her husband providentially dies in an automobile accident and the charmed atmosphere of "the room" is soon reconstituted in her new establishment.

The real danger to "the room" lies not in adult reality but in a counterenchantment; not in Agathe and Gérard but in Dargelos, a heartless, older schoolboy hopelessly adored by Paul. It is this external factor that originally sets the plot in motion and finally brings it to its catastrophic conclusion.

In a prologue to the novel, set in the enchanted light of a winter's afternoon, Paul wanders through an abandoned courtyard searching for his idol, Dargelos. Suddenly he is struck full in the chest and seriously hurt by a snowball that Dargelos has thrown. Unable to return to school, he lives from then on under Elizabeth's watch in "the room." At the close of the novel Dargelos happens to meet Gérard in the street, ironically asks after Paul, and, as a test of his own powers, sends Paul a package of poison—a "black pellet" counterbalancing the snowball of the prologue. Paul takes the poison, and a last-minute struggle sets in between Agathe, Elizabeth and the absent Dargelos for the final possession of Paul's soul.

At first it seems that Agathe will win out, for she arrives upon the scene before Paul dies, and Elizabeth stands by in impotent fury while the two lovers unravel the subterfuges that have hitherto kept them apart. In an access of rage Elizabeth seizes a revolver, then suddenly controls herself, and with a feverish lucidity, a supreme effort of the will, rediscovers the magic words, associations and memories that will restore the charmed atmosphere of "the room." Paul's expression of hatred gives way to curiosity, curiosity to complicity, as Elizabeth, her finger on the trigger of the revolver, waits for her brother's death spasm. Paul's head falls back. Elizabeth presses the revolver against her forehead and pulls the trigger. But she has struck too soon. Paul is not yet dead, and Elizabeth, falling, brings down a screen hiding the window.

As the corrupt Danish court, in the last act of *Hamlet,* disintegrates at the sound of Fortinbras's martial trumpets, the perverse enchantment of "the room" is dissipated, for evermore, by the pale light of the frosty windowpane, by the ghostly spectators that lurk outside. Paul recognizes these spectators—the noses, the cheeks, the red hands, the capes, the scarves of the memorable snow fight of several years before—and resumes, in his last moments of consciousness, his original quest for Dargelos.

Les Enfants terribles, in striking contrast to Cocteau's earlier and more impressionistic novels, has the rigorous economy of means, the geometrical construction, the almost claustrophobic *unité de lieu* of a classical tragedy. As Cocteau himself reminds us in a number of incidental references, the theme is somewhat similar to that of Racine's *Athalie*—a pattern better adapted to Cocteau's purposes than that provided by a nineteenth century novelist's treatment of the theme of adolescence. That necessity of a "rigorous equilibrium" for those who reject the conventional equilibrium, seems to apply not only to the poetic sensibility but also to the technique of novel-writing. This most ordered of Cocteau's novels also has the strongest poetic impact.

The basic ingredients are as down to earth, as credible, as one could wish. But they are also capable of unlimited expansion. "The game," "the room," are perfectly familiar childhood rituals; but they are also poetic sacraments. Elizabeth is entirely understandable as a passionate young girl who refuses to relinquish her childhood; but she is also the savage priestess-queen of *Athalie*. Dargelos is a thoroughly recognizable classroom criminal; but he is also the angel that preys on poets—the "Ange Heurtebise" of Cocteau's poem and of his *Orphée*. In contrast again with Cocteau's earlier novels, the universal and the particular, the poetic and the novelistic, are here indissolubly fused.

Les Enfants terribles was written in three weeks during a "cure." And the experiences that Cocteau describes, "the game," "the room" and the breath-taking poetic ascension that precedes the double suicide, are very similar to his descriptions of the effects produced by opium. It would thus seem possible that Cocteau, in his struggle to abandon opium, momentarily recovered the childhood reality for which opium had acted as an artificial substitute. "All children," Cocteau writes, "have a fairy-like power to change themselves into whatever they want. Poets, in whom childhood is prolonged, suffer greatly from losing this power. Indeed this is one of the emotions that drives them to use opium." This momentary return to childhood may provide the key to Cocteau's best novel; but it also shows the limitations of this novel, of the novel form itself as used by Cocteau: an incapacity to carry the poetic vision into the enlarged and more complex realm of adult consciousness.

Cocteau is somewhat prone to idolize this element of childhood in himself. "If I have not remained young," he wrote in 1937, "I have remained a child, and I hope to remain one until I die." Even so, the theme of childhood plays no more than a minor role in Cocteau's most successful poems and plays. It may well be that the theme, though not the attributes, of childhood is somehow written into the very nature of the poetic novel. Perhaps childhood is the only satisfactory means of reconciling the conflicting demands of the poet's imagination and the novel reader's sense of the plausible in human life. Other novelists, Alain-Fournier, Giraudoux, Bosco and Queneau, have used it in that way.

This theme, if taken literally, has certain dangers. As a character in one of Giraudoux's last novels remarks: "To adore childhood is the worst heresy." Yet, it is only in his last two novels that Giraudoux himself fully accepts the challenge of adult reality. And in these two novels Giraudoux the poet is displaced to some extent by Giraudoux the philosopher.

One would mistrust a similar evolution in Cocteau. Despite, perhaps even because of, his deliberate limitation of its scope, *Les Enfants terribles* remains a remarkable example of the exciting new air-borne vehicle that Cocteau calls "the poetry of the novel."

Jean Giraudoux's Elusive Garden of Eden

It is easy to remember that Giraudoux was born in the provincial town of Bellac, celebrated in so many of his plays and novels. It is easy to remember that he had a brilliant school career, graduating first in his class from the Ecole Normale Supérieure in 1905, for Giraudoux is obviously an intellectual, with all the important qualities and the incidental limitations that the word implies. But here, for all purposes of literary interpretation, his biography comes to an end. Only casually, or in his less successful novels, are we reminded that Giraudoux entered the French Foreign Service in 1910, that he fought and was twice decorated in World War I, that he was at one time a protégé of the Quai d'Orsay official, Philippe Berthelot, and that he was Minister of Information in the Daladier cabinet of 1939, in short, that Giraudoux played an active role, of sorts, in the political events of his age. Whatever ideas or emotions these events may have produced are so filtered, chastened, by Giraudoux's particular brand of literary alchemy that an event itself is hardly recognizable as such.

The war of 1914, as seen by Giraudoux, dwindles down to that series of charming vignettes, *Adorable Clio,* 1920—a strangely endearing epithet for the contemporary muse of history. To convey the real tragedy of modern warfare, Giraudoux must go back to the *Iliad*. Germany, for Giraudoux, is more a product of German legends and fairy tales than the observations of an embassy officer at Berlin. With the passage of time, the link between Giraudoux's literary and public existence becomes weaker still. His delicate fantasy *Intermezzo* coincides with Hitler's rise to power in 1933; *Ondine* just precedes the French declaration of war in 1939.

This literary retreat from life was no doubt encouraged by Giraudoux's sudden immersion in the theater. Indeed, after his meeting with Jouvet and the performance of his first play, *Siegfried,* in 1928, Giraudoux all but ceased to use his previous novel form. And it may well be that his particular approach to literature was better suited to the theater than the novel. This highly intellectualized type of fantasy—an ironic exploitation of all the tricks of classical rhetoric—is perfectly adapted to the conventions and illusions of the stage. In a novel, particularly the impressionistic type of novel that Giraudoux wrote, it is more like a literary exercise—artificial, repetitive, at times monotonous, and always disconcerting. There is a conflict here between the reality of the subject matter and the unreality of the manner. For Giraudoux, the novelist, however, this conflict of art and life is in itself a literary theme, an extremely intimate and complex theme that determines the substance as well as the surface mannerisms of a Giraudoux novel. In the plays, based for the most part on ancient legends or personal fantasies where life itself is elevated to the realm of art, this conflict is no longer apparent, and the theme must disappear.

Giraudoux's play *Siegfried* is undoubtedly more effective than the somewhat meandering novel from which it was derived. It is also less ambitious. In adapting his novel for the stage Giraudoux stripped it of all its melancholy, semiautobiographical ruminations on the nature of human existence, leaving us with an amusing, well-constructed, and extremely simple statement of the Franco-German problem. This, if we are to believe Giraudoux, is due to the nature of theater itself. "Good theater," he wrote in an essay on Racine, 1939, "is a heaping up of perfections, and if the reader seeks for revelations in his book, the spectator wants only enjoyment in his spectacle. . . . Great theater convinces minds that are already convinced, moves souls that are shaken, dazzles eyes that are already illuminated. . . ." Giraudoux probably mastered this art more successfully than any of his contemporaries. Yet at the very height of the dramatist's success he returned to his original novel form to write what seems to be his last important work: *Choix des élues* (The Chosen One) 1938. He apparently wanted to convey a meaning that would have been inaudible at the Athénée theater, a meaning that demanded the finer acoustics of the printed page.

The novel, as used by Giraudoux, demands a good deal of his readers. Not only must they be able to grasp the meaning of the text, which is thick with literary allusions; they must also be able to hear the novelist's exact tone of voice, to know when he is smiling, when he is pretending and when he is really in earnest. This is often a perilous undertaking. Sartre, for example, once considered this problem and came up with a strictly literal interpretation: The result was his portrait of Giraudoux as a twentieth century Aristotelian: a man who has managed to persuade himself that existing reality is actually shaped into the neat outlines of intellectual concepts and nicely ordered in the pigeonholes of intellectual categories. This is an interesting portrait, but it looks less like Giraudoux than like an upside-down portrait of Sartre himself.

We have, to be sure, a conventional schoolbook, in fact rather Aristotelian, version of the universe in many of Giraudoux's novels. This is a version that Giraudoux finds extremely charming but one that he does not appear to take very seriously. In the opening pages of *Suzanne et le Pacifique* (*Suzanne and the Pacific*), 1921, Suzanne observes: "In Bellac the properties, the movements of the universe only appeared in an orderly fashion, and were so visible that they were inoffensive. January was always cold, August always torrid, each neighbor had only one quality or one vice at a time; and we learned to know the world properly by spelling it out into distinct seasons and sentiments." This is the universe that Suzanne has learned about at school and that she gradually unlearns on her desert island: "All those judgments that I had learned to apply mechanically to the vices, the virtues, were suddenly of no further value."

In this case, as in most others, we are given fair warning. Even so, Giraudoux's ironical treatment of the conventional schoolbook maxims is so affectionate, so polite, so devoid of bitterness and sarcasm, that many readers are inclined to swallow it whole. They quote his description of a triumphant lycée career as a charming eulogy of the French educational system: "I had come there to weld on to myself the past of great men, of little men, of the universe. It was done, solidly done. The future would have to pull very hard on me to detach it." In his later novels Giraudoux tells us more explicitly what he really thinks of the "great men." But the inadequacy of these schoolbook maxims is already suggested in the final sentence of the passage.

Here, indeed, is the central problem of Giraudoux's novels: the discovery that things are not really the way they have been described by our primary and grade school teachers, who, for Giraudoux's heroes and heroines, generally take the place of mothers and fathers. "Dolores, console me," cries Bernard the Weak of *L'Ecole des indifférents* (The School for Indifference). "'I have lost all confidence. I find nothing in life of what my teachers and nurses told me.'" How then can we accept Sartre's accusation that Giraudoux, rather than attempting to discover the real nature of things, merely covers them with a coating of pre-existing human concepts?

As a matter of fact, in *Juliette au pays des hommes* (Juliette Visits the Land of Man), 1924, Giraudoux accuses a fictitious writer of this identical crime—of laboriously memorizing the correct term for every existing object and human sentiment and of thus covering the universe with a reassuring verbal crust that hides the depths of chaos lying beneath. Giraudoux does not totally condemn the man— one has to live in this world as best one can—but wonders, "Why had he to choose the only profession where words are no longer beautiful labels, where they come to the mind as soft as sponges, and sticky, and indefinite? Why did he have to be a writer?" The problem of seeing things as they really are, encountered by most of Giraudoux's characters, is the crucial problem of the writer and, consequently, of Giraudoux himself. Once we have discovered that things are not as we were taught at school, how are we to know them?

In his early *L'Ecole des indifférents,* 1911, and in *Simon le pathétique* (Simon the Pathetic), 1918, Giraudoux shows how this intangible complex of contradictions, oneself, disintegrates under the pressure of introspection. And again with his unhappy writer of *Juliette au pays des hommes* he shows us the disastrous nullity of the "stream of consciousness" technique. Suzanne wisely abandons any attempt at self-description: "As soon as I place a piece of white paper before me, two dissimilar persons flee, like shadows under a street light, but of myself nothing remains." Nor is there much to be learned from observation, unless the subject observed is removed, protected by the enigma of sleep or, still better, death. The Psyche theme in which one person contemplates another's sleep recurs frequently in Giraudoux's novels. And Giraudoux, recognizing the same theme in his favorite poet, La Fontaine, observes: "As for myself, I know what this emotion is. . . . To be face to face with a secret, even if one does not understand it, is still the best way for men to understand it."

Giraudoux's interpretation of the Psyche legend suggests that reality is only visible, only true and only real when we succeed, by means of some device or subterfuge, in abstracting it from its context of time, space, external causality, and giving it a momentary semblance of divinity. These devices and subterfuges have been used, although less consciously, by poets; they have also been used, although less explicitly, by philosophers. A number of Giraudoux's critics have questioned whether they are suitable for a novel. They seem to forget that allegory was the original novel form: *Le Roman de la Rose,* for example, and *Don Quixote.*

It is true that allegory creates a certain distance between the reader and his text, that it filters many of the grosser sentiments and passions, that it remains aloof, obscure, ambiguous. But, it is not, when properly treated, a mere petrified form, the overpowering and thickly varnished picture of Victory embracing Justice. True allegory is immortal, eternal, and yet it is alive, a sort of halfway resting point between gods and men. This, at any rate, is the explanation that Giraudoux offers for one of the greatest masterpieces of allegory, La Fontaine's fables: between the living but inconsequent inhabitants of this planet and the immortal but lifeless figures of Greek mythology La Fontaine has discovered "a third race which by its eternity, its immortality, would have the poetic value of the second, by its life, the reality of the first . . . : animals."

Giraudoux's idealized, like his schoolbook, version of reality should by no means be taken at face value. Such a misinterpretation has given Giraudoux the totally unmerited reputation of apologist for human reality, human limitations and human happiness. His choice of an allegorical medium already implies a certain dissatisfaction with the existing state of things—an attitude not dissimilar to that of Sartre, even though his ultimate conclusions are very different.

It would be possible to trace this quarrel between Giraudoux and Humanity back to World War I. Giraudoux mentions this event in the famous "Prayer on the Eiffel Tower" of *Juliette;* Jérôme Bardini gives it as a cause of his "revolt"; these are the very years that Suzanne passes on her desert island. But such an interpretation is too limited. The real origin of Giraudoux's difficulties dates back to the story of Eve and her apple, man's fall from grace and consequent declaration of war on God, on nature and on himself. This is the key to Giraudoux's distrust of the "great men": "The great man is generally great in proportion to his degree of consciousness of individual existence and to the extent that he has emphasized the differentiation of man from the other forces that surround him, as regards Nature, as regards God. There are no great men, there are only great conflicts." The great man is, after all, only a larger version of man himself, whom Giraudoux condemns for the very quality that most contemporary writers have exalted as his chief virtue: the deadly sin of pride.

We here encounter in Giraudoux a mystical element which, like the allegorical forms that he has used, seems nearer to the medieval than the modern mind: a belief that pride is not simply a moral flaw but a scale before our eyes that prevents us from seeing the real nature of things. In *Juliette au pays des hommes* Emmanuel's entire establishment, a truly Spenserian palace of sin, is subject to this petrifying influence: "Throughout all of the house, silence. In analogy to the birds without a cry, the dogs without a bark, the ornaments, the furniture, seemed to have lost their language." Jérôme Bardini, one of Giraudoux's prime sinners, appears as a shadow to the young girl, Stéphanie, "because he was covered with a coating and a sort of absence on which nothing took."

Certain of Giraudoux's sinners attempt to escape this deadly nothingness secreted by themselves, to regain episodically, or even artificially, the lost innocence of Eden. The Bernard the Weak of *L'Ecole des indifférents* has discovered the trick of inventing a newly created universe, of imagining that each natural event is occurring for the first time. This device is typical of Giraudoux himself. Jérôme Bardini flees to America. And the man who delivers the "Prayer on the Eiffel Tower" boasts that he has personally saved a few corners of the world from the universal malediction: "I am a small Messiah for tiny objects and animals. I use certain words . . . as Adam used them. I am a small Messiah for three or four sentences. I alone am able to perceive, here and there, the being, the insect, the patch of sunlight that, in its own category, has had my happy fate and has escaped the accursed word."

This is all very well, but these few recaptured corners of Eden have the disadvantage—an important disadvantage for the novelist—of being totally destitute of human life. To proceed from these miniature revelations to the enlarged canvas of the novel, Giraudoux had to invent a member of the human race who was not altogether human. The word "man" is specific as well as generic. And Giraudoux, slyly exploiting man's tendency to represent humanity *in toto*, suggests that he has found one form of human life on this planet that has been exempted from man's fall from grace, the allegorical

"third race" that La Fontaine discovered in animals: woman herself
before the creation of man, or a young girl. This allegory, like any
allegory, immediately invites the question: Is Giraudoux's young
girl a nymph or spirit in disguise, or is she really a young girl? No
doubt, as in any allegory, the truth lies somewhere between the two
extremes. She certainly touches the earth very lightly, if at all, and,
like Suzanne, seems more at home when she is perched on the top
of a tree or diving under the water. But whether divine or mortal or
halfway in-between, she casts about her a steady, incorruptible light
in which all human vanities, pretensions and impurities are merci-
lessly exposed and judged.

Giraudoux encountered his heroine in one of his earliest stories,
Allégories, 1909: a beautiful, naked girl who turns out to be Truth.
But naked Truth, however beautiful, is a little too near the nether
end of allegory to command the undivided attention of a novel
reader. Not until twelve years later, with *Suzanne et le Pacifique,*
did Giraudoux succeed in giving Truth the recognizable features of
a sensible provincial schoolgirl.

Suzanne is a young girl from Bellac who is shipwrecked on a
desert island and there witnesses, without fear or dismay, the gradual
unfolding of a newly created universe: first, fishes, flowers and birds;
on a neighboring island, mammals, a few traces of man; on a more
distant island, gods; then dead men, victims of a torpedoed boat;
and finally living man himself, in the shape of her rescuers, if one
can speak of being rescued, from Eden. Thus abstracted from civilization, "the only person not to have a thousand men on my right, a
thousand men on my left, with women in-between for extra padding,
everything that came from nature or from my heart reached me at
the first shock and overwhelmed me."

In this favored position Suzanne delivers Giraudoux's most famous
and, in its casual common sense, its matter-of-fact simplicity, perhaps
most devastating judgment of man: her personal opinion of Robinson Crusoe as revealed to her by Defoe. "But I, searching this book
for precepts, for advice, for examples, was stupefied by the poverty
of the lessons that my elder, man, was giving me. . . . This puritan,

prostrated by reason, with the certainty that he was the sole concern of Providence, never, for a single minute, committed himself to her care. At each instant, for eighteen years, as if he were still on his raft, he tied strings, he sawed logs, he nailed boards." So Suzanne, who had originally hoped to profit by Crusoe's experiences, now feels impelled to take the poor man by the hand and guide his faltering steps, to tell him: "Don't work for three months making yourself a table: Squat down. Don't waste six months making a prayer stool: Kneel down."

Is this, we ask again, a divine or a female judgment? And again, no doubt a little of both, is the reply. Another woman, Virginia Woolf, has viewed this same man with something of Suzanne's fond despair. "Nature must furl her splendid purples; she is only the giver of drought and water; man must be reduced to a struggling, life-preserving animal; and God shrivel into a magistrate whose seat, substantial and somewhat hard, is only a little way above the horizon." And yet it is not quite the same, for Robinson Crusoe, as seen by Virginia Woolf, is simply Robinson Crusoe, one perspective among many others. For Suzanne he is man himself, just as Suzanne, in her judgment of Crusoe, becomes the voice not only of woman but of divine innocence and divine candor.

As in the case of many first novels, that is, a novel in which the author for the first time encounters his real hero or heroine, *Suzanne et le Pacifique* is one of Giraudoux's best. Until his last novels, *Aventures de Jérôme Bardini* (The Adventures of Jérôme Bardini) and *Choix des élues,* Giraudoux has little to add to what he here has said. Perhaps for this reason he then turned to a different and more terrestrial subject: allegories based on a series of national, political or racial antitheses. These were interrupted by only one novel, reminiscent of *Suzanne: Juliette au pays des hommes. Siegfried et le Limousin* (*My Friend from Limousin*), 1922, is based on the Franco-German antithesis; *Bella,* 1926, which contains a very transparent portrait of Poincaré and of Giraudoux's personal mentor, the radical socialist Berthelot, on the antithesis of the two Frances; *Eglantine,* 1927, on the antithesis of East and West as embodied in the persons of Fontranges, a simple-minded country gentleman, and Moïse, a rich Jewish banker.

These political and social antitheses are neither very original nor very profound; nor do they lead to any very new or arresting conclusions. In a number of instances Giraudoux does try to reconcile his two terms in a final synthesis: the Germano-Frenchman, Siegfried; Bella's death on the altar of French unity. But we cannot take these efforts very seriously. Giraudoux has already weighted the scales too heavily in favor of France and Berthelot. As a matter of fact, undisguised, venomous hatred, absent in all of Giraudoux's other writings, creeps into his portrait of Poincaré. This may be politically justified; it is not allegorically valid. Giraudoux can raise French virtues, even French faults, far above the faults, even the virtues of Germany. He can applaud Berthelot and despise Poincaré. But the reader may be disinclined to identify France and Berthelot with absolute, unadulterated truth.

Giraudoux seems partially aware of this, for the subjects that he has chosen twist themselves around in his hands. Geneviève becomes not so much a delegate of France as a delegate of Truth; Bella, already a delegate of Truth, pushes forward to the center, even the title page, of a novel constructed around the Poincaré-Berthelot feud; and in the last of these novels the idyllic relationship of Fontranges and Eglantine completely displaces the antithesis of East and West.

And so we are back to our original story: What happens to Truth in a highly imperfect world? One or the other of these two must give way, and the existing world is not very likely to do so. Truth must either adapt herself to human reality or else depart therefrom. In other words the young girl cannot always remain a young girl. She must either die, as is the case with Bella, or else she must become a grown woman, as is the case with Suzanne and Eglantine. The latter transition is accomplished when she falls in love, or becomes ready to fall in love, and thus sacrifices her divine estate, her omniscience, her secret relations with ghosts, gods, plants and animals in exchange for humanity.

This is an old and venerable legend: the goddess who through love of man abandons her divine prerogatives; the sleeping beauty who is awakened by a prince; the virgin who is sacrificed to a monster; and, Giraudoux even implies, the story of the Messiah. But each of us must decide for himself whether this is a happy or a tragic legend; whether the illusion, created by love, of man's divinity is worth the sacrifice of divinity itself; whether the young girl who becomes a woman has lost or found her true destiny.

Giraudoux, as usual, is evasive on this point. We have every reason to rejoice in Suzanne's return to France, to humanity, and, we are led to believe, her future husband. We do rejoice, we are rejoicing. Then comes that famous final sentence: "I am the controller of weights and measures, Mademoiselle. . . . Why are you weeping?" The final paragraphs of *Eglantine* are even more disturbing. It is the last night of Eglantine's innocent relationship with the Quixotic old country gentleman, Fontranges, and as she watches his sleep, Eglantine realizes that "this wake is thus the wake that precedes one's entry into the terrible convent of human beings. She trembled, but she saw how useless and cruel it would be to resist. . . . He was now turned toward her. Both had their hands around their heads and seemed to be supporting a heavy burden, as do all humans, standing up or lying down, sitting or kneeling, caryatids of nothingness. . . ."

A chronological account of Giraudoux's development would no doubt indicate an ultimate decision in favor of the human race. Most of Giraudoux's novels are earlier than his plays, and his plays—his successful plays at any rate—generally point to this conclusion. What is *Amphitryon 38*, 1929, what is *La Guerre de Troie n'aura pas lieu* (*Tiger at the Gate*), 1935, if not a triumphant vindication of married woman? How grandly Alcmène, the faithful wife, rejects Jupiter's gift of immortality! How far Andromaque, in all her stubborn blindness, stands above the virgin prophetess Cassandra because she loves her husband, because she is going to have a child! In Giraudoux's later play, *Ondine*, 1939, the picture becomes less clear, the struggle between the divine and human factions more balanced.

Even so, the most eloquent lines of the play are not given to Ondine; they are given to her imperfect lover, Hans. "I demand for men the right to be left a little more to themselves on this earth."

This very human protest against the impossible aspirations that lead men to their destruction was written by an older and a wiser man than the author of *Suzanne* and *Eglantine*. But it was also written by a dramatist, that dramatist who believes that "if the reader seeks revelations in his book, the spectator wants only enjoyment in his spectacle." Although the word "enjoyment" must be given a broad interpretation in this context, it is nonetheless firmly opposed to "revelations." And those of us who seek a revelation of Giraudoux's deepest meaning are thus warned to leave his theater, even the theater of his maturity, and turn to his last two novels.

Although separated by eight years, *Aventures de Jérôme Bardini,* 1930, and *Choix des élues,* 1938, are in a sense companion pieces: the twin panels of Giraudoux's Last Judgment. In both novels he abandons the familiar paths thus far explored. With Jérôme he returns to the male hero of *L'Ecole des indifférents* and *Simon le pathétique.* But whereas the earlier novels were written in the first person and showed a certain degree of sympathy for the narrator hero, Jérôme Bardini is seen objectively and far less indulgently, first by Giraudoux, then by a young girl, and finally, after his encounter with a child Messiah, by Jérôme himself. *Choix des élues* starts out at the very point where Giraudoux previously concluded his novels. Edmée is not a young girl who returns to humanity but a grown, married woman who succeeds, provisionally, in escaping therefrom.

The action of both novels is set neither in France nor on a desert island but in America, which to French eyes, in particular to Giraudoux's, must seem the least likely setting for a supernatural event. Did not Moïse, the incarnation of the Orient, speculate on the very high improbability of a saint or a Messiah appearing in America? Yet Jérôme encounters a child Messiah at Niagara Falls, and Edmée, who lives in Hollywood of all places, is a saint. Giraudoux is now avoiding all possible ambiguities and double meanings.

He is deliberately sacrificing the pastoral charm, the early morning freshness, of his earlier novels and facing up to the crucial problem that Cocteau, the novelist, avoided: that of extending his poetic visions into the realm of adult consciousness.

We cannot expect Jérôme, who is a sinner, to take us very far in this direction. He is dissatisfied with life but he is incapable of anything more than life. The best he can attain is self-knowledge—a recognition of his own presumptuous egotism. In the final pages of the novel old Fontranges of *Bella* and *Eglantine* names Jérôme's sickness. It is the deadly sin of pride, which is (and it is no coincidence that Giraudoux uses the very term Sartre has since made so famous) "a nausea at the idea of creation, a repulsion for our way of living, a flight from our dignities, a terrible modesty." And Fontranges concludes: "But I have no fears, even for you, Jérôme. I know that God's punishments are invisible. That is their greatness. They affect neither our happiness nor our conscience. They are a silence of God."

The sin of pride is a fairly common affliction among the adult male population of Giraudoux's novels. But no previous Giraudoux hero ever saw himself so clearly. This is an important step forward. To proceed from the negative revelation of human reality to the positive revelation of reality itself, however, we must turn to Edmée.

Edmée, the chosen one, first becomes conscious of her call at a birthday dinner given in her honor by her adoring family: her all too human husband, Pierre, who is a successful engineer; her all too human son, Jacques; and her definitely non-human daughter, Claudie. From the outset of his novel Giraudoux emphasizes a strong sex division in this quartette, the male elements being characterized by a pedantic respect for, the female elements by an ironic indifference to, the schoolbook incarnations of humanity: our old friends "the great men."

It is during this disastrous birthday scene that Edmée sheds two tears, tears that the male members of her family, like Suzanne's controller perhaps, erroneously suppose to be tears of happiness.

Soon afterwards, accompanied by her confederate, Claudie, Edmée escapes; at first to a park, then on a week-end visit, and finally altogether. She still carries with her, to be sure, a single and rather brittle tie with humanity: her maternal love for Claudie. But this tie is severed when Claudie suddenly grows up and becomes an average young girl; her father's daughter, she does well at school, hangs up portraits of great men, likes to sew, weeps over poetry and music, and finally judges, condemns and deserts her mother in exchange for humanity.

Edmée, thus totally abandoned, goes through a period of uncertainty and dark despair. The unseen presence who has thus far directed her destiny, has so relentlessly chosen her and severed her from all human ties, remains silent, unresponsive. Unlike Judith, unlike Jeanne d'Arc and the official saints, she has no visions, no ecstasies or stigmata. It is not until her son Jacques returns to her that the veil is lifted, that she understands: "This was her destiny: an intrigue without words or gestures, but lasting, but intimate, with a presence manifestly not that of man."

We stumble, toward the conclusion of this novel, over the curious resemblance of Edmée, the saint, and Jérôme, the sinner; of her revelation and his sense of nothingness. Jérôme, like Edmée, has abandoned his family, his home, his place in the world; he suffers from the same apprehensions, the same anxiety; for him, as for her, the material world has become invisible. The distinction between Jérôme and Edmée is almost imperceptible; it is nonetheless the very dividing line between heaven and hell: the absence or presence of grace. To Jérôme, God's silence is empty; to Edmée, it is full of meaning. Jérôme's accursed indifference reduces the universe to nothingness, but Edmée's divine indifference makes the universe transparent.

It is easy to see where Giraudoux found the story of Edmée. It is the legend of Psyche, the woman who was loved by an invisible god. Giraudoux, as we have seen, is particularly fond of this legend. "It was with the eye of Psyche" that Eglantine contemplated and lost the sleeping Fontranges. Juliette, a deluded Psyche, believes that her human lover is a god when she sees him naked for the first time. Stéphanie, a Psyche in reverse who supposes that she has contracted an infernal liaison with a demon lover, discovers, as she watches his sleep, that Jérôme is only a man. But Giraudoux has never before carried this legend so far—all the way back to its Platonic origins, to a belief that the soul can find true happiness only when, escaping from the prison of the body, its desires and its senses, "she passes," according to Plato's *Phaedo,* "into the realm of purity, and eternity, and immortality, and unchangeableness, which are her kindred; and with them she ever lives, when she is by herself and is not let or hindered."

It is characteristic of Giraudoux, the novelist, that he conveys this austere and fragile message through the down-to-earth and all-too-familiar theme of the eternal triangle. Nor does he spare his heroine the familiar and semi-ironic frustrations implied therein, as they are implied in the eternal dualism of mind and existence. Had Giraudoux been writing a poem, he would perhaps have permitted her to remain forever, like Psyche, in her celestial paradise. Had he been writing a play, he would probably have given her the dignity of a tragic end. But Giraudoux was writing a novel, which is the cruelest form of all; for the novelist can escape neither the inadequacy nor the implacability of life. Just as Suzanne returned to France, just as Juliette returned to her fiancé, just as Eglantine returned to the world of eligible young men, Edmée, abandoned by her invisible lover, must return to her legitimate husband. But we now know what we previously only suspected: This return is not a triumph for humanity; it is a cruel defeat for Giraudoux's heroine—the human soul.

And so the novel concludes, as it began, with another family dinner. Edmée's eyes, this time, are dry, but she suddenly notices that her daughter's eyes are full of tears. This is the unkindest cut of all. "Well, well," Edmée reflects bitterly, "he is certainly losing no time. The mother gave him a taste for it; now it's the daughter's turn. There now. . . . He is beginning with Claudie."

Louis-Ferdinand Céline: Ulysses Again

By 1932 surrealism had been fairly well domesticated. The more talented younger writers, Malraux and Saint-Exupéry, were now fleeing the literary atmosphere of postwar Paris. The war itself, which they had not experienced, was being relegated to the past. Then, like an unexploded bomb that had been neglected in the rubble, came the sudden blast of Céline's *Voyage au bout de la nuit* (*Journey to the End of the Night*).

The first shock came from Céline's use of spoken language on the printed page. In America, where *Huckleberry Finn* is counted as a children's classic, the public is used to this. In France it was an unprecedented innovation. And the distance between the written and the spoken language is far greater there than in America. As with Mark Twain, Céline's use of ungrammatical, spoken language as a narrative technique would seem to be a sort of verbal realism, a tearing away of the hypocrisies and artificial refinements of civilized discourse and a getting down to the spontaneous reactions of the living human organism. This is an important source of Céline's savage verbal humor—particularly in the opening chapters of the novel where the abominable carnage of World War I, as seen by Céline's narrator, is contrasted with the absurd commands of the superior officers and the patriotic clichés of a civilian population brought up on Déroulède and Barrès.

Actually, this use of spoken language as a written narrative technique is in itself an artifice. People do not ordinarily write words as they speak them; they tend to lose their ear for language. And Céline's written transcription of contemporary Parisian slang is as conscious, in its way, as Gide's attempts to purify his style of all such surface relief. Among the writers who have been influenced by Céline, Sartre was attracted by the verbal realism, a fitting vehicle for his own existential philosophy. More word-conscious writers, like Queneau, were attracted rather by the humor and the oral poetry of Céline's literary style.

With Céline himself, the realism, the humor and the oral poetry are combined in a hallucinatory account of Ferdinand Bardamu's flight through existence. The "voyage" of Céline's narrator is literal as well as metaphorical. He spends his whole life escaping from one environment to another. From that moment in the opening chapter of the novel when Bardamu, exhilarated by wine and military music, enlists as a soldier, the chase is on. "They had surreptitiously closed the door behind us, the civilians! We were done for, like rats." From now on, there is no turning back. Door after door swings closed behind the fleeing Bardamu until he is finally cornered.

Since the novel opens with Bardamu's experience of World War I, one might imagine that he now has seen the worst of it. One is soon corrected. Bardamu's subsequent adventures are even more atrocious, as he himself occasionally observes. These include a period of detention in an insane asylum, with the probable alternatives of execution, return to the front, or permanent confinement; a further period of enforced detention in a solitary outpost of the African jungle; a trip to America as a galley slave; and Bardamu's life in America, first as a bum and then as a worker on the Ford production line.

These experiences, which comprise the first half of the *Voyage*, are much in the style of the traditional picaresque novel. Indeed the rather improbable galley slave incident points to a deliberate parallel with some of the narratives in *Don Quixote*. Yet, as we read, this galley seems no more incredible than the Western Front or the Ford production line. As with Cervantes himself, this use of a mock heroic form gives a sharp satirical bite to Céline's whole denunciation of contemporary civilization: A naïve and astonished observer is pointing out the scandalous absurdity of war, of colonialism, of modern industrialism.

With Bardamu's return to France and his sordid existence as an unsuccessful doctor to the poor, the novel takes a somewhat different turn. The naïve amazement of a Bardamu still "unviolated by horror" gives way to the sullen resignation of a man who takes the worst for granted. Bardamu's indignation is no longer directed against the structure of Western civilization but against the actual quality of human existence—in any form. His dramatic leaps from continent to continent degenerate into a series of petty moves from one section of Paris to another or from Paris to Toulouse and back again. Bardamu is now almost twenty years older than the Bardamu who enlisted in the first world war. He has learned that travel as he may, he will never escape from life—or from himself. Even his momentary escapes from conscious existence, such as the accesses of fever that made his African adventures endurable, the humble dream worlds of the movies and the brothel that illuminated his existence in America, become more rare. Bardamu is no longer even able to sleep at night. The "world has closed in" around him, and the only remaining exit, death, is barred by an unreasoning animal instinct for physical survival.

Throughout this voyage, Bardamu has been accompanied by a mysterious fellow wanderer, befittingly entitled "Robinson"— a sort of alter-ego who always manages to be one step ahead of Bardamu himself. When Bardamu encounters Robinson in the front lines of the war, it is Robinson who first conceives the possibility of escape. When Bardamu arrives at his solitary outpost in Africa, Robinson is already there and preparing to abscond with the company's funds. When Bardamu arrives in Detroit, he finds that he has been preceded by Robinson. With their return to France, Robinson is the first to shake off all remaining traces of human self-respect. He leads a shameless gutter existence, agrees to murder an old lady in exchange for a thousand francs, and when this enterprise falls through, lives on the money of a young girl in the south of France.

At the end of the novel Robinson finally murders the old lady, this time without any financial inducements, abandons the young girl and returns to Paris, where he lives on what he borrows from Bardamu. And when his erstwhile fiancée finally tracks him down, he provokes her to such a degree that she shoots him in a taxi. Robinson's final diatribe is at once the cause and justification of his death. The young girl, Madelon, imagines that Robinson's insults are aimed against herself, but Robinson's disgust is aimed rather against the physical aspects of love, of humanity, of life in general.

Here again he has outdistanced Bardamu, whose general revulsion against life has not yet hardened into an ascetic philosophy that can stand up against death. "I wasn't ready to take any more of it any longer myself! . . . But as for me, I hadn't even gone as far as Robinson in life! . . . I really hadn't succeeded. I hadn't found one single solid idea, like the one he had found for getting himself bumped off. Even bigger than my big head, bigger than all the fear inside of it, a beautiful idea, wonderful and very convenient for dying. . . . My own ideas were just knocking around in my head with a lot of space in between, it was like a lot of measly little spluttering candles, trembling all through my life in the midst of an abominable universe, something really horrible."

From this, we see perhaps the major defect of Céline's novel. Bardamu stands midway between his two near contemporaries: Giraudoux's Jérôme Bardini and Sartre's Roquentin. As with Bardini, Bardamu's revulsion against life takes the form of an unsuccessful escape from life. Like Roquentin, Bardamu expresses this revulsion as a sort of physical revulsion against the obscenity of carnal forms. Unlike Bardini and Roquentin, however, Bardamu has no clear, even if unattainable, conception of his heart's desire—and consequently, he has no real sense of loss. He meets no sybil and no child Messiah. His revelation of existence is not illuminated by a counterrevelation of nonexistence. The best he can manage is an occasional lapse of sentiment over an old soldier who is using his life's earnings to send an orphan to a respectable school, a warmhearted prostitute or the merry laughter of unsullied childhood. One almost prefers his out-and-out pornography.

It is true that these lapses of sentiment are not an important aspect of the *Voyage au bout de la nuit.* But in a novel of this length we feel the lack of something else. And it is not necessarily a more explicit treatment of the "metaphysical anguish" implied in so many passages of Céline's novel. Indeed, after Malraux and Camus one is almost relieved not to have to interpret Bardamu's experience of the war, his trip to Africa, the inferno of the African jungle or of the Ford production line as conscious symbols of "man's fate." What is lacking is an intellectual framework of some sort on which Céline can hang his story.

In the first half of the novel we are carried along by the movement of the story, which flows forward as swiftly and relentlessly as the omnipresent waters of Bardamu's sea journeys: the flight to Africa, the flight down the African coast, the flight to America. And the novel concludes, impressively, on the banks of the Seine with another image of this relentless flow of life. "Far off, the tugboat has whistled; its call has passed the bridge, another, the lock, another bridge, far off, still further off. . . . It was summoning all the barges of the river, all of them, and the whole city, and the sky and the country and ourselves, everything that it was carrying away, the Seine as well, everything—so that we can drop the whole subject."

During the second portion of the novel, when the vanquished Bardamu is stranded in Paris, this movement is arrested. The story drags on, but wearily, monotonously and somewhat pointlessly. Céline's roar is here degenerating into the compulsive whine of the concierge. As Bardamu himself has put it, "You get overwhelmed with the subject of your whole life when you live alone. It knocks you out. To get rid of it you scrape it off on the people who come to see you, and it bores them."

This confession really applies to Céline's later novels, such as *Mort à crédit* (*Death on the Installment Plan*), 1936, and *La Bande de Guignol* (*Guignol's Band*), 1943, which often seem nearer to psychotherapy than literature. Taken all in all, the *Voyage au bout de la nuit* is well worth the fare. The novel seems too long for what it has to say, but Céline has a prodigal vitality often lacking in the more efficient novelist. Queneau, perhaps, and Sartre, undoubtedly, are better novelists than Céline. Yet, not only the language but many of the scenes of Queneau's novels are taken from this *Voyage*. The noisy, lunatic gaiety of a cheap amusement park in *Pierrot mon ami* (*My Friend Pierrot*) is closely modeled on Bardamu's trip to the Batignolles fair. And that repulsive, slimy quality that Sartre has given to

existence is inspired not only by life itself but by life as filtered
through the imagination of Céline's Bardamu.

Raymond Queneau: The Sunday of Life

Raymond Queneau, like Aragon, is an ex-surrealist. As one reads
his novels, one understands why he was attracted to that particular
experiment. Queneau is a born experimenter. One also understands
why he could not produce these novels until he had escaped the
confines of surrealist dogma. Queneau's experiments are strictly literary experiments and, as such, concerned with problems of literary
style and literary form that the surrealists themselves deliberately
ignored.

Céline, whose *Voyage au bout de la nuit* appeared a year before
Queneau published his first novel, *Le Chiendent* (Fly in the Oint-
ment), 1933, provided the necessary stimulus. Inspired by the example of "the first important book in which the use of spoken French
is not limited to the dialogue," Queneau proceeded to develop a
theory of linguistics that must have astounded Céline. According to
Queneau, the gap between written French, as this was established
in the seventeenth century, and contemporary spoken French has
now become as wide as the gap between classical Latin and the
Romance languages; modern literature, if it is to survive as a living
language, must therefore imitate the spoken rather than the written
form. Obedient to this theory, *Le Chiendent* originally started out as
an attempt to translate Descartes's *Discours de la méthode* into
modern slang, and it still contains a slangy approximation of
Plato's *Parmenides*.

The resulting effect, as Queneau must surely be aware, is not,
however, one of increased intelligibility. If anything it is the reverse—
a sense of comic surprise at seeing these venerable abstractions fitted
out in the racy fashions of contemporary Parisian slang. Queneau's
subsequent novels, moreover, are by no means confined to this form
of speech. He is just as apt, on the contrary, to give absurdly literary
pretensions to his spoken dialogue—by the use of complicated sub-

junctives, the preterite past, or highly specialized nomenclatures. His characters, for example, habitually refer to the movies as the *cinématographe*.

Queneau's language, both dialogue and narrative, is sometimes a phonetic reproduction of ungrammatical or slangy spoken French; sometimes it rises to the heights of epic poetry; sometimes it lies between the two. But at all times, and whether vulgar or sublime, it follows a fairly unified pattern of rhythmic rhetoric, full of puns, coined words, polysyllables, alliterations and phonetic ornaments that cannot be classified under any heading other than that of "Queneau-ese." It would thus appear that Queneau's scholarly concern for the ever widening gap between written and spoken French is, at heart, simply a pretext for upsetting the rules and regulations of the written language. To this extent he is really nearer to Joyce, whom he has acknowledged as an important influence, than to Céline.

The influence of Joyce is also apparent in Queneau's second experiment, which is an experiment with form. This, still more than his linguistic innovations, shows how far he has departed from his surrealist past. We are tempted to call *Nadja* an anti-novel because of its very shapelessness. Queneau has called his own novels anti-novels because he deplores the anarchical status of the existing novel form: "As for myself," he has written, "I really cannot submit to such free and easy ways. If the ballade and the rondeau have perished, it seems to me that in opposition to this disaster an increased rigor should be shown in the use of prose."

Queneau's boasted "rigor" is not always very evident in the novels that he has written. This is because most of his rules are completely invisible to even the most sympathetic of readers. Here, for example, is a partial explanation of *Le Chiendent:* "I could not bear to allow accident determine the number of chapters in these novels. It is for this reason that *Le Chiendent* is composed of 91 (7 x 13) sections, 91 being the sum of the first 13 numbers and its 'sum' being 1, it is thus at once the number of the death of beings and their return to existence. . . ." If this type of rule escapes us, as it certainly would if Queneau had not spelled it out, we cannot feel that we have suffered a very great loss. Yet, although Queneau's novels are not very rigorously constructed—that is to say, if we overlook the number magic that has occasionally obsessed him—neither are they totally devoid of form.

A poet as well as a novelist, Queneau has written one novel, *Chêne et Chien* (The Oak and the Dog), in verse form and has also incorporated verse passages into his prose novels. More important than this, however, is his extension of certain poetic conventions to the novel form itself; not, as with the surrealists, the convention of metaphor, which he uses sparingly, but that of repetition. "One can rhyme situations and characters," he declares, "as one rhymes words; one can even be content with alliterations." A sentence, perhaps a single word, recurs insistently. Characters alone or in groups of two or three (Queneau is especially fond of the conventional fairy tale trilogy) advance and retreat at regular intervals and mirror each other's words and gestures. Our final impression is that of a dance, at times stately, at times wildly orgiastic, but always ceremonial in nature.

This atmosphere of ceremony is due in part to Queneau's choice of subject matter. The whole action of *Saint Glinglin* (Doomsday), 1948, revolves around an annual spring dish-breaking festival; that of *Pierrot mon ami*, 1942, arises out of the conflicting claims of an amusement park and a "Poldavian" prince's grave. Almost all human activity in Queneau's novels is ceremonial rather than practical in nature—assiduous movie attendance, shopkeeping (devoid of profit), walks (devoid of destination), conversations (devoid of meaning), quests (devoid of objects), courting rites (generally devoid of consummation), not to mention the many funerals scattered through his pages. And the contrast between the gravity and the vanity of these occupations suggests a meaning more subtle than that of satire. Is this, we wonder, a kind of comment on the nature of existence, and, if so, of what kind?

Queneau has studied philosophy and, what is more, has suggested that a solid grounding in philosophy is an important prerequisite for any serious novelist. One philosophic problem that keeps rising to the surface of his novels is that of existence, of nonexistence, and the relation of the one to the other. So universal is this problem that we cannot pin it down to any one school of philosophy. The recent critical orgy of *reductio ad existentialismum* will of course point triumphantly to Sartre. But aside from the fact that many of Queneau's novels antedate Sartre, one could equally well point to Plato's *Parmenides* which, it will be remembered, Queneau transcribed in *Le Chiendent*. As a matter of fact, Queneau is especially intrigued by pre-Socratic logic-chopping of this type. In *Le Dimanche de la vie* (The Sunday of Life), 1952, the Captain's response as to why a certain private is not listed among his soldiers is worthy of an early Greek, if not of the Red Queen herself: "How, my dear lady, would you expect me to know? If he were listed, I would be able to give you the reasons for which he would not have been listed, but in a case where he is not listed, I really do not see how I could give you the reasons for which he would be listed."

One could also point to certain aspects of Hegel. Queneau, like the existentialists, has reflected on Hegel's phenomenology. But whereas the characters in a novel by Sartre or Simone de Beauvoir seem to have reached and to have become inextricably stuck at that moment of Hegel's dialectic when consciousness for the first time becomes aware of its enemy, the non-self, Queneau's characters seem barely to have emerged from the lowest category of subjective mind: the moment when the mind is hardly aware of itself as such, when the distinction between the self and the non-self is still vague, and when, as with children, prophets, poets and dreamers, meaning is not a function of discursive reason but of pattern, ritual, ceremony and habit.

Simone de Beauvoir prefaces her novel, *L'Invitée* (*She Came to Stay*), with Hegel's gloomy statement: "Each consciousness seeks the death of the other." The title of Queneau's *Le Dimanche de la vie* is taken from a very different phase of Hegel's philosophy: ". . . it is the Sunday of life that levels everything and banishes all that is evil; men gifted with such good humor cannot be fundamentally evil or vile."

This "Sunday of life" suggests an early moment in the history of human consciousness, but it also suggests that margin of purely ceremonial activity in which man's weekday struggle for recognition, prestige and material goods is provisionally abandoned. Queneau's novels reveal a vista of uninterrupted suburban Sundays, and often in the literal as well as the figurative sense of the word. Pierrot, Petit-Pouce and Paradis, one of Queneau's most alliterative trilogies, are thus irresistibly attracted to "L'Uni-Park" (Luna Park) "into which this June Sunday poured beautiful weather and a crowd, coalesced into a dark and noisy seething, sprinkled by the fires and music of more than twenty attractions." The *cinématographe,* where personal identity is so easily merged with the fictitious identities projected on the screen, is another Sunday or, for children, Thursday afternoon activity. Queneau has devoted an entire novel, *Loin de Rueil (The Skin of Dreams),* 1945, to the adventures of a schoolboy, Jacques, whose identity becomes inextricably confused, both for Jacques and for the reader, with the identities of a series of conventional moving picture heroes. The novel concludes, or rather completes its circle, when Jacques himself becomes an actor and is shown in a film, *The Skin of Dreams,* acting out this entire process.

If, with the significant exception of a successful arms manufacturer, Queneau's principal characters tend to linger in this innocent Sunday of life, this is not entirely due to stupidity or laziness. "The man who works," says Queneau, "violates nature; his action is a crime as regards her. . . . Thus goes human action according to Hegel's dialectic. There have always been certain sensitive souls who are saddened by this process that goes from one necessary destruction to another." These sensitive souls—the type of person who wonders if oysters on the half shell are still alive—are none other than Pierrrot, Jacques and Valentin, the unlisted soldier of *Le Dimanche de la vie.* Even their gay harlequinades betray this throbbing note of sadness: the pangs of unrequited love, the remorseless passage of time that carries all things in its wake, the inexplicable existence of fleas, the tremulous reproach of the oyster. It is difficult to become totally innocent of conscious existence.

A number of Queneau's characters have come close to this dividing line: Jacques, the movie-goer of *Loin de Rueil,* who is dreamily dispersed in the identities of a dozen fictitious characters; Valentin, the unlisted soldier, who by contemplating the passage of time has for several minutes at a stretch accomplished the difficult feat of not thinking of anything at all. But when they actively aspire to sainthood, "the absolute and gratuitous innocence of the idiot," they are beset by a number of familiar logical and psychological difficulties.

In the first place, the idea of nonexistence is in itself a proof of existence. In the second place, the moment we are convinced of our humility we are guilty of the sin of pride. When Jacques explains that his constant preoccupation with the idea of death is a means of humiliating himself, his girl friend remarks: "But you look rather pleased with yourself." To which Jacques replies: "Alas, how right you are! There's no end to it. One can't extricate oneself from it. I would so like to be nothing at all and not even be able to boast of it." And Valentin, who experiments with sainthood in the army, similarly abandons all hope when he finds that he actually enjoys latrine duty—a task he had voluntarily assumed in the interests of self-humiliation. To Descartes's triumphant "I think, therefore I am" Queneau seems sadly to reply: "Alas, yes. There's no getting away from it." So Jacques and Valentin, like most of Queneau's characters, continue to wander in that twilight zone inhabited neither by men of the world nor by saints but by dreamers and poets.

The most interesting and the most ambitious of Queneau's novels, as regards both form and content, is *Saint Glinglin,* a novel that was at least fourteen years in the making, since the final version, published in 1948, incorporates and expands two earlier novels: *Gueule de pierre* (Stoneface), 1934, and *Les Temps mêlés* (Mixed Weather), 1941. *Saint Glinglin* departs from the curious but recognizable context of Queneau's other novels to enter the fabulous realms of mythology. It is, briefly, a saga of the various exploits of the three sons, Pierre, Jean and Paul, and the feeble-minded but prescient daughter, Hélène, of the mayor of the "Native City," a secluded and backward town, which, owing to the beneficent presence of a "cloud-disperser," enjoys perennial good weather. As the novel is divided, the four lyrical monologues of these four central characters alternate with three narrative chapters describing three different versions of the traditional spring festival of Saint Glinglin. Here, as in the potlatches of the Kwakiutl Indians, the leading citizens of the town vie with each other in providing the expensive crockery which is ceremonially smashed to pieces by the collective population of the town. The plot, if plot there is, arises out of Pierre's revolt against his father, who, after an epic flight through the "Arid Mountains," falls into the "Petrifying Springs." Pierre then replaces his father as mayor, does away with the annual dish-breaking ceremony, institutes a new religion revolving around the petrified form of his father, and throws the cloud-disperser into the communal dump (which doubles as burial ground). The previous period of perennial good weather is thus supplanted by a period of perennial rain that dissolves the petrified father-image, and the angry villagers oust Pierre as mayor in favor of his brother Paul. At the close of the novel fine weather is restored by a new contraption, and Pierre hurls himself into the communal dump.

Any attempt to analyze this novel in terms of plot is doomed to failure, so largely is plot subordinated to pattern. Yet when we start again and attempt to understand the pattern, we are thrown into a state of wild confusion. We can track down, to be sure, the familiar problem of existence and nonexistence. Pierre, in his original reflections on marine existence, discovers that there are two different modes of life: the marine and the non-marine, the obscure and the luminous; the one a source of happiness, the other a source of anguish; the one corresponding to the embryo, the other to man—a theme he develops further in a lecture to the inhabitants of the Native City. Is it possible that Pierre's destruction of the cloud-disperser implies an attempt to restore his "Native City" to the water-bound environment of the embryo, and his ultimate disappearance in the primeval slime of the communal dump, a desperate return to the womb?

But Pierre's revolt against his father, his ascent to the summit of the Arid Mountains, the subsequent petrification and dissolution of the father-image, also have distinctly Freudian implications, an interpretation reinforced by certain parallels with the frankly psychoanalytical *Chêne et Chien*. In contrast with *Chêne et Chien*, however, these implications are depersonalized and broadened into a general commentary on nature, society, politics and religion. Like the *Ulysses* of Joyce and Flaubert's *Bouvard et Pécuchet, Saint Glinglin* seems to be one of those heroic efforts to sum up and systematize an enormous fund of human knowledge and experience.

We are confronted here with an aspect of Queneau that is less apparent in his other novels than in his critical essays: the encyclopedic curiosity of the man. Like most novelists, Queneau reads many novels; but he is also interested in mathematics, linguistics, anthropology, psychology, biology, agriculture and entomology. The last-named subject, as one might guess from the intense insect activity of *Loin de Rueil* and of Hélène's soliloquy in *Saint Glinglin,* is one of his favorites. A life of beetles, in his mind, "outdistances, and by a long shot, the *Cent vingt jours de Sodome* by the Marquis de Sade. The habits of these little beasts are repellent, horrible, unspeakably vile." A life of grasshoppers, meanwhile, contains "the germ of countless meditations; and if philosophers, for the two thousand and a few hundred years that they have existed, had, helped by an exact science, reflected on animals instead of dreaming about the soul, maybe their writings would have acquired a practical human value."

Queneau has militated for a re-alliance not only of natural science and philosophy but also of natural science, philosophy and poetry. His principal contribution here is his *Petite Cosmogonie portative* (Portable Cosmogony), 1950, a lengthy poem devoted to the history of the world in which Man himself, the usual subject of poetry, is dismissed in a single couplet wedged in between the primates and the development of machines:

The monkey effortlessly the monkey becomes man
who slightly later disintegrates the atom.

Now the obvious model for this portable cosmogony is Lucretius's
Of the Nature of Things. Like Lucretius, Queneau is apparently
using cold scientific facts as the subject of his poem, a process justified by Mercury, the god of science as well as eloquence, in the third
section of the poem:

Instead of the buttercup or else the convolvulus
he has taken calcium and the alveolate bee
Get it? instead of the bench and the springtime moon
he has taken the cell and the phenol function
Get it?

As with Lucretius, Queneau's poem is divided into six sections, and
it contains an invocation to Venus, the source of all higher organic
life. These apparent similarities merely serve, however, to underline
the basic dissimilarity of the two poems. *Of the Nature of Things* is
first and foremost an attempt to supply an objectively scientific account of the universe. Poetry, here, is not an attitude of mind but a
superficial sugar-coating on Lucretius's bitter pellet of materialism.
Queneau's cosmogony is poetic in spirit as well as form, for his treatment of the physical sciences is fully as fanciful as if he were writing
of buttercups and springtime moons. With a charming and highly
unscientific anthropomorphism he bemoans the fate of the planet
Neptune, "distressed to be navigating so close to the edge of infinity,"
admires "the audacity" of the first living cell "who threw life against
the ramparts of death" and respects "the modesty" of the electronic
calculating machine, "pulverizing the records established by bipeds."

This type of speculation may not give a very accurate picture of
the external cosmos, but it gives a wonderful picture of our own
feelings about this cosmos. No human being, not even the scientist
himself, entirely escapes the strange and sometimes terrifying emotions engendered by his nonhuman environment. And although we
seldom formulate the questions, What does it feel like to be the

planet Neptune? the first living cell? the electronic calculating machine? these questions are lodged somewhere in the back of our
minds. Only the poet, however, with his gift of sympathetic con-
templation and his miraculous ability to merge his identity with any
external object that excites his curiosity can find the answers—answers that previously took the form of the ancient mythologies.

It is this combination of Queneau's scientific curiosity and poetic
sensibility that determines the strangely compelling atmosphere of
Saint Glinglin. *Saint Glinglin*, in contrast to the *Petite Cosmogonie*,
is Homeric in form as well as feeling. Style, subject matter and characters, as well as the general spirit of this novel, suggest that Queneau
is attempting to create a modern mythology. The complex and mul-
tiple themes of this mythology somehow fail, however, to add up
to a meaningful whole. Poetry and science, philosophy and psychology, linguistics and numerology, astrology, anthropology and entomology are thrown together in a semi-ironic, semiserious conglomer-
ation of ideas and analogies that never crystallizes into an intelligible
statement about life.

Our suspicions about the general structure of this novel are perhaps unfairly aroused when we perceive that Queneau has incorporated a previously autonomous whole, *Gueule de pierre*, into his
larger unit with only superficial readjustments. (*Les Temps mêlés*,
which is much inferior to its predecessor, is considerably revised.)
Queneau has explained that the structure of *Gueule de pierre* resembles that of a helix, since the novel opens with Pierre's reflections
on fish and concludes, with the flight through the "Arid Mountains,"
under the zodiacal sign of the Fishes. The reader is free to approve
or disapprove of this particular device, but the fact remains that
if it gives unity to *Gueule de pierre*, it necessarily cuts the longer
Saint Glinglin in two. And again, while *Gueule de pierre* is
frankly dominated by the central figure of Pierre, *Saint Glinglin*
hesitates between this original emphasis and a tendency to divide
the parts more equally between the three sons and the daughter.
To be sure, the final narrative section, which is called "The Saint
Glinglin," links up with the opening soliloquy through Pierre's an-

guished reiteration of certain key phrases. But this is a slender link for a novel of such scope and such complexity. And the hurried, last-minute thematic modulations of this concluding section fail to bring the novel to a satisfactory conclusion.

The particular seduction of *Saint Glinglin,* for seduction there is, lies less in the total structure than in the individual parts, certain of which rise to heights of poetic intensity that are rare in any novel. Pierre's opening soliloquy on fish, written in a sort of subaqueous prose where each stubby "b" is systematically replaced by a sinuous "s," is as compelling, in its way, as Pascal's reflections on outer space. To fit a nugget such as this into a larger unity is no doubt a fearful undertaking. And even though *Saint Glinglin* proves a partial failure when taken as a whole, it is one of those rich and adventurous failures that invites applause.

RETURN TO MAN

There is a watershed that throws the French novel of the inter-war years on two different courses: backward to the first world war or forward to the second world war. Chronologically speaking, Queneau and Aymé are the contemporaries of Malraux, Saint-Exupéry and Sartre. Yet something about their novels—a certain air of detachment, a certain kind of irony—places them on the other side of the watershed even, as is the case with Aymé, when they are writing about the second war.

The distinguishing characteristic of these backward-looking novelists is briefly this: World War I was not their war. They had not foreseen it; they saw no sense in it; they would have no part of it at all. Their one desire was to dissociate themselves from this appalling catastrophe and, insofar as they could, from the civilization that had made it possible. Giraudoux's Suzanne flees to a desert island; the adolescent hero of Radiguet's *Le Diable au corps* (*Devil in the Flesh*) flirts with a soldier's wife behind the lines; the hero of Queneau's *Un rude Hiver* (A Hard Winter) spends most of his time at the movies; Céline's Bardamu finds temporary refuge in an insane asylum. The only enthusiastic participant in sight is Cocteau's Thomas the Impostor; but Thomas is prone to a mysterious illusion that he has wangled a front-row seat at a particularly festive display of fireworks.

It has become fashionable to despise these literary isolationists. At the time, however, it was the only possible literary attitude. The year 1914 had in many cases severed the bonds that united the novelist with the society in which he lived, and it was necessary for him to show that this had happened. The novel under these circumstances was eminently asocial. But it was alive, it was fertile, and, above all, it was an act of liberation whose consequences are still apparent today.

Still, no literary attitude, however understandable, however fertile, can last forever. Malraux's *Les Conquérants* (*The Conquerors*) appeared in 1928 and, three years later, Saint-Exupéry's *Vol de nuit* (*Night Flight*). The French novel was beginning to take a new direction. It still carried the heritage of 1914, to be sure. Malraux and Saint-Exupéry, Sartre and Camus, are still at heart as skeptical and solitary as their predecessors. Unlike their predecessors, however, they can no longer endure this state of spiritual isolation. The more desperate their predicament—adrift in an absurd and unintelligible universe—the more urgent their desire to believe, to belong, to sense, however fleetingly, that they are part of some human society.

It is this conflict between the intellect and the emotions that gives these forward-looking novelists so tragic an intensity. Incapable of Romains's cheerful *camaraderie* and the savage misanthropy of Céline, they are driven on extreme and desperate courses. Some, like Malraux, take part in far-off revolutionary actions; some, like Saint-Exupéry, were among the pioneers of commercial aviation; others flirt with Communism, like the early Malraux and the later Sartre. The intellectuals of the twenties were attracted to Communism because they viewed it as a vast destructive operation—a sort of political adjunct of surrealism. To the intellectuals of the thirties and the forties, Communism offered a sense of participation, of belonging—the privilege of sharing common risks.

When war broke out in 1939, these novelists were prepared to participate in the event. And in France it took the form of a spontaneous Resistance movement in which the intellectual could play an active role. It was less the war itself than its depressing aftermath that provided the real spiritual ordeal for this generation of writers. The danger once past, the fragile community of the Resistance days was torn asunder, the sense of participation and solidarity irrevocably lost. Saint-Exupéry's *Pilote de guerre* (*Flight to Arras*), 1942, Malraux's *Les Noyers de l'Altenburg* (*The Walnut*

Trees of Altenburg), 1943, Sartre's *Les Chemins de la liberté* (*Roads to Freedom*), 1945–1949, and Camus's *La Peste* (*The Plague*), 1947, are still borne on the impetus of wartime aspirations. Saint-Exupéry, who died in action, did not live to see the end of the war. But Malraux's last novel, part of which was destroyed by the Gestapo, remains unfinished; Sartre has not yet concluded his *Les Chemins de la liberté*. Camus waited nine years before publishing another novel. And the final pages of *La Peste,* which show the disintegration of the Oran community after the plague is ended, seem almost to mark the end of another literary era.

This was an era of political violence and, from the point of view of the novelists discussed here, of political defeat: the defeat of the Comintern in China, of the Loyalists in Spain, of France in 1940. Yet in the novel it produced a sense of personal exhilaration, a triumphant rediscovery of human solidarity. This sense of exhilaration could not survive Hiroshima and the dubious victory of 1945. The ideas of political violence and political defeat have now become too vast, too terrible, to serve as literary stimuli. As Camus seems to realize, although he may not yet have solved this problem, contemporary fiction has now to find a new direction.

André Malraux: Maker of Myths

"La tragédie, maintenant, c'est la politique."

Malraux is fond of quoting this statement of Napoleon's. There was a time when we too might have been tempted to use it in a discussion of Malraux's three major novels: *Les Conquérants* (*The Conquerors*), 1928, which is based on the Canton insurrection of 1925; *La Condition humaine* (*Man's Fate*), 1933, which is based on the Shanghai insurrection of 1927; and *L'Espoir* (*Man's Hope*), 1937, which is based on the first year of the Spanish Civil War. Today we are inclined to doubt the applicability of Napoleon's phrase and to believe that the real political tragedy of our times remains as yet unwritten.

It is true that Malraux was the first contemporary novelist to sense that he had been born into an age of political violence. Popular legend has made him an important figure in the Chinese revolution; and even if popular legend exaggerates the actual facts of the case, Malraux's publication of *Les Conquérants* at a time when most people were still thinking in terms of the League of Nations was an important literary event. The passage of time has given a prophetic aura to Malraux's choice of subject matter; however, it has also permitted us to view his treatment of this subject matter with a greater degree of personal detachment. It now seems fairly obvious that Malraux was concerned not with the political fact of revolution but with a certain mythology of revolution that, largely thanks to Malraux himself, prevailed during the thirties and the early forties. As is already apparent in the titles of his novels, Malraux has seen the shape of man in the revolutionary cause; the inimical factors that control his destiny in the antirevolutionary cause; and in the conflict between the two, man's eternal struggle against his fate.

Politically speaking, this is something of a simplification. Yet, had Malraux taken the theme of revolution as an abstract symbol rather than as the living substance of this drama, he would never have been able to give it so much intensity and power. The spectacle of men chained to each other and executed one by one that Pascal uses as an image of man's condition—a passage that inspired the title of Malraux's second novel—has re-emerged as a horrible fact, a fact more difficult to understand and to accept than the abstract idea of death. Malraux has found in revolution not only a fundamental myth to embody his conception of man's position in the universe but also dramatic means of expression: the urgent pressure of events and foreshortening of time, counted not by weeks and days but by hours and minutes; the total disruption of the normal relations between things; the violent contrasts of noise and silence, of light and dark, of the heroic choice and the fatal mechanism of events.

All of these elements are real. In Malraux, they take on the wider significance of a terrifying dream come true. In his marginal notes to Gaëtan Picon's study of his works, Malraux repeatedly insists—with regard to his own novels as well as the novels of Dostoevski,

Stendhal and Balzac—on the nonreality of fictional worlds. "I am going to suggest a game. Tell three or four of the greatest novels to yourself, supposing all the while that 'this has happened.' Really happened. You will see the resistance offered by the *fairyland* of the novel—the real creation." The "fairyland" of a Malraux novel lies in this dramatic intensification and enlargement of existing human reality. And it is to Malraux, more than to any other novelist, that we owe the legendary figures of the thirties and the early forties.

In later life he himself called *Les Conquérants* an "adolescent" novel, but few characters in modern fiction have so gripped the imagination of the contemporary reader as his cynical adventurer, Garine. To him Emmanuel Berl dedicated his *Mort de la pensée bourgeoise* (Death of Bourgeois Thinking); Camus obviously had Garine in mind when he described "the conqueror" of *Le Mythe de Sisyphe* (*The Myth of Sisyphus*); and it is Garine who haunts so many of the minor Resistance novels. To be sure, there was something in the spirit of Garine, his courage, his toughness, his passionate negation of existing European values, that corresponded to the spirit of the times. Yet when confronted with Berl's dedication, with Camus's portrait of "the conqueror," we are almost inclined to believe that this fictional character had flesh and blood existence. As Malraux has said of the eighteenth century novelist, Laclos, the real problem here is that of the means used by the artist to make us believe his myth.

In *Les Conquérants* Malraux has used an obvious technique. Garine does not appear until the middle of the novel. Up to this point he is seen entirely in the light of legend, police reports or personal recollection. And even when he appears, he is seen in the enlarged perspective of the narrator—a younger and apparently admiring man. *La Condition humaine* uses a new device. Unlike *Les Conquérants* and Malraux's earlier novel *La Voie royale* (*The Royal Way*), it is never dominated by a single overpowering presence. The scene is divided among a number of different men, and these are not presented in the light of legend or the admiration of a younger man. Yet they too are transfigured, more subtly magnified; for Malraux contrives striking visual effects in certain of his scenes, "pictures," one might say, rather than descriptions.

There are not many of these in *Les Conquérants,* perhaps only one that we remember: the dead bodies of four hostages lined up against the wall; a woman on her knees hanging onto one of the bodies. The effect of this scene depends largely on the eerie fact that the dead bodies, already stiff, are *upright* (a word that Malraux italicizes in the text). As with so many of Malraux's pictures, it is magnified by our memory of other pictures; it is composed as a crucifixion. From the dramatic opening scene, in which Tchen murders a sleeping man in a hotel room, up to the majestic closing scene, in which the vanquished revolutionists are awaiting execution, *La Condition humaine* is full of such pictures. And these have a common trait that is an important element of Malraux's visual style: They are nocturnal scenes composed in such a way as to offer a dramatic play of light.

Certain of Malraux's critics have emphasized the "authenticity" of his descriptions and attributed this to his personal experience of the events depicted in his novels. This comment is founded on the popular assumption, neither confirmed nor denied by Malraux himself, that Malraux participated in the Canton and Shanghai insurrections. Wilber Frohock, in his excellent study, *André Malraux, the Tragic Imagination,* has thrown much doubt on the assumption. Whatever the truth of the matter, it seems extremely unlikely that the major events of the Shanghai revolution took place in carefully composed scenes, and always at night, with a dramatic play of light. The night scenes may well have been inspired by certain of the painters that Malraux loves so well: Rembrandt, El Greco, Goya and de la Tour, of whom he has said, "This unreal light suscitates, between the forms, relations that are no longer real." In the opening hotel room scene Malraux in fact interpolates the conscious intention of an anonymous painter: "The only light came from the opposite window: a great rectangle of pale electricity, cut by the window bars, one of which made a line across the bed just below the foot, as if to accentuate its volume and its life."

Yet both the narrative technique of *Les Conquérants* and the more subtle visual effects of *La Condition humaine* are simply literary means of expression. The essential aura of the Malraux hero lies in the actual structure of events portrayed, in a sense of inescapable doom. We know from police reports given early in the novel that Garine is doomed, that he is to die of the fever contracted in China during his service in the revolutionary cause. All his words, all his gestures, thrown against the blank wall of approaching death are thus magnified, and increasingly so as the novel nears its end. The principal characters of *La Condition humaine,* who elect to remain in Shanghai after the city has been abandoned to Chiang Kai-shek, are similarly enlarged. As Frohock points out, Malraux has here deliberately changed the course of history to create the sense of doom so necessary for the structure of his novel: The Communist decision not to oppose Chiang was already apparent a year before the Shanghai insurrection and could not have come, the way it comes in Malraux's novel, as a disastrous surprise. Even here, the characters who escape destruction eventually fade in significance. Those who emerge as the real heroes of the novel are Tchen, who dies in his suicidal attempt to assassinate Chiang Kai-shek; Kyo, who poisons himself; Katow, who is executed in a particularly horrible manner. And Malraux's concluding chapters, which carry the novel beyond this point and show the respective fates of the political survivors, bring a certain sense of anticlimax.

L'Espoir, in contrast with the novels on the Chinese revolution, reflects a number of diverging aims and methods. Malraux is telling the story of the men who fought the Spanish Civil War, but he is also attempting to describe the events as they occurred—a problem that demands considerable ingenuity when these events take the shape of a major war. He has solved the problem by using a multiplicity of rapidly changing perspectives. Now we are in Barcelona, now in Madrid, now with the aviators, now with the ground forces. The numerous characters are thus important not only as characters; they also supply the different perspectives from which events are viewed.

It is true that *L'Espoir*, like *La Condition humaine*, is far removed from the objectivity of a historical document, but Malraux's departures from history serve different ends. Whereas he deliberately changed the course of history to give a tragic conclusion to *La Condition humaine*, he seems to have taken an unduly optimistic view, both in his selection and presentation of events, of the first year of the Spanish Civil War. We never see the Fascist victories in Africa and in the south of Spain. In the battles that Malraux has described, the Republican tanks and planes always arrive at the last minute and just in time to save the day. The ignorant, undisciplined mobs, when properly harangued, burst into the "International" and become efficient fighting forces. And the bitter power struggles between Communist and non-Communist factions, which so greatly weakened the Loyalists, are transmitted only as abstract discussions between highly civilized, disinterested intellectuals.

It is possible to see a propagandistic intention here. At the time that he was writing this novel Malraux was also attempting to win world opinion over to the Loyalist cause. But if by propaganda one means coldly calculated means to a desired end, the word does not apply. It is rather that Malraux seems to have felt during the Spanish war, and perhaps for the first time, the real horror of organized violence aimed at innocent and helpless victims. Whatever may be true of Malraux's earlier novels, this is an eye witness account of a particularly cruel war. In contrast with *Les Conquérants* and *La Condition humaine*, the esthetic distance that makes tragedy endurable is often lacking. And since tragedy would be unendurable, it is generally averted. Alvéar's son will recover his sight; the English boy's legs will not be amputated; the Republican planes will arrive in time.

Yet, on three occasions the tragic myth that we have seen before in *Les Conquérants* and in *La Condition humaine* breaks through the surface. These are the execution of Captain Hernández, where, as in Katow's recollection of an execution scene, the victims are outlined against the horizon; the nocturnal conversation between the Italian aviator, Scali, and the old Spanish art lover, Alvéar, in a hotel room during the bombing of Madrid; and the descent of the wounded

aviators from the mountain during the battle of Teruel—a sort of
Descent from the Cross, although Malraux does not say so. On
each of these occasions Malraux reverses the hopeful forward movement of his novel. Hernández, like the principal characters of
La Condition humaine, has chosen to remain in Toledo after it has
fallen to the Fascists—the only military defeat in the novel. The
conversation between Scali and Alvéar takes place during what they
believe to be the last night before the Fascist seizure of Madrid, and
Alvéar has chosen to remain in Madrid. The descent of the wounded
aviators from the mountain top is in a sense a Republican victory—
but it is no victory for these wounded heroes.

  L'Espoir gives the impression of two different novels that have
been woven together: the hopeful daylight romance, built out of
the historical events on which Malraux felt so deeply and which is
dominated by Communist figures like García and Manuel; the desperate nocturnal dream, dominated by the doomed figures of Hernández, Alvéar and the mutilated aviators—men who can survive
neither a Communist victory nor a Communist defeat. The first of
the novels concludes with the triumphant organization of the Republican army and is focused on the figure of Manuel, now a full-
blown Communist leader. The other novel concludes with one of
the most beautiful and moving passages in all of Malraux: the elegiac
descent of the wounded aviators into the world of happiness where
they have no place. It is as if Malraux, the man, were trying to tell
us, "It is not too late, we still have hope," while Malraux, the artist,
keeps reiterating, "All, all is vanity." Whatever Malraux's actual intentions may have been, it is the latter message that prevails—for it is
treated far more effectively.

  Had Malraux been writing a political tragedy, the concluding
chapters of *L'Espoir,* and the concluding chapters of *La Condition
humaine* as well, might have conveyed that return to order and equilibrium we feel at the conclusion of Shakespeare's *Julius Caesar.* But
this return to order supposes a natural political order of some sort,
a set of fundamental rules that may be transgressed during the
development of the action but that automatically reassert their au-

thority at its conclusion. With Malraux, it is the very absence of this idea of a natural political order that creates the tragedy. And in this he is typical of his age. Each individual hero lives in a private world of his own making, unsupported by any external norms. And the game of revolution becomes an end in itself—meaningful not because of its political consequences but because of its effects upon the players.

The word "lucid," which Malraux sometimes applies to the heroes of his early novels, has frequently been applied to Malraux himself. Nonetheless, when we come to examine the meaning of his text, we find that he is very far from lucid as this word is generally understood in France. All the words that Malraux loves so well, that he uses over and over and over again—fraternity, destiny, fate, eternity, centuries-old, millenary—are just the resonant type of word that sets us dreaming. Whatever precise contents these words may originally have had is soon dissipated by incessant reiteration. Yet there is something in these vague and shapeless words, and in the emotions that are clustered around them, that is essential to Malraux's meaning. Malraux truly believes—and he has become increasingly explicit on this point in his later writings—that the really important, fundamental aspects of human experience are mysteries that cannot be elucidated but only revealed. Death is a mystery; human fraternity, a mystery; art, a mystery; and behind them all, the great impenetrable mystery of man himself. "The word 'to know' as applied to human beings has always stupefied me. I believe that we know no one." But we do have, according to Malraux, an immediate intuition of this mystery in certain moments that transcend our normal experience of life. And the vague abstractions, progressively depleted of rational content during the unfolding of a Malraux novel, are suddenly brought to life at the end, by the impact of approaching death. Death gives the dimension of the absolute to that which was relative, the depth of eternity to that which was transient. And the emotional illumination is reinforced by the strange nocturnal lighting effects that are characteristic of so many of Malraux's climactic scenes.

It is at this moment that the reader is suddenly confronted with

an extremely curious fact: Although Malraux's whole myth of revolution is apparently constructed around man's heroic revolt against
his fate, the climactic scenes invariably suggest an act of mystical
surrender. Tchen, after he has killed a man for the first time, states
that he feels his terrorist vocation not as an anguish but as a "fate."
When Kyo is talking to Communist officialdom at Hankow, he
affirms that what he respects in Communism is not the sense of a
fate but the exaltation of a will. Yet in the moments immediately
preceding the execution of the vanquished revolutionaries, Kyo has
the following revelation: "The fate, *freely accepted by them,* rose
with the murmuring of wounded men like the *peace* of the evening,
covered Kyo, *his eyes closed,* his hands crossed on his *abandoned*
body, with the majesty of a dirge." In *L'Espoir,* during the Battle of
Teruel, Magnin senses that his men are united by a "fraternal fate."

Still more revealing, although the idea of fate is suggested and not
explicitly stated, is the sudden spurt of eloquence in Malraux's
UNESCO speech on "Tragic Humanism": "As with England during the Battle of London, let us say: 'If this should die, may all
civilizations die as beautiful a death!'" But did they ever really say
it? This is an exact inversion of Churchill's famous speech which
urged heroic survival, not a spectacular Twilight of the Gods.

There is a hidden attraction in this idea of "fate," not only for
Tchen and Kyo but also, apparently, for Malraux himself. The overpowering and inevitable catastrophe toward which they are impelled
seems to have the mystical power of translating individual and
mortal men into a transcendent unity called Man—at the cost, however, of their individual and mortal lives. It is this veiled emotion,
much more than the explicit idea of revolt, that determines the
psychology of Malraux's myth of revolution.

The sacred mystery of human sacrifice no doubt lies buried deep
in some dark corner of the human mind, but it has generally been
disclaimed by the great poets of Western civilization. Malraux, however, has merged this ancient, Oriental rite with the Western concept
of tragedy; he has resurrected the barbaric gods and spirits, so avid
for human blood and human sacrifice, whom the Greeks purged

from their art and literature. If Malraux has changed their names, he has not changed their fundamental nature. The terrorist religion of Hong and Tchen, cruel, bloodthirsty, irrational; the insatiable power lust of Garine; the erotic sadism of Ferral—this whole complex of emotions carries us back to some primitive scene peopled with fanatic priests and inhuman despots. It is true that Katow and Kyo die not for the gods of Hong and Tchen but for human dignity and human fraternity. Even so, human blood must be shed and human sacrifices amassed. Malraux has put these Western concepts into Oriental terms, and the Old Testament Jehovah still rumbles in the distance and must be appeased.

With *L'Espoir* we seem to be arriving at the New Testament. There is compassion here, and hope, and the ever-present figure of Christ, who is crucified again, as so often in the past, by churchly officialdom. The hymns of hate formerly sung by the revolutionists are taken over by the Fascists. It is true that the emotion of human fraternity is still limited in time and space to the chosen race that is fighting the revolutionary cause. But in the background the spectacle of the silent misery of the people of Spain gives birth to a new emotion, an emotion that stretches back over the centuries, and includes the present moment in a timeless vision of the human race. "Eternal," "centuries-old," "millenary"—words that recur so often in *Les Noyers de l'Altenburg* and *Les Voix du silence* (*Voices of Silence*)—are sounded here for the first time.

This new emotion is connected with Malraux's discovery of the common people of Spain. These common people, like the heroes of his earlier novels, are not seen as ordinary men and women; they are seen as pictures: "Behind silent groups passed wagons humped with baskets and bags, where the scarlet flash of a bottle glittered for a moment; then, on donkeys, peasant women, faceless, but whose fixed eyes one nonetheless imagined, and their centuries-old distress of the Flights into Egypt." And, as with Christianity itself, one wonders if it is the men and women or the paintings they suggest that stands uppermost in Malraux's imagination.

The problem is brought out into the open in the nocturnal conversation between Scali and Alvéar, a conversation that is framed around the question: What still holds in the face of human suffering and human death? Alvéar, who has devoted his life to art, insists that art and art alone survives. Scali, although a cultivated man who has made an important study of Piero della Francesca, replies: "No picture holds in the face of spots of blood."

In *L'Espoir* Malraux leaves this problem hanging in the air, but in his later novel, *Les Noyers de l'Altenburg,* 1943, he has apparently attempted to defend the humanist religion of Scali. As this novel was intended to be only one part of a larger unit, its meaning is never altogether clear. It would seem that this meaning is related to Malraux's discovery of the Common Man—the unshaven, ignorant soldiers who play an important role both in the narrator's experience of the early months of the second world war and his father's experience of the first world war. The reason for their presence here is Malraux's new belief that uneducated people are more eternal, more continuous, than educated people.

In an intellectual colloquy that takes place in the central section of the novel one speaker advances this argument as proof of the continuity of the human race. His antagonist replies that these common people have no significance. Man is of interest only to the extent that he is civilized, and to the extent that he is civilized he is always changing. In the passages that follow, Malraux seems to be asserting that the continuity of common men is more important than civilization; however, his treatment of this argument inadvertently supports the opposing thesis. In order to give his common soldiers an aura of eternal truth, he is obliged to see them as works of art, to disguise them as Gothic statues, medieval wood carvings and Breughel paintings. He has tried to justify the Scali point of view; nonetheless, it is Alvéar who has prevailed. This victory is uncontested in Malraux's subsequent publications, which are all devoted to the study of art.

Malraux has still, however, to refute the skeptic of *Les Noyers de l'Altenburg* and show that human civilizations are not wholly mortal. This is the central thesis of his epic study of the psychology of art, *Les Voix du silence,* 1947-1950. Malraux's theme, as he himself has emphasized, is particularly appropriate to the present age. Now, for the first time, the amassing of pictures and statues in museums, and, still more important, in reproductions, has permitted us to become familiar with the art of all times and all places and to see this art not as the expression of a particular civilization but as an end in itself.

To rescue the idea of art from history and from the mortal civilizations of which history is made is to create a new absolute and, in a sense, a new religion. Like Pascal's thinking reed, a single work of art is greater than the surrounding universe because it subjects this universe to its own laws. Unlike the thinking reed, however, a work of art is eternal, or as eternal at any rate as the human race, because it is reborn again and again as it is rediscovered and seen in different ways by different civilizations of men.

This religion does not really answer the question raised in *L'Espoir:* How can we look at paintings when men are suffering and dying around us? And although Malraux has asserted that the idea of art as an eternal value is the basis of a "universal humanism," this humanism leaves many human questions hanging in the air. Are the Egyptian pyramids worth the suffering that was necessary for their construction? The Aztec images, the children sacrificed thereto? But these questions become irrelevant when art is no longer seen as the expression of a religion but as a religion in itself. The violent urge to find a sacred absolute, no matter what the cost or the result, is purified when we are no longer thinking in terms of human agony and human blood—and this is one reason why Plato was probably right in ejecting the poets from his Republic. After *Les Voix du silence* we see Malraux as the passionate and single-minded artist that he is; not as the humanist that he is not.

Antoine de Saint-Exupéry: Knight-Errant

Saint-Exupéry, like Malraux, is one of those legendary figures of French fiction: a novelist who looks more like the hero of a novel.

His two early novels, *Courrier-Sud* (*Southern Mail*), 1929, and *Vol de nuit* (*Night Flight*), 1931, are based on a firsthand knowledge of the pioneering age of commercial aviation in North Africa and South America. *Terre des hommes* (*Wind, Sand and Stars*), 1939, *Pilote de guerre* (*Flight to Arras*), 1942, and *Lettre à un otage* (Letter to a Hostage), 1943, are directly autobiographical. Malraux, the revolutionist, has come to typify the twentieth century adventurer; but Saint-Exupéry, the air pilot, is more of a knight-errant. His life, as we see it in his writings, seems to have consisted of a series of quests. And a quest, as distinguished from an adventure, is a search for something that remains elusive but that is known to be of great value.

As a commercial air pilot, Saint-Exupéry explored parts of the African desert and the southern Andes hitherto unseen by human eyes; he was among the first aviators to explore the night; and, more important still, he explored ways of seeing and feeling the whole planetary system that were previously no more than suppositions of the poetic imagination.

The true purpose of the quest is not merely a search for new horizons, new antagonists, new metaphors and new sensations—intriguing as these may be. Saint-Exupéry is seeking a new aspect of the self, a spiritual power that will enable him to pierce through the shell of outward appearances. We are close to Giraudoux here, but to a Giraudoux who has engaged his body and his senses, as well as his mind, in this search for the invisible meaning of things.

The theme of the quest is most explicit in Saint-Exupéry's first novel, *Courrier-Sud*. Here he shows us the underside of his story: the personal aspirations that have driven his aviator hero to his dangerous calling and eventual death. *Courrier-Sud* is ostensibly the story of Jacques Bernis's flight from Toulouse to Cape Yubi, as narrated, and in most part imagined, by a friend awaiting his arrival in Cape Yubi. Although the novel is set within the temporal framework of a single flight, the central and longest section goes back to Jacques's brief love affair with a married woman during a two-month vacation prior to his departure. And since Geneviève, the woman in question, is a childhood friend of both Jacques and the narrator, this episode carries us still further back in time.

Jacques Bernis, since earliest childhood, has been a treasure seeker—a "water diviner who carries his trembling hazel stick all over the world." His adult existence as an air pilot is simply an extension of his childhood explorations of the garden and the attic and carries the same anticipation of mysterious, otherworldly revelations. When Jacques returns to Paris on leave, the familiar faces and places, so charged with emotion in his memory, seem opaque and meaningless. Then he rediscovers Geneviève. Geneviève has always had a magical insight into the terrestrial order of things. Even as a child, the narrator reflects, "you seemed eternal to us by being so closely tied to things. . . ." And speaking of her present relations with Jacques, he says: "She came to him as a delegate of things. . . . She was giving him back those chestnut trees, that boulevard, that fountain. Each thing again carried that secret in its core that is its soul." This is not really what Jacques is seeking. Geneviève's unhappy marriage and Jacques's loneliness draw them to each other, but they cannot live together. Geneviève must return to her own native element—her house, her garden, her trees—and Jacques to his.

With the concluding sections of the novel we return to the story of Jacques's last flight. His plane is lost in the desert, and when the narrator discovers Jacques's body, we learn that he has been crucified by a band of dissident Arabs. The novel ends with the narrator's apostrophe to his dead friend. From this passage, which is closer to poetry than prose, it is clear that this last flight is the triumphant conclusion of Jacques's lifelong quest for the invisible meanings of things. It is a final severance of the terrestrial ties that were gradually loosened during the course of his flight, and a final discovery of the hidden treasure "in the star the most vertical to him."

This astral treasure is private, episodic, a fragile ray of poetry that flashes and is gone. Saint-Exupéry's second novel, *Vol de nuit,* conveys a similar dissatisfaction with our terrestrial order of things, but the search is for a wider and more enduring realm of meaning.

Rivière, the director of an air transport line in Buenos Aires, is sitting up all night to wait for three planes which are carrying mail from three different points in South America. As he waits, he wonders about the value of his enterprise. In order to compete successfully with other forms of transport his planes must fly by night as well as by day. Night flights in the southern Andes are at this time almost prohibitively dangerous. Yet, in the face of much official criticism, Rivière stubbornly continues the costly work. What is the meaning of it all? Why should brave men risk their lives for the sake of a commercial air line? Because, Rivière reflects, a man is saved only when he believes that something is of greater value than his own life. "We do not ask to be eternal, we ask not to see actions and things suddenly lose their meaning. The void around us then becomes visible. . . ." "The end perhaps justifies nothing, but the action delivers from death."

There is an important element of truth in Rivière's message, and we now can see that Saint-Exupéry is attempting to convey a meaning that he perceived more clearly in his later writings: the meaning of a civilization. But since Rivière divorces this concept from the natural content of human emotions and needs and obligations, it seems little more than an empty form—the ritual of a dead religion. His message is somewhat similar to that of the priest overheard by Jacques in *Courrier-Sud*: "Come to me, you to whom action, which leads to nothing, was bitter. Come to me, you to whom thought, which leads only to laws, was bitter. . . ." And can we not say of Rivière, as Jacques said of this priest: "What despair! Where is the act of faith? I did not hear an act of faith but an utterly desperate cry." Rivière is not telling us that he is helping his pilots to discover the true meaning of actions and things. In his eyes there is no meaning, and we are surrounded by void. He is merely—and to a cynic this is perhaps the very art of government—giving them an illusion that such meanings exist.

In *Vol de nuit,* as in *Courrier-Sud,* Saint-Exupéry allows a "delegate of things" to plead her cause. She is the woman whose husband, Fabien, is lost in the Andes. It is true that Rivière is moved by this woman's anguish; yet her presence seems little more than a necessary element of resistance to the essential message of the novel. Far from shaking Rivière, she helps him to discover his convictions. The reader, however, may feel inclined to give this woman greater weight than Saint-Exupéry intended. Her reasons are not necessarily better than those of Rivière, but they are at least true reasons that give real meaning, rather than simply an illusion of meaning, to actions and things.

Saint-Exupéry's most convincing answer to this delegate of things lies not in the realm of reason but again, as with *Courrier-Sud,* in the more elusive realm of poetry. Fabien, like Jacques, is something of a treasure hunter who ultimately discovers his treasure in the stars. After flying for several hours in complete obscurity, Fabien sees a hole in the clouds and soars upward into a brilliant nocturnal sky. This is a direct transgression of the laws of flying, and Fabien knows he now is doomed. "Still a hundred dim arms had released him. His ties had been unknotted, like those of a prisoner who is allowed to walk alone, a little while, among the flowers."

The novel form in *Courrier-Sud* and *Vol de nuit* is a very thin veil cast over an amalgam of deeply personal memories. The key situations that recur so often are the very situations that Saint-Exupéry has described most feelingly in his personal letters: the sensations of a pilot starting out for the first time on a new route, his first inkling that he has lost his way, his sense of triumph when he has completed a difficult mission—or the terrible vigil of those who are waiting for a missing plane. The male characters in these novels spring directly from Saint-Exupéry's own life as an air-pilot; and the women characters, who plead for the terrestrial order of things, from the deeper past of Saint-Exupéry's early childhood. Even this thin veil seems to have impeded the natural progress of his thought, for after *Vol de nuit* he cast it off entirely. With *Terre des hommes,* 1939, *Pilote de guerre,* 1942, and *Lettre à un otage,* 1943, Saint-Exupéry found his true voice. The conflicting voices of poetic, heroic and terrestrial truths are now resolved into a mature and eloquent reflection on the nature of human existence.

Terre des hommes is made up of a series of reminiscences, sometimes about Saint-Exupéry himself, sometimes about his comrades.
What holds the book together, and what also distinguishes it from
its predecessors, is less the subject matter than the point of view.
Although published in English as *Wind, Sand and Stars,* its title is
"*Man's Earth.*" The airplane is here used as a means of rediscovering
rather than escaping from this planet. Saint-Exupéry remarks in his
introductory chapter: "The earth teaches us more about ourselves
than all the books. Because it resists us. Man discovers himself when
he measures himself with an obstacle. But in order to act upon the
obstacle, he needs a tool. He needs a smoothing plane or a plow. The
peasant, in his labor, gradually wrests a few secrets from nature, and
the truth he uncovers is universal. In the same way the airplane, the
tool of airlines, plunges man into all the old problems."

The air pilot is here again presented as a treasure seeker, but one
whose treasure is hidden not in the sky but in the earth, whose heroism consists not in accepting but in combating death. The two heroic
episodes are combats of this kind: Guillaumet's solitary descent from
a mountain peak, where his plane had crashed, in subzero weather;
Saint-Exupéry's struggle for survival after an accident in the Sahara.

In *Terre des hommes,* as in his novels, Saint-Exupéry still produces occasional passages of dazzlingly nonterrestrial poetry. Here,
for example, he describes a flight over the desert at nightfall: "This
death of the world takes place slowly. And it is only gradually that
I notice the fading light. The earth and the sky gradually merge.
This earth rises and seems to spread out like a vapor. The first
stars tremble, as in green water. I should have to wait for a long time
for them to change into hard diamonds." The treasure no longer
lies hidden in the stars; these are the enchantresses who attempt to
turn the pilot from his course, the temptation to be resisted. The true
meaning of things lies in human laws, obligations, needs and emotions. It lies in those very ties that Jacques and Fabien cast off when
they ascended to the stars, the ties which give a sense of direction to
the aviator lost in the sky—Guillaumet lost on his mountain top,
Saint-Exupéry lost in the desert. Since this sense of direction must

be personally rediscovered, or experienced, in order to be consciously known, it too evades the possibilities of prose analysis. Saint-Exupéry again conveys his meaning primarily in terms of imagery. We feel the pull of a civilization, that magnetic field of intangible relationships, as a blind man who senses the direction of a fire; a nomad, a spring of water. Saint-Exupéry's terrestrial poetry is nonetheless a universal poetry, intelligible to all men; it is much more than a personal revelation.

This sense of belonging to a civilized community of men seemed almost fatally threatened in 1940 by the German defeat of France. In *Pilote de guerre,* the description of a perilous and militarily useless reconnaissance flight during the last days of the French defeat, Saint-Exupéry tells us how he almost lost but ultimately recovered his sense of direction.

The problem is somewhat similar to that of Rivière: What is the true justification of this apparently useless sacrifice of human lives? Saint-Exupéry realizes that his reconnaissance flight, even if successful, will in no way serve his country. As he starts out he finds no answer to this problem; he is simply doing what is expected of him, as a man who has lost his faith might say his prayers: "It is hard to exist," he reflects. "Man is no more than a knot of relationships, and now I find that my ties are no longer worth very much." This initial incredulity gains ground as he flies over the devastated countryside. The whole French defense effort, the pointless destruction of bridges, houses and trees, the pathetic hordes of refugees streaming along the roads, seem like a cruel and senseless ritual.

The very vulnerability of his position, the slow hours of dangerous inaction, turn him back to childhood reveries: his house, his garden, his nurse. All are invested with the mysteriously important meanings that childhood gives to things. These memories are no doubt delegates of the terrestrial order of things, but delegates as far removed from Saint-Exupéry, the air pilot, as Geneviève from Jacques, or Fabien's wife from Fabien. Saint-Exupéry has had a fleeting vision of the invisible meanings out of which a civilization is made, but he is no longer part of a civilization. In order to become so, he must undergo the exact reverse of his previous experience, pass from inaction to action, from childhood to maturity, from a sense of vulnerability to a sense of victory. And this is what happens at the climactic moment of the flight when Saint-Exupéry and his crew are directly above Arras, an insolently simple target for the German anti-aircraft fire. Yet the target escapes destruction.

A number of writers, including Tolstoi and Hemingway, have observed that when a man has survived the first enemy attacks, fear suddenly turns into courage, the passive victim into an active agent. This birth of confidence can be put to many different uses. With Saint-Exupéry it has the effect of remagnetizing that field of intangible relationships of which a community is built. On the return trip from Arras, Saint-Exupéry is no longer alone. He is part of the crew in his airplane; he is part of his division of the air force; he is part of France.

How much has been written of this particular moment of history. And how little of it has survived! *Flight to Arras* is an exception. The quality of a revelation, even in so tragic a moment, can after all be no different from the quality of the man: We can discover only what is already latent in ourselves. Saint-Exupéry observed when he set out on his mission: "An illumination suddenly seems to throw a destiny on a different course. But the illumination is merely the sudden vision of a route that has been slowly prepared."

Saint-Exupéry's discovery of his civilization, like Proust's discovery of past time, seems to be the very crux of this development. The Arras anti-aircraft fire, which "broke through the shell of outward appearances," is the climax not only of *Pilote de guerre* but of Saint-Exupéry's entire literary output. *Courrier-Sud, Vol de nuit* and *Terre des hommes* are each steps which will eventually lead to this triumphant rediscovery of the self.

There is no doubt a touch of Malraux in Saint-Exupéry's illumination—in his realization that it is only through the sharing of a common risk that we discover we are part of a community of men. Malraux, who tends toward emphasis and abstraction, is speaking of a transcendent concept: Man. Saint-Exupéry, who tends toward the understated and the concrete, is speaking of a real community to which he feels that he belongs. Thus during his stay in New York after the Fall of France, he observed: "France, truly, was for me neither an abstract goddess nor a historian's concept, but a real substance on which I depended, a network of ties that regulated me, a group of poles that determined the inclinations of my heart."

In *Lettre à un otage,* from which this passage is taken, Saint-Exupéry uses the memory of a Jewish friend living in Occupied France as his principal magnetic pole. It is characteristic of Saint-Exupéry that he should appeal not to the idea of fraternity but to a friend. Even when he was writing his previous books, so similar at times to his personal letters, he seemed to need to feel that he was communicating with a friend—Guillaumet, to whom he dedicated *Terre des hommes;* the members of his combat division, to whom he dedicated *Pilote de guerre.* And if the final pages of *Pilote de guerre,* in which Saint-Exupéry attempts to elaborate a whole philosophy of life, fall far below his description of the flight itself, it is perhaps because we no longer feel this note of direct communication. In an earlier moment of the story Saint-Exupéry remarks: "To know is not to demonstrate, nor to explain. It is to have access to the vision. But in order to see one must first participate." And, as he himself implies, the nature of his illumination, thus abstracted from the circumstances of the illumination, loses a great deal of its meaning.

One cannot always have access to the vision, however, and the years he spent in America and then in North Africa, plunged in the debilitating milieu of political expatriates, were, spiritually, a far more difficult ordeal than the perilous flight to Arras. *Lettre à un otage* still reflects the light of Saint-Exupéry's earlier illumination, but *Le Petit Prince (The Little Prince),* 1945, and *Citadelle (The Wisdom of the Sands),* published posthumously in 1948, are scarred by this ordeal.

Le Petit Prince, because it is a fairy story and ostensibly written for children, is the type of book immediately pigeonholed as "charming." And, in a sense, what could be more appropriate a vehicle for the poetry that Saint-Exupéry apprehended in his solitary flights than a fairy story about an astral prince! There is, nevertheless, more poetry in Saint-Exupéry's descriptions of his actual flights. And the charm of *Le Petit Prince* is sometimes blighted by a desperate, solitary sadness that no child would ever understand. It is also overshadowed at times by a series of rather ineffectual attacks upon the human race in general. That the human race is somewhat coyly referred to as "grown-ups" does little to relieve the sadness of the message. Indeed this very complicity with the world of childhood produces an uncomfortable impression.

Citadelle, which was begun in 1936 but written for the most part after 1940, is an enormous treatise on the concept of civilization. An old desert prince is instructing his son in the art of government—a problem that reaches down to the very foundations of human values. The various truths that Saint-Exupéry discovered during the course of his life, in particular the themes of the final pages of *Pilote de guerre,* are brought together and further elaborated in this volume. It might well be interpreted as Saint-Exupéry's literary testament.

Many obvious defects, the repetitions, the long-windedness and the monotony, can be attributed to its unfinished state. But this book also has a fundamental defect. As with the final pages of *Pilote de guerre,* Saint-Exupéry's use of a didactic rather than a narrative form takes away some of the power of his message. The treasure, thus abstracted from the quest, appears as lifeless as the prose summary of a poem. And one cannot help but feel that for Saint-Exupéry, as well as for the reader, the vision has become less clear. Friendship, that "certain quality of smile" for which he fought in 1940, is conspicuously absent. The desert prince is not really a part of his own community. He is merely the sovereign who has founded this community for the betterment of his ignorant subjects. A super-Rivière, he stones the adulteress, strangles the false prophet, chastises his quarrelsome generals—and regularly observes the outward rituals of what seems to be a dead religion.

Had Saint-Exupéry lost contact with his own civilization at this time? Perhaps his desperate efforts to persuade a reluctant officialdom to allow him to return to active service as an air pilot were efforts to recover the friends and the community that he had lost. We have no record of Saint-Exupéry's experience of these last flights. He was shot down by the German air force in 1944. It nonetheless seems inappropriate to look to *Citadelle* for the truest expression of his message. Of all the writers of his time, Saint-Exupéry most closely approached and most clearly apprehended a true and positive faith in human existence on this planet.

Jean-Paul Sartre: The Search for Identity

Sartre published a first novel, *La Nausée* (*Nausea*), in 1938, but his sudden rise to fame took place several years later during the final months of World War II. This was an exciting literary event, as those who saw the excellent performance of *Huis clos* (*No Exit*) in the unheated Vieux-Colombier theater during the winter of 1944–45 may well remember. The four-year intellectual blackout had finally come to an end. The clandestine writers of the Occupation years could at last come out into the open, and a famished reading public, full of hope, enthusiasm and uncertainty, was eagerly casting about for a new intellectual leader to provide a framework, or perhaps a foil, for their pent-up emotions and ideas.

Sartre, a man of unusual intelligence and literary ability, was a natural choice. A relative newcomer, with few prewar commitments, he had sided with the Resistance forces since the early days of the Occupation. Had he not even succeeded in having an obviously anti-Vichyite play, *Les Mouches* (*The Flies*), performed in Paris under the very noses of the German police? In addition he was a philosopher whose monumental *L'Etre et le néant* (*Being and Nothingness*), also published during the Occupation years, seemed to correspond to the needs of the times. This treatise was no doubt more talked about than read in Paris intellectual circles, but a vague impression gained currency that the existentialist philosophy of Sartre effectively demolished the costly illusions of the prewar era and cleared the ground for a more realistic approach to present problems.

At a fairly early stage in his career Sartre thus found the enthusiastic public that many writers have never known. A mixed blessing, perhaps, as this was also an impatient public, avid for simple directives, capsule solutions, and more interested on the whole in ideological than literary problems. The triumphant discovery in Sartre of a "philosophical" novelist and dramatist—as if philosophical problems ordinarily had no bearing on human problems—was something like M. Jourdain's discovery that he had been speaking prose all his life. Critics began to treat Sartre's novels and his plays as a special form of literature to be judged not on its own merits but on the philosophical ideas contained therein. And since these ideas are of a controversial nature, sides were then taken, insults exchanged, and the scene prepared for a dreary battle of the books that has not yet subsided.

The crux of Sartre's existential philosophy insofar as it affects his creative writing, lies in his interpretation of human reality as an inner experience rather than as an objective fact. This has a number of advantages, in particular its revelation of the liberty of mind. Deterministic views of man always imply the distorted perspective of the outside observer. Sartre's inside perspective also distorts the picture, but in different ways. In the first place, it must necessarily lose in breadth what it has gained in depth. How can any one man, be it Kierkegaard or Heidegger or Sartre, offer an objective and comprehensive description of the actual experience of the human mind—an experience that can be apprehended only through the highly subjective process of introspection? And this very process of introspection tends, in and of itself, to color our perceptions. The mind turned inward does not behave in the same way as the mind turned outward. It becomes doubtful, undecided and, frequently, depressed.

In the second place, this inside view of mind is highly incompatible with the structure of human thought and language—its precision, its stability, its "either-or" rigidity. And after all, the structure of human thought and language is as much a part of human reality as the inner experience of mind. In choosing this inside view of man, Sartre found an excellent vantage point for exposing the "thingish" unreality of most objective descriptions of the mind—from Descartes to Freud. His critical insights are always illuminating. When it comes to furnishing a positive description of the mind, though, his sharp-edged tools are turned against himself. This, no doubt, is why Sartre's terminology is so abstruse and unwieldy, why he is so inclined to take refuge in negative formulations, and why he so often seems inclined to contradiction.

There is nothing to be gained, however, in reproaching Sartre, the novelist, for the subjective impurities or logical fallacies of Sartre, the philosopher. A novelist is not judged by the objectivity and consistency of his thought. He is judged by his credibility, or his creative power. Indeed what appears as an outrageous innovation in *L'Etre et le néant* is quite in keeping with current literary trends. Since the turn of the century, novelists have been seeking new techniques for suggesting a concept that neither the philosopher nor the psychologist is able to convey: the living reality of the individual human mind. Whatever we may think of Sartre's conception of this reality, there is no denying his ability to make it live. It is this disturbing intellectual realism, this way he has of taking ideas out of the textbook and putting them back in the mind, that accounts for much of his originality both in the novel and the theater. His appeal goes beyond the quality of the ideas expressed.

Sartre's first attempt in this direction is the strange intellectual experience of Roquentin, the hero of *La Nausée*. Roquentin, after traveling extensively in central Europe, the Far East and North Africa, retires in 1932 to the provincial town of Bouville-sur-Mer to complete his research on an eighteenth century nobleman, the Marquis de Rollebon. These facts, given in an introductory notice, are the only objective information we have concerning the person of Roquentin, for the novel itself, written as a journal, is devoted to Roquentin's investigation of his inner life. The outward context is admirably suited to the inward subject matter, however, as it offers no relief or distraction of any kind. Bouville, apparently drawn from Sartre's impressions of Le Havre, suggests, phonetically, both the muddy torpor and bovine complacency which Paris intellectuals, from Flaubert on down, associate with small town life in France. Roquentin, living alone in a rented room, working in the anonymous atmosphere of a public library, whiling away his leisure hours on the depressing streets or in the equally depressing cafés of Bouville, is soon reduced to that state of solitary boredom wherein the mere process of thought leads to introspection and wherein introspection leads to dangerous discoveries.

Roquentin's personal discovery stems from a sudden consciousness of the inhuman, meaningless and loathsome aspect of material objects. His journal reflects his efforts to describe and, if possible, elucidate his resulting sense of personal anxiety. This grows from a flickering apprehension to a series of attacks of physical nausea as his new perception of things intensifies, spreads out. Gradually the whole of existence—objects, other people and himself—is reduced to a sickening, amorphous mass that has no reason to exist aside from the arbitrary fact that it is there. Roquentin finally reaches a crisis when he becomes convinced that his present intuition of reality corresponds with the actual nature of reality, that all the distinctions, qualities and categories that give intelligibility to our perception of things are simply excretions of the human consciousness.

In one sense Roquentin is a typical twentieth century novel hero. He is the intellectual or artist whose urgent desire for order, form and necessity is cruelly belied by the quality of life around him. We meet him in Proust, in Gide, in Giraudoux, in Malraux, and, after Sartre, in Camus. What is new here is Sartre's hallucinatory personal imagery, his ability to reveal Roquentin's sickening conception of the fundamental nature of existence in the most innocuous and familiar objects—a stone picked up on the beach, a doorknob, a hand, one's own face in the mirror. What is also new is Sartre's willingness to push Roquentin's experience to its extreme limits, his uncompromising rejection of all previous escapes.

When Roquentin rails against the respected props of Bouville society who, in their role of civic leaders, captains of industry, doctors and professors, have convinced themselves that they have the "right" to exist, he is following a well-worn literary path. But Roquentin's destructive operations go much further than this. To anyone familiar with contemporary fiction in France, *La Nausée* reads at times like a veritable literary graveyard. Malraux's discovery of Eastern adventure and Eastern art, Proust's rediscovery of lost memories and Giraudoux's revelation of unincarnate forms are all dragged forth, investigated and duly emptied of content.

There remains, of course, the "humanist" argument for the solidarity of man, the warmth of the crowd, the invigorating fraternity of left-wing political groupings—Jules Romains, in short. Sartre reduces these well-intentioned generalizations to a sickening medley of pretentious verbiage and maudlin sentiment simply by putting them in the mouth of a secondary character, his simple-minded *Autodidacte,* an office clerk whose principal life effort seems to be that of reading the entire contents of the public library in alphabetical order.

What then is left? A frail, a minute, an apparently incongruous ray of hope: Roquentin's pleasure when he hears a certain recording of the jazz tune "Some of These Days." This recording (and one wonders which it may be) reveals another form of existence, another aspect of time, which is crystalline, finite, and governed by a rigorous internal necessity.

At the conclusion of the novel, after Roquentin has finally abandoned all hope of finding some justification for his existence, has dropped his abortive research on the Marquis de Rollebon and prepares to leave the town of Bouville, he hears the tune for the last time. And he realizes that all his life he has wanted to achieve the same effect: "to chase existence out of me, empty the moments of their fat, wring them out, dry them, purify myself, harden myself, so as to give out finally the clean, precise note of a saxophone." Perhaps he might be able to put into a book what the composer of this melody has put into a song? But will he be able to do so? One tends to doubt it. Sartre, unlike Proust, does not imply that his own novel is the very novel his narrator eventually will write. Roquentin's discovery of the world of music does not give meaning to his past existence but merely accentuates its shapelessness.

What then is the real conclusion to this novel? We have some reason to suspect it is insanity. In the introductory notice to the novel the "editors" affirm that "these notebooks were found among the papers of Antoine Roquentin," and we have the impression that Roquentin is no longer on the scene. He might conceivably have killed himself, but, despite his horror of existence, there is no evidence he ever contemplated suicide. There is some evidence, however, that Roquentin, judged by ordinary standards of behavior, would probably appear insane. On the few occasions when he becomes conscious of his effect on other people, Roquentin realizes this himself. Once the reader is aware of this possibility, the intense and anguished tone of Roquentin's journal, his scrupulous analysis of his every mental and emotional reaction, reads like a desperate struggle to cope with impending insanity. This interpretation in no way lessens the impact of the novel: If you, my readers, tried consistently to see things as they really are, Roquentin seems to be telling us, you also would become insane.

If *La Nausée* is to be interpreted as a "metaphysical" novel, it will not bear very close inspection. This is partly because of Sartre's almost passionately subjective bias. In addition he resorts to a number of literary techniques that would seem suspect in a philosopher. At one point in his journal Roquentin points out the artifice involved in telling a story: Events are not related as they were actually experienced but in the light of future events. Insignificant details acquire a dubious prestige simply because they are included in the story and apparently point to the anticipated conclusion. Now Sartre is obviously using Roquentin's journal to show that the actual experience of human existence is utterly meaningless. Events succeed each other in time, and that is all there is to it. But Sartre is not writing a journal. He is telling a story. And in so doing he must select, relate, interpret and impose a recognizable meaning on this succession of events: Roquentin's gradual revelation of the utter meaninglessness of human existence.

Or, to take another example, the brute fact of existence, as revealed to Roquentin, is loathsome because it evades all our categories of understanding. As Sartre says in *L'Etre et le néant,* the being of a phenomenon is transphenomenal. But if existence were truly transphenomenal, how could it ever be described? The attributes that Roquentin applies to existence—"soft, monstrous masses in a state of disorder . . . naked, of an obscene and frightening nudity"— are extremely unpleasant, but they are nonetheless attributes.

In either case Sartre has run headlong into his usual obstacle: the stubborn necessities of human discourse. He can describe neither the total meaninglessness of human existence nor the total formlessness of material existence. He can only pretend to describe them. Whatever view we take of this as philosophy, it is an extraordinary example of the art of writing. The progressive stages of Roquentin's journal really do convey the arbitrary, nonselective quality of immediate experience. And his final revelation of existence really does seem to offer a terrifying glimpse into forbidden realms of meaning.

The basic technique here is an indirect use of negative formulations. Sartre has woven two excellent examples of nonexistence into the underlying structure of his novel: history and music. Roquentin's journal is constantly contrasted in our minds with his attempted biography of the Marquis de Rollebon; his impressions of existence with his impressions of a jazz tune. To the question, What is existence? Sartre can thus reply: Existence is the opposite of nonexistence. Almost every positive attribute that he applies to existence —soft, disorderly, naked—implies an *absence* of the intellectual clarity and intellectual rigor found in historical reconstructions of the past or in the world of music.

Sartre has also used this device in *L'Etre et le néant;* but since he is now writing a novel, no holds are barred. He can give free rein to his fertile imagination, his highly concrete and suggestive formulation of abstract ideas, his unrivaled talent for evoking unpleasant physical sensations. The technique is consequently far more effective. When Sartre, the philosopher, informs us that we have an immediate intuition of existence in the sensations of boredom and of nausea, we tend to raise an eyebrow. But when Sartre, the novelist, describes this situation, we are almost convinced.

La Nausée, if not necessarily the best, is by far the most original and, from the point of view of literary construction, the most finished of Sartre's fictional works. But La Nausée once written can never be written again. Sartre has here carried a fictional theme to a point that will admit no further qualifications, reinterpretations or literary sequels. He had to find a new subject. The fact that the world changed so greatly between 1938 and 1945—the year of publication of the first two volumes of his novel cycle, Les Chemins de la liberté (Roads to Freedom)—no doubt encouraged him to do so.

From the earlier period there remains Sartre's short story collection, Le Mur (Intimacy and Other Stories), published in 1939. Sartre is here primarily concerned with the mind's relation, not to material existence, but to other minds. His psychological insight is by no means weakened thereby: One marvels at his ability to install himself so successfully in the minds of so many strange and different characters. Yet the spell is somehow broken. As with his later studies of Baudelaire and of Jean Genet, these stories read like a series of psychological case histories; they are brilliantly reconstructed, extremely credible, but convey an uncomfortable impression that the author is out to prove a theory. This is perhaps because the characters, unlike Roquentin and the three damned souls of Huis clos, do not discover the ideas that Sartre is wishing to convey; they merely serve as passive illustrations. The complex play of consciousness on consciousness, which he handles so effectively in Huis clos, thus tends to degenerate into a series of predictable devices: the urge to be oneself and somebody else at the same time, the unpleasant sensation that someone is looking at the back of one's neck, the temptation to exist in terms of some recognizable category of existence. This is one reason why these stories are such a fertile quoting ground for a certain type of Sartrian criticism.

The subject matter of Sartre's unfinished novel cycle, *Les Chemins de la liberté,* suggests that Sartre has attempted a history of the French experience of the last war. *L'Age de raison* (*The Age of Reason*), 1945, covers the phony peacetime era that ended with Munich; *Le Sursis* (*The Reprieve*), 1945, the uneasy Munich days; *La Mort dans l'âme* (*Troubled Sleep*), 1949, the French defeat in 1940; and *Drôle d'Amitié* (Strange Friendship), the chapters of the unpublished concluding volume which have thus far appeared, take place in a German prison camp. Sartre is not really exploring the meaning of these historical events, however. At no point does he ask, as Tolstoi asked, What really happened? Why did it happen as it did? Could it have happened otherwise? These questions are in fact outlawed by Sartre as unjustifiable intrusions of the omniscient novelist. Like the Orestes legend in *Les Mouches,* history in this novel cycle exists not as an objective fact but as a personal opportunity: a chance to quit the inconsistent void of subjectivity and find positive existence in a concrete situation.

When Sartre's Orestes returns to Argos, he longs for an action that will give him the freedom of the city and finds such an action in the murder of his uncle. In this, he is very similar to the French intellectuals who seized the opportunity of political commitment provided by the French resistance to the German Occupation forces. Sartre is a sufficiently skilled dialectician, or, to put it more crudely, he is enough of a word-juggler, to name this opportunity a "road to freedom," thus countering a natural impression that he is retreating from the original premises of his philosophy. Strictly speaking, it seems more like "a road away from freedom" as freedom is defined in Sartre's earlier writings: a means of reassuming some of the concrete human loyalties that Sartre, the philosopher, found incompatible with the corrosive liberty of mind.

The first volume of the cycle, *L'Age de raison,* is set in the summer of 1938 and is deliberately apolitical. The central figure is an ineffectual lycée professor called Mathieu, a man who has not even the courage of Roquentin's despair. The two marginal characters who anticipate the possibility of a European war—Gomez, a Spanish loyalist who is fighting in Spain, and Brunet, a Marxist—merely represent two possibilities of political commitment that Mathieu has somewhat guiltily rejected. Mathieu himself is occupied with the more intimate problem of whether to marry his pregnant mistress, Marcelle, or encourage her to have an abortion. At the end of the novel this problem is taken out of his hands by a homosexual called Daniel, who, for a number of complex personal reasons, woos, wins and marries the girl himself.

This unexpected resolution of the plot—Daniel's dramatic entry in the crucial final scene, settling all existing complications, unraveling all accumulated misunderstandings—seems more in keeping with a conventional Parisian farce than with a serious novel. But the central problem here, as is already indicated in the title of the volume, is not so much the problem of disposing of Marcelle as the problem of growing older.

Mathieu, now in his early thirties, has reached the age when he realizes that he cannot enjoy the privileges and immunities of uncommitted youth forever. All the human contacts he experiences during the course of the novel remind him of the fact—his conversation with his "bourgeois" brother, Jacques, his abortive flirtation with a much younger Russian girl, Ivich, his brief encounter with the Marxist, Brunet; and, hanging over him throughout, his unwitting conception of a child. Nevertheless, he is unable to commit himself. His personal liberty, so carefully guarded up to now, weighs on him like a jealous mistress. Nor is the problem of growing older restricted to Mathieu himself. It haunts, although in different ways, the awkward and incongruously pregnant Marcelle, the childish Ivich and her childish brother, Boris, and Boris's aging mistress, Lola, and thus provides the sense of urgency and deadline that outward history thus far has veiled.

Only the few weeks of the summer vacation elapse between *L'Age de raison* and *Le Sursis,* but in *Le Sursis* the situation is suddenly reversed. The various characters previously assembled in Paris are now dispersed in different parts of France. Each has ceased to exist primarily in terms of his relation to the others, for each must now be concerned with his relation to the crucial world problem: Is there to be a European war? To accentuate this change of outlook, Sartre borrows the Dos Passos technique of continuously shifting, sometimes in the middle of a paragraph or a sentence, from scene to scene and from mind to mind.

Sartre's new technique, however justifiable in theory, unfortunately collides with his basic technique of novel writing. Since Sartre can view events only through the minds of the characters depicted in his novels, his novels are necessarily based on a subjective sense of time. This subjective sense of time, of which we are so conscious in *L'Age de raison,* is here totally fragmentized by the objective timetable of the fatal Munich days. The fragments are never reunited in a meaningful pattern. The rapid and apparently inexplicable shifts of perspective merely prevent us from establishing any one perspective as a coherent point of view. We have hardly begun to feel at home in one character's mind when we are brutally expelled therefrom and forced to adapt ourselves to a completely new environment. In order to find our way about at all, we are forced to reconstruct the very breaks and omissions that Sartre deliberately suppressed—a tedious process that destroys the intended effect of the novel.

In its third volume, *La Mort dans l'âme,* Sartre's novel reaches a crisis. We are confronted not with an anticlimax, whether public or private, but with a vast human tragedy—the French defeat in 1940. This subject presents a technical problem somewhat similar to that of describing the Munich crisis, but Sartre uses a simpler and more effective narrative technique that allows him to explore the tragedy in depth as well as breadth. The first half of the volume shows the French defeat fairly consistently through the eyes of Mathieu, a private on the northern front, with only occasional breaks to give the contrasting perspectives of the other characters of the cycle. The second half is devoted entirely to the Marxist, Brunet, who is taken prisoner by the Germans.

These two consecutive points of view—for Brunet takes up the story of the defeat at the very point and place where Mathieu drops it—offer two different examples of political commitment. Mathieu, instead of waiting to be taken prisoner by the Germans, joins a band of soldiers in an abandoned church tower and dies in a desperate attempt to slow down the German advance. Subjectively, this gesture is important. As he shoots at the German soldiers Mathieu is avenging a whole lifetime of hesitations, scruples and ineffectual introspection. For the first time he is totally committed, and for the first time, paradoxically, he feels that he is free. But seen objectively, this is a futile and irresponsible gesture. The German forces have been delayed only a quarter of an hour, and it is possible that they will take reprisals on the helpless population of the town.

In contrast with Mathieu, who even when committed to heroic action is motivated by personal considerations, Brunet, the Marxist, has apparently been trained to resist subjective motivations of this kind. Rather than making a symbolic gesture of resistance, he allows himself to be taken prisoner, because he believes that he can perform an important political function in the German prison camp. His Marxist limitations—an ill-disguised contempt for human weaknesses, a certain lack of critical sense, a dogmatic self-assurance, all the irritating qualities of the overly zealous eagle scout—are revealed to him by a mysterious fellow prisoner, Schneider, a man who shares many of Brunet's aspirations but none of his illusions. In the concluding chapters of the volume Brunet has become much more sympathetic as an individual, much more effective as a leader, but, one is inclined to suspect, a good deal less reliable as a Communist.

In the two brief excerpts from the unpublished concluding volume these suspicions are confirmed: Brunet, at odds with party officialdom, is forced to choose between his friendship with Schneider, his influence over his fellow prisoners, his personal values and convictions, and his existence as a member of the Communist party. He thus begins to know something of the private hell experienced by so many men of his generation.

For Sartre's final judgment on the problem of human liberty we must await the still unpublished conclusion to his cycle. The fact that this conclusion was once postponed—the proposed three volumes were later expanded to four—and then considerably delayed gives some indication that Sartre has had difficulty in forming such a judgment. And the volumes that have thus far appeared seem to show a shift of judgment during the actual writing of the novel. At the end of the first section of *La Mort dans l'âme* Sartre has disposed of his major character, Mathieu, and his major problem, the problem of human liberty, without at the same time being able to conclude his novel. The scene shifts instead to Brunet, who played only an incidental role in the earlier volumes.

One has the impression that Sartre has run into an obstacle of some sort; that he first attempted to bypass this obstacle, but after changing the direction of his novel again found the same obstacle lying in his path. This obstacle consists perhaps in the following contradiction: Sartre is still committed, both as a philosopher and as a novelist, to a purely subjective interpretation of reality. Everything outside the minds of his fictional characters is ruled out of bounds. Actions and events exist not as objective facts but as the contents of some individual consciousness; they are evaluated in terms not of their external but of their internal consequences. At the same time, however, Sartre believes that literature should take a stand upon the practical problems of its age; that it should again assume a "social function." This is a natural consequence of Sartre's experience of the war, and we can sympathize with his position. The problem nonetheless remains: How is it possible to give a "social function" to purely subjective events?

It seems probable that when Sartre first conceived his novel he believed that he had found a solution: The mere fact of political commitment would have not only subjective value as "a road to freedom" but also objective value as a political stand. But Sartre does not really believe that all political commitments are equally valid. He must thus assume a "situation" where only one alternative—the alternative that interests Sartre—is possible. The German defeat of France provided him with such a situation. That the mere fact of political action was so highly honored during the Occupation years was no doubt because the only possibility of political action lay in resistance to the German Occupation forces. The situation itself automatically determined the direction of action.

The problem of political commitment no longer seems as simple as it did during the Occupation of France—a fact that Sartre himself pointed out in his exchange of letters with Camus. And this, perhaps, is why he shifted his novel from the straightforward alternatives of resistance or appeasement to the more complex problems of a French Communist during the time of the Hitler-Stalin pact. Brunet, unlike Mathieu, is involved in a moral conflict, but this is not a conflict between two different forms of political action; it is a conflict between political action and political inaction. Sartre may admit that times have changed, but he still betrays a latent nostalgia for the political clarity of the Occupation years. By tacitly assuming that the existing structure of Western society is not a living political organism but a frozen historical fact, he has recreated the same type of one-way situation that existed at the time of the German Occupation of France. The Communist party, under these circumstances, appears as the only possible form of political action.

For all his manipulation of history, Sartre's fundamental problem remains unsolved: He can see political decisions only as subjective events, and can evaluate these decisions only in terms of their subjective consequences. Mathieu's last stand against the German soldiers, as Sartre probably recognized, has no political relevance. But the same is true of Brunet's political dilemma: "If the party is right, then it is only I who am crazy; if it is wrong, *all men* are alone and the world is done for." This may sound as if Brunet were putting the human race ahead of his own intellectual security. Its real meaning is very different: Brunet prefers the idea of a crazy Brunet to the idea of a meaningless world. And his reluctance to accept a meaningless world is actually as personal in motivation as Mathieu's last stand against the German soldiers, or, to go back to one of the minor characters of the cycle, Daniel's sudden conversion to Christianity.

Now it is true that here, as elsewhere, Sartre is a keen political psychologist. The political psychologist, though, is necessarily something of a political debunker. The very fact that he interprets political decisions in terms of their internal motivations rather than their external consequences disqualifies them as political decisions. And Sartre has recognized this in many of his writings. The *autodidacte* of *La Nausée,* the fascist adolescent who emerges from one of his short stories, even the troubled hero of *Les Mains sales* (*Red Gloves*), are unmerciful exposures of the fallacy of personal salvation through politics. Mathieu and Brunet, however, are unintentional examples of the same disease.

We are less conscious of this weakness in Sartre's first effort in the direction of political commitment, for in *Les Mouches* contemporary history is disguised as ancient legend. With this disguise removed, Sartre can no longer use so simple a solution as a symbolic murder. And when the clear-cut alternatives of the Resistance years give way to the complexity and ambiguity of postwar politics, the symbol loses much of its significance. It is possible that Sartre perceived this truth while he was writing *Les Chemins de la liberté;* and that because he was reluctant to accept it, he abandoned his novel for the oversimplified, didactic moralism of his postwar essays and certain of his postwar plays.

How natural that the vulnerable, solitary, guilt-ridden core of being that Sartre reveals in us should long for the hard, protective shell of a concrete identity! This search for a tangible identity of some sort, whether, as in *Huis-clos,* through one's relations with other people or, as in *Les Chemins de la liberté,* through political commitment, is Sartre's real theme—not, as he has suggested in his critical writings, the actual outcome of the search. Failure is written into the very nature of the Sartrian search itself. The mind turned inward is painfully aware of its need for faith, for commitment, for a stable and tangible identity, but it is in no position to make the necessary moves. The act of introspection is an interrogation, not an affirmation, of the self. Mathieu as seen by Daniel, Brunet as seen by Mathieu, the political actor as seen by the political observer, may seem a most enviably solid and resistant entity. Each one as seen by *himself,* and consequently as seen by Sartre, dissolves into a fluid mass of inconsistent possibilities. No novelist has ever stated this contradiction more powerfully than Sartre. But, the very power of Sartre's destructive genius precludes all possibility of reconstruction.

Albert Camus: The Two Sides of the Coin

Camus is the only literary figure in postwar France who, for ability and reputation, can stand comparison with Sartre. Like Sartre, he is a Resistance intellectual whose rise to fame coincided with the retreat of the German Occupation forces; like Sartre, he has exercised considerable influence over a certain body of French opinion—by means of newspaper and magazine articles as well as books; like Sartre, he has known both the rewards and penalties of sudden glory. There was a time when their names were generally pronounced in unison, like those of two twin deities. In recent years, however, Sartre and Camus have drifted in opposite directions. This development was made all too clear by their exchange of letters, or, more properly, of insults, in a 1952 issue of Sartre's *Les Temps modernes*—an unfortunate occurrence that could, and should, have been avoided. Yet it somehow seems more natural than their earlier alliance, for although Sartre's first novel, *La Nausée,* and Camus's first novel, *L'Etranger (The Stranger)*, have a certain air of family resemblance, never were two men more opposed in temperament, in background and in general outlook.

Sartre, the Parisian, is an erstwhile professor of philosophy with an extremely unprofessorial knack of giving life to his ideas. His scope as a novelist is wide and varied; yet mind and existence remain the two fixed poles of his conception of reality. As such, he may be seen as a direct, if somewhat distant, descendant of Descartes. Camus, the North African, has also studied philosophy, but less as an intellectual discipline than as the expression of a certain type of sensibility. His range as a novelist is far more limited than that of Sartre; his attack, far more direct. Camus is guided mainly by those reasons of the heart of which Pascal has spoken—reasons that often fly directly in the face of logic and experience, that are less reasons, perhaps, than an impassioned cry.

We have here the fundamental theme of Camus's writings: at once a bitter protest against the injustice of man's position in the universe and an examination of the ethical problems which this implies. Camus, even in his earliest writings, instinctively rejects the amoralistic views that might seem to be the logical consequence of his sense of the absurdity of human existence. From the very outset he is seeking an intellectual foundation of some sort for his deep-seated ethical convictions.

In his early writings—his first novel, *L'Etranger,* 1942, his first essay, *Le Mythe de Sisyphe* (*The Myth of Sisyphus*), 1942, and his plays, *Le Malentendu* (The Misunderstanding), 1944, and *Caligula,* published in 1945 but written before the war—Camus states the nature of his problem, showing the inhuman consequences of certain forms of existence implied in a philosophy of "absurdity."

In his second novel, *La Peste* (*The Plague*), 1947, his second essay, *L'Homme révolté* (*The Rebel*), 1951, and his later plays, *L'Etat de siège* (The State of Siege), 1948, and *Les Justes* (The Just), 1949, he attempts to resolve this conflict and move toward the establishment of a more positive ethic. The moral limits beyond which, as is already implied in Camus's earlier writing, man loses all humanity are here explicitly marked out. Camus's third novel, *La Chute* (The Fall), 1956, is a passionate denunciation of the all-or-nothing approach to human problems which Camus described in *Le Mythe de Sisyphe* as a form of the consciousness of absurdity.

It is true that this development has taken place in the field of Camus's personal emotions rather than in his fundamental outlook on the world. His sense of the absurdity of human existence and his ethics are founded on an identical act of revolt against the existing structure of the universe. And, for a self-styled agnostic, the one seems just as arbitrary as the other. Were Camus merely telling us that moral values cannot be grounded on pragmatic facts, nor political right upon political might, it would be easy to accept his point of view. He seems rather to be telling us that moral values are incompatible with pragmatic facts, that political morality is incompatible with political efficacity. In other words, he must suppose not only an amoral but a directly antimoral universe—a highly anthropomorphic pagan deity of some sort—as a fitting object of revolt. There would be little point in shaking our fists at blind, insentient matter.

The whole argument, as set forth in *Le Mythe de Sisyphe* and in *L'Homme révolté,* almost invites a refutation. For all the faulty reasoning and the lack of realism, however, we know instinctively what Camus means: The eternal moralist, within us, cannot accept the universe that modern science has revealed. Although men, habitually, are attracted by material power and material success, there remains a mighty human prejudice—expressed so forcibly in all of Camus's writings—in favor of the victims, of the vanquished, of the men who fought upon the losing side. It is our only way of contesting the fundamental rules of the game.

There is something of this protest in Christianity, tempered, however, by faith in the ultimate justice of the Christian God. Camus's general attitude toward life resembles that of a Christian who believes in an unchristian God. He has retained the protest, but rejected the consolations of the Christian faith. It is nonetheless a religious attitude toward life. The emotion comes first, the intellectual justification of the emotion second, just as two of Camus's novels, *L'Etranger* and *La Peste,* antedate the two essays to which they are related. Camus's expression of what amounts to a personal religion in these two parables is much more persuasive than his subsequent efforts to ground his religion on logical syllogisms, to express it as a practical code of behavior, to "prove" that it is valid.

L'Etranger, which is narrated in the first person, is the story of a young man at odds with society. This is not due to a conscious revolt. Like a child, Meursault is simply unaware of the emotional reactions expected of him in different social situations. He is completely oblivious of the fact that he is expected to express certain sentiments at his mother's funeral; to allow a certain period of time to elapse before establishing a liaison with a girl; to tell this girl that he loves her, when he simply wants to make love to her; to appear anxious to rise to a higher position in his office.

The psychologist no doubt has a name for Meursault's peculiar apathy toward life. But the dry and disconcerting humor of Camus's novel is aimed less at its hero than at society. Meursault's mind is so constructed as to record all the separate details of life he observes around him, but to censor the usual interpretations attached to these details and the usual connections established between them. This point of view is reflected in the brief, disconnected and purely descriptive statements of Camus's narrative style. And the reader, once he has become accustomed to the one-way mind of Meursault, begins to wonder whether these interpretations and connections are not merely arbitrary conventions designed to give a superficial veneer of logic and familiarity to the inexplicable fact of human existence.

These conventions, however unfounded, have a certain survival value, and it is to be expected that society, when confronted with so dangerous an enemy as Meursault, should be on its guard. Halfway through the novel, due to a series of highly irrational circumstances—Meursault's passive "friendship," with a rather shady character involved in a feud with some Arabs, his equally passive acquiescence in a plan to spend the day at the beach, the effects of the merciless midday sun—Meursault kills an Arab. The fact is clear, but the severity of the sentence depends on whether or not the murder was premeditated. As is obvious to the reader, the murder was not premeditated. Yet when the jury is informed of Meursault's behavior during and after his mother's funeral, the prosecutor has no difficulty in obtaining a death sentence. Meursault, unable to find any relation between his previous actions and the crime as it is reconstructed in the courtroom, has meanwhile followed his trial with the dispassionate curiosity of an outside observer. He is left with the impression that he is condemned to die because he did not express the proper emotions at his mother's funeral.

It is only after his trial and condemnation—a concrete symbol of the arbitrary, unmeaning death to which we all are sentenced—that Meursault becomes fully aware of the fundamental absurdity of man's position in the universe. His puzzled incomprehension of social norms now turns into a conscious revolt. In the legal procedure to which he has been subjected, he recognizes a concrete symbol of the arbitrary, unmeaning death to which we all are sentenced. This final revelation also brings to the level of consciousness his sense of physical solidarity with the existing world. And Camus's novel ends, not on the negative note of Meursault's consciousness of absurdity, but with its complement—his positive recognition of all the earthly happiness he had previously taken for granted. "As if the great burst of anger had purged me of evil, emptied me of hope, before this night laden with signs and stars, I laid myself open, for the first time, to the tender indifference of the world. To feel it so similar to myself, so fraternal really, I sensed that I had been happy, that I still was happy."

Camus's second novel, *La Peste,* the story of a modern city, Oran, afflicted with the bubonic plague, is somewhat longer and more complex. It is narrated by one of the central characters, Dr. Rieux, whose identity, however, remains unknown until the closing pages of the novel. Dr. Rieux habitually speaks of himself in the third person and when describing the general effects of the plague, uses the first person plural. Camus no doubt intended to combine the inside understanding of a participant with the objectivity of an observer. The device is on the whole successful, although the fiction of this anonymous but omniscient narrator occasionally becomes a trifle strained.

The central subject of this novel is a whole community, temporarily cut off from civilization by an unforeseeable disaster. The general structure of the novel follows the course of the plague itself, from its onset to its final disappearance, as the narrator relates in minute detail the physical and moral consequences for the citizens of Oran.

The crucial events of both *L'Etranger* and *La Peste*—Meursault's trial and condemnation and the arbitrary mass murder brought about by the Oran plague—are obviously symbols of a more universal human fate. Other contemporary writers have used them as well.

L'Etranger can be compared to Kafka's *The Trial,* and Camus found the symbol of the plague in Antonin Artaud's essay, *Le Théâtre et son double,* as well as in Defoe's *Journal of the Plague Year.* Whatever literary stimuli may be at work, these symbols are also tied to Camus's personal experience of life, and he has used them in an entirely personal way. The theme of execution has absorbed many novelists, including Dostoevski, Stendhal, Hugo and Balzac, but for Camus, it goes back to the shock he experienced as a child on hearing his mother describe an execution attended by his father. The impact of this shock on the later development of Camus's thinking can be inferred from the fact that Tarrou, in a leading passage of *La Peste,* attributes his own moral crisis to a similar experience. Moreover, Camus's elaboration of the symbol of the plague is based, in its details as well as in its larger implications, on the more generalized shock of the German Occupation of France.

It is also characteristic of Camus that the fictional credibility of these symbols lies less in a nightmarish blend of fact and fantasy of the kind that Kafka conveys than in their meticulously matter-of-fact presentation as objective events. In *The Trial* we feel the insidious pull of a frightening dream; in *L'Etranger,* the resistance of a material object. Although Camus's symbols are equivalent to all the age-old images of divine injustice, they are no less painfully recognizable as human events. If it is shocking to realize that nature can imitate the cold-blooded procedures of a modern bureaucrat, it is still more shocking to realize that human societies can imitate the inhuman laws of nature. Should we not, on the contrary, be doing our utmost to denounce, to resist, and, insofar as possible, to mitigate the workings of these natural laws?

The primary emotion gives the key to Camus's consciousness of "absurdity": his belief that since all men eventually must die, human existence is utterly meaningless. The secondary emotion provides the basis for Camus's ethical convictions: his belief that men who are fighting together against a common evil, even though they are fighting a losing battle, can give some meaning to their lives and achieve a sense of human solidarity.

Camus's philosophy of absurdity is most apparent in *L'Etranger;* his ethical convictions, in *La Peste*. Although they lead to opposite conclusions, the two are closely intertwined. In *L'Etranger* the symbol of human justice points to the divine injustice of the universe; in Camus's second novel the divine injustice of the plague points to the arbitrary, wholesale slaughter of modern war. In neither case can we divorce the meaning from Camus's symbolic expression of his meaning. The physical universe, as seen by Camus, retains a quality of almost human malevolence; and human society, the blind indifference of a material force.

This symbolic marriage of natural and social evils, of metaphysical and moral problems, creates a certain element of ambiguity in Camus's novels. Why, for example, do we remain indifferent to Meursault's irrational murder of an Arab, and yet feel so strongly about his condemnation to death? It is true that Meursault is unjustly accused of a premeditated murder, but given the antilegalistic context of Camus's thinking, this is something of a technicality. The novel itself fails to resolve the contradiction between his philosophy of "absurdity"—in view of the fundamental injustice of the universe, "everything is permitted"—and his ethical convictions.

In *La Peste* this contradiction is removed, but Camus can be charged with evading an important moral issue. The material and moral effects of the plague—the quarantine, the separations, the rationing, the black market, the terror, the anxiety and the boredom —inevitably bring to mind the effects of the German Occupation of France. But Camus has substituted an abstract evil for an enemy of flesh and blood; although the plague retains a quality of almost human malevolence, it raises no moral difficulties. The essential, if painful, question of whether or not it is legitimate to oppose violence with violence is raised by Tarrou, in connection with his experience of revolutionary action, and answered, rather briefly, in the negative. It is never raised in Camus's novel, however. Tarrou's account of his experience of revolution, even though it seems to explain the central symbol of the plague, does not correspond to the situation created by the plague itself.

Were Camus's novels actually concerned with the practical problem of political or social organization, these objections would have considerable weight. But it seems wiser to interpret them merely as the expression of a fundamental human revulsion, not so much against violence itself as against the cold-blooded, rationalistic organization of collective violence that Camus reads into the physical structure of the universe and that is implied in the very nature of the modern state. Both nature and society, as seen by Camus, are evil; both, certainly, are powerful; and both exact the same sort of sinister idolatry from their victims. It is against this spiritual sanctification of material force, and the ignorance and the illusions on which it thrives, that Camus speaks. The priest and the judge, insofar as they are acting in their official capacities, are morally equivalent: the twin antagonists in both of Camus's novels.

When viewed in this light, the antithesis between *L'Etranger* and *La Peste* is overshadowed by an antithesis between Camus and the very novelist who at first glance invites comparison—André Malraux. Camus and Malraux are both guided more by sensibility than by sense. What is more, the shade of Malraux can be clearly seen on certain pages of *Le Mythe de Sisyphe*. There is a residual nostalgia here for certain of the heroic and defiant attitudes of Malraux's heroes. But Camus's novels seem not only independent of but also antagonistic to this literary influence. The problem posed is not that of transcending oneself, of discovering some absolute to throw in the teeth of death and destruction. It is that of seeing these enemies for what they are and holding them at bay as long as possible. As Tarrou puts it: "To do everything possible to cure oneself of the plague. . . . This is the only thing that can unburden men, and if it cannot save them, at least it can let them do as little harm as possible and even a little good sometimes."

There is another important contrast with Malraux, with certain aspects of *Le Mythe de Sisyphe* and of *L'Homme révolté,* too:

Camus does not suggest that this intellectual and moral struggle
against the existing structure of the universe is man's primary goal
on earth. The affirmative side of Camus's thinking lies rather in the
positive quality of life itself, in the occasional moments of earthly
happiness which, however ephemeral, however gravely menaced, are
as real and as important an aspect of human existence as the symbolic plague. At the conclusion of *Le Mythe de Sisyphe* he writes:
"The struggle toward the summits is enough to fill the heart
of man. One must imagine that Sisyphus is happy." But in Meursault's final recognition that he has been happy, in Rieux's discovery during his nocturnal swim with Tarrou that both "are
filled with a strange happiness," the idea of happiness is not purely
imaginary.

The problem of individual happiness has obvious ethical implications. But in *La Peste,* as is not always the case in his newspaper
articles, Camus generally has the discretion to avoid the preacher's
pulpit. In striking contrast to the usual type of the greatest-good-of-
the-greatest-number moralist, who in his enthusiasm for the general
welfare so often forgets the humble individuals involved, Camus
does not indicate that the collective end automatically justifies any
and every private means to that end.

His narrator, Dr. Rieux, shows a certain degree of sympathy for
a Parisian journalist marooned at Oran who attempts to bypass
the quarantine regulations in order to rejoin his mistress. It is
true that the journalist eventually decides to remain in Oran and
help to fight the plague, but this decision does not erase the significance of his previous remark: "As for me, I've had enough of
people who die for an idea. I don't believe in heroism; I know that
it's easy, and I've learned that it's murderous. What interests me
is to live and die because of what one loves." Even Tarrou, the
character most intimately concerned with moral problems, admits:
"Of course a man must fight for the victims. But if, elsewhere, he
ceases to love anything, what is the use of his fighting?"

In this respect, the discipline, the sacrifices, even the occasional
heroism of the citizens of Oran are not treated very differently from

the petty regulations imposed upon them by the city government. All are simply necessary and on the whole unpleasant means to a desired end: the reduction of human suffering on earth.

This is rather far removed from the attitudes and aspirations of the French novel since the publication of *Les Conquérants*. How is it possible even to think of individual happiness in the world as we know it today? The whole thing is simply another "bourgeois" opiate, and the only satisfaction left to man is that of protesting against his impossible predicament. This, on the whole, is the fundamental message of the thirties and the forties.

If Camus has been able to revitalize the theme of individual happiness, to snatch it from the jaws of habit and convention and make us feel its insistent pull on the human heart, it is not because he has any illusions on the subject. It is perhaps because Camus—one of the few French novelists of any stature to have known the real meaning of the word poverty—has had an especially intimate experience of the obstacles standing in its way. With the exception of his early *L'Envers et l'endroit* (The Two Sides of the Coin), 1937, which has never been republished, Camus seldom speaks directly of these personal experiences. They have nonetheless given him a special sensitivity to certain forms of human suffering as well as a deep aversion for any attempt to justify or to exalt them in the name of some superior value—whether this be an act of resignation to the will of God, an act of faith in some political ideology or a belief that men who risk their lives in some collective cause can transcend their individual and mortal limitations.

But like Meursault after his death sentence or the inhabitants of Oran after they have been struck down by the plague, this intimate understanding of the underlying tragedy of human existence brings an acute and painful awareness of man's temporal bond with the world he lives in. This is what Camus calls "the other side of the coin." The lyric element in Camus's sensibility emerges most strongly in an early collection of essays befittingly entitled *Noces* (Nuptials), 1938. In the novels it is restrained and guided by Camus's sober insistence on the cruel indifference of the world to which he feels so

closely bound. It is never altogether lost from view. The special resonance of Camus's writing lies neither in its stern lucidity nor in its
latent sensuality but in the equilibrium maintained between the two.

It is significant that Camus's novels are situated respectively in his
native Algiers and Oran, two cities that he regards with a curious
blend of affection, sympathy, contempt and horror. Bleak and barren,
mediocre and uninteresting, these modern metropolitan deserts, so
utterly devoid of man-made beauty, of nature and of history, seem
to symbolize the stifling prison of the twentieth century mind itself.
Herein, perhaps, lies the secret of their special attraction for Camus.
If the blank, expressionless stones of Oran offer him no hope, neither
do they offer him any illusions. Here, at last, one can find solitude—
the solitude, as Camus says elsewhere, that gives everything its price.
And then there is "the other side of the coin," the surrounding
countryside of arid mountains and shining beaches, so sharply separated from the city that it has all the splendor of a revelation. This
fundamental antithesis between the stifling limitations of the city
and the sudden liberation of the sea is intensified by a further contrast between the pitiless, inhuman light of day and the sudden deliverance of nightfall and the evening breeze—the nocturnal sounds
and smells that awaken the unconscious Meursault to life, the sea
breeze that marks the end of the Oran plague.

The brutal oppositions of city and sea, of noon and evening, of
death and life, of the cruelty and beauty of the world, which give
so clean and hard an outline to these two novels, are no doubt characteristic of North Africa itself. They seem to suggest a geography
and climate that leave no room for all the vague, transitional
zones of feeling experienced by a northern European. For a man
less responsive to the quality of life around him, these autobiographical factors would have little relevance. But with Camus, sensibility and thought are inextricably bound together. The geography
and climate of North Africa are reflected not only in the subjects he
has chosen for his novels but also in the very structure of his thought:
a continuous and often painful effort to maintain a human equilibrium between two contradictory extremes.

With *La Chute* (The Fall), 1956, Camus abandons the Mediterranean world. The novel is set in Amsterdam and generally at night or in the late evening: land and water, sea and sky, light and dark, merge to form a colorless, indefinite and murky limbo which is contrasted, in one brief passage, with the precision and clarity of the Grecian coast. The narrator himself suggests that the concentric circles formed by the canals are comparable to the different circles of Dante's hell, and he has made his headquarters in a sordid bar, frequented by the flotsam and jetsam of the whole of Europe, which is situated within the very last of these circles: the hell reserved for traitors to God.

La Chute is written as a long monologue or, more properly, as one side of an extremely one-sided dialogue. The narrator, Jean-Baptiste Clamence, picks up a young Frenchman in a bar, gradually insinuates himself into his confidence, and, much in the manner of Dostoevski's *Notes from the Underworld,* proceeds to tell him the story of his life, or "fall," during five successive encounters.

Clamence describes his present occupation as that of "judge-penitent," a title explained only at the close of his confession. He had previously been a successful and prosperous Parisian lawyer specializing in the defense of widows and orphans. Perfectly at home with the world, with society and with himself, unusually magnanimous and courteous in his relations with the underprivileged and the oppressed, he had then seen himself as an incarnation of total human perfection and had lived on the exhilarating summits of complete self-satisfaction. One night as he was crossing a bridge over the Seine and had paused to enjoy his sense of both physical and moral elevation, he heard a burst of laughter behind him that seemed to "put things in their place." This was the beginning of his "fall."

It had actually begun three years earlier when, crossing a different bridge over the Seine, he had seen a slim young woman in black leaning over the parapet, had heard the noise of her body falling into the water and her repeated cries, and had gone on his way without attempting to save her. But Clamence had forgotten all about the incident. It is only after he hears the laughter that his conveniently bad memory is awakened. From this time on, prodded by continuing bursts of laughter, he begins to re-examine his previous image of himself and to plunge slowly downward into an abyss of total self-contempt. His ferocious introspection gradually destroys all the motivations and feelings to which men habitually give value—generosity, courtesy, friendship, love—until he finds nothing within himself but a satanic will to power and a monstrous hypocrisy.

At this point Clamence's entire existence is given over to a series of abortive efforts to escape the intolerable sense of guilt generated by his new image of himself. He first tries to expose his own lies, to show himself for what he really is. He then flees the company of men, who judge our weaknesses, for that of women, who enjoy them, experimenting unsuccessfully with romantic love, chastity, and finally debauchery. His last invention is his vocation of "judge-penitent": a man who loudly and compulsively confesses his guilt for all to hear but so arranges his confession that it will apply to his interlocutors as well as to himself and contaminate them with his own sense of guilt. This procedure is actually illustrated during the whole course of the novel as Clamence finds point after point of resemblance with his interlocutor and insidiously begins to use the word "we" rather than the word "I." In thus drawing one damned soul after another into his own inferno of guilt and abjection, he experiences the dizzy elation of God on the morning of the Last Judgment—a fitting substitute for his previous summit of self-satisfaction, although Clamence's feverish and almost defiant assertion of his new-found well-being in the final pages of the novel suggests an actual state of inner desperation.

In *Le Mythe de Sisyphe* Camus had already described the "incalculable fall from the image we have of ourselves" as a form of the consciousness of absurdity, but without further comment. In *L'Homme révolté* he denounced this type of moral extremism, which can find no mean between a sense of total innocence and a sense of total guilt, as one of the most murderous aspects of contemporary European thought. "This," he wrote, "is why humanitarian verbiage is just as unfounded as cynical provocation. Man, at bottom, is not

entirely guilty, since he did not begin history; nor altogether innocent, since he continues it. Those who go beyond this limit and
affirm their total innocence end in the fury of definitive guilt."

Jean-Baptiste Clamence, this "false prophet who cries in the wil-
derness and refuses to leave it," is obviously a prophet of the all-or-
nothing type of mind that Camus describes in *Le Mythe de Sisyphe*
and denounces in *L'Homme révolté*. He is a man who is incapable
of accepting his human limitations and can live only on the summits
of total innocence or in the depths of total guilt. He is a man incapable of establishing distinctions or degrees of any sort and must
thus plunge from the extremes of humanitarian sentimentalism to
those of total nihilism. As a lawyer, he pleaded that all men, even
the guilty, were innocent; as "judge-penitent," he argues that all
men, even the innocent, are guilty.

Clamence apparently sees himself as a typical modern European,
an image somewhat in line with Camus's denunciation of modern
Europe in *L'Homme révolté*. Camus's judgment, in each case, seems
excessively harsh. It no doubt applies less to the modern European
as such than to the modern European intellectual and in particular
the more destructive type of intellectual from Nietzsche on down
through Sartre. These destructive thinkers, which Camus discusses
at considerable length in *L'Homme révolté*, at one time had an important influence on Camus's thought and apparently still haunt his
mind today. For all its ironic detachment, there is a savage violence
in *La Chute* which suggests that Camus is wrestling with his personal demons, demons that he instinctively locates in the murky fogs
of northern Europe and banishes from the luminous clarity of
Greece.

Camus has called *La Chute*, and now his two previous novels as
well, a *récit*, or "tale"—a title used by Gide to emphasize his own
ironic detachment from the scene. When *L'Etranger* was first published, the French reading public often tended to equate the Stranger
with Camus himself, both as regards the ideas expressed in the novel
and the manner in which it was written. The simplicity and frank-
ness of Meursault's particular form of expression were admired as

a new literary style per se. Since the publication of *La Peste* and, to a still greater extent, *La Chute,* this interpretation is no longer possible. It is Dr. Rieux, the conscientious chronicler of *La Peste,* who seems to approach Camus's personal convictions most closely. And Rieux has little in common with either Meursault or Clamence. In *L'Etranger* and *La Chute* Camus, like Gide, uses the novel not as a means of expressing his personal point of view but of pushing certain attitudes of mind—attitudes for which he feels both fascination and revulsion—to their extreme consequences and thus revealing their ultimate implications.

Each one of these novels is written in the first person, and each is written in an entirely different style: a sort of linguistic equivalent for the different forms of being depicted in the different novels, which reveals Camus's extraordinary gift for verbal mimicry as well as his talent as a writer. Indeed the only point of resemblance between the brief, disconnected and purely factual sentences of *L'Etranger* and the ingratiating and diabolically man-of-the-world tone of Clamence's confession lies in the fact that each constitutes a recognizable literary style.

Camus, with Gide, is one of the few contemporary novelists to have maintained the esthetic distance of a literary style. This esthetic distance seems to correspond with Gide's own personality, but it is something that Camus has had to conquer. Both the verbal mimicry of *L'Etranger* and *La Chute* and the judicious and somewhat formal sobriety of tone that is typical of *La Peste* are disciplines that he has imposed upon an unusually ardent sensibility—a capacity to feel the underlying tragedy and the intermittent pleasures of human existence more deeply and more intimately than most of us are able, or will perhaps allow ourselves, to do. It is this very literary distance, apparent in everything that Camus writes, that most infuriates the Sartrian clique of intellectuals. And when, as in his newspaper articles and in certain of his essays, it is combined with a didactic form, it really does become a trifle pompous. One has the impression in the concluding pages of *L'Homme révolté* that Camus is a little overly aware of his Mediterranean heritage: Merely because he happened to be born in North Africa and not in France, he seems to think he has the right to drape himself in the spotless garments of an ancient Greek and stand in solemn judgment on "the desperate convulsions" of "those little Europeans." But when, as in *La Peste,* Camus treats North Africa as a context, not as a rostrum; when his mind and his emotions are focused on a concrete situation, and not dispersed in generalities; when he is using a narrative, not a didactic, form—then this quality of personal detachment becomes an impressive literary achievement. It has permitted Camus to offer us something that no one of his contemporaries could offer: a sober yet sympathetic appraisal of his age.

Neither Malraux, who has turned to the study of art, nor Saint-Exupéry, who died in the war, nor Sartre, who still clings to the emotional climate of the Resistance days, has yet acknowledged the truth that Camus has made evident in the whole narration of *La Peste:* We are now looking backward on an era that ended with the dubious victory of 1945. The time has passed for seeking the hidden meaning of these events, for justifying the terror and the violence in the name of abstract ideologies or subjective illuminations. We should only be making meaningless speeches before the tombs of unknown soldiers. It is time to assume the humbler role that history has assigned us. It is time to pause, to reflect, to evaluate and to remember. Thus, in the midst of the official celebrations marking the end of *La Peste,* Camus's narrator decided to write his chronicle—"in order to give evidence in favor of the stricken, to leave some reminder of the violence done them, and simply to say what one learns in the midst of a disaster: that there is more to admire than to despise in men."

AN END AND SOME
BEGINNINGS

Camus's *La Chute,* 1956, was really a liquidation of the past. It had been preceded, two years earlier, by Simone de Beauvoir's *Les Mandarins (The Mandarins),* which, it has been said, is the fitting conclusion to Sartre's unfinished *Les Chemins de la liberté. Les Mandarins* was barely disguised autobiography, a not altogether impartial account of the post-liberation years. It is tempting, though dangerous, to substitute well-known figures for the protagonists. Dubreuilh, Anne, Henri, and Scriabine came uncomfortably close to Sartre, Simone de Beauvoir, Camus, and Koestler. The "novel of commitment," in Beauvoir's hands, was turning into personal testimonial. Simone de Beauvoir wisely carried it to its logical conclusion in her memoirs. Sartre is rumored to be doing likewise. In spite of, perhaps because of, its many imitators, the "committed" novel slipped out of existence.

For a few years it seemed that the novel itself was in eclipse. Not one of the well-known novelists of the thirties and forties survived the fifties. Gide and Colette carried away with them the last vestiges of a past age when they died. Romains, Duhamel, Mauriac, Giono, Green, and Bosco continued to write but seemed unable to catch the mood of the time. Martin du Gard remained silent until his death in 1958. Malraux was absorbed in his grandiose meditations on art. Sartre, involved more and more deeply in philosophical and political debate, abandoned fiction for the stage. Camus, with

L'Exil et le royaume (*Exile and the Kingdom*), 1958, a collection of short stories, was experimenting with new themes and techniques in preparation for a vast novel, *Le Premier homme* (The First Man). He died, in January 1960, before the novel was finished.

Meanwhile a veritable avalanche of novels was bursting from the Parisian presses. Commercialized novel-writing turned into a profitable, almost standardized, business. Publishing houses, avid for publicity, discovered prize-winning novelists by the dozen. The atmosphere of the interwar years and of the forties was a thing of the past. The French novel, then, had primarily been a reassertion of the inner reality of man. The novelists of this period had been deeply concerned with the pressing problem of giving an individual life its full dimension, its full measure of spiritual significance. This is what gave them their weight and their authority. Liberation from all the bonds of routine and the slow access to an inner world of beauty and spiritual plenitude is the theme of the greatest novel of the twentieth century, one of the greatest of all times, Proust's *A la recherche du temps perdu*.

After Sartre one has the impression that the quest for unrestricted personal autonomy had reached a point of diminishing returns, a point where both inner and outer reality threatened to dissolve under the corrosive action of the human mind. As the fifties moved into the sixties, the atmosphere of daily life increasingly diverged from that of the twenties, thirties, and forties. The routines and conventions of the past had been shattered and were no longer serious antagonists. The individual, emerging from the experience of the Occupation, from German prisoner-of-war or concentration camps, no longer saw himself in the guise of a "conqueror." The revolt against the existing conditions of life was now turning into a convention itself. The Algerian war, the atomic bomb, the advent of the Fifth Republic raised new questions. A new generation, torn between anxiety and the satisfactions derived from the booming Common Market, was looking away from the past, out of sympathy with the intellectual theories and extremist attitudes of its predecessors.

The change of mood was first apparent in an upsurge of technically sophisticated but rather lightweight "uncommitted" novels, traditional in type. Most of the major writers of the thirties and the forties had assumed that modern politics, to be effective, must in some way tie up with an indictment of the existing order. As with the postwar writers of the twenties, the idea of political commitment was now satirized in novels like Jean-Louis Curtis's *Les Forêts de la nuit* (*The Forests of the Night*), 1947, and *Les Justes Causes* (Just Causes), 1954. Marcel Aymé, a successful satirist of the thirties, hit the best-seller lists again with his ferocious *Uranus* (*The Barkeep of Blémont*) in 1948. Imaginative, picaresque novels like Roger Vailland's cynical *La Loi* (*The Law*), or Romain Gary's unashamedly idealistic *Les Racines du ciel* (*The Roots of Heaven*), used the political scene for purely novelistic ends. Except for writers in France's former colonies, particularly in North Africa, politics and the novel tended to part company.

The sudden upsurge of the "feminine" novel, with Françoise Sagan, Françoise Mallet-Joris, and Christiane Rochefort in the lead, was perhaps another reaction against the conscious "virility" of the novel of commitment. And it is true that the very sound of the word "virility," when coupled with "lucidity," "fraternity," and other such abstractions, began, in the fifties, to grate upon the ears. But the postwar "feminine" novel, often a minute and personal exploration of the patterns of emotional and sexual relationship, excessively analytical and ungraced by the wonderful feline subtlety of Colette, sometimes seems to justify the invidious connotations often attached to "women's novels." To be an artist, Virginia Woolf observed, one must be neither male nor female; one must be androgynous.

From concentration and prisoner-of-war camps, from long days lived in close contact with physical and moral misery, some few novelists emerged with a bewildered but real feeling of human charity. This is apparent in their treatment of certain inherited

themes. One of these is a recurrent and rather frightening animal
symbolism: the violent insect activity we find in some of Queneau's
novels and in the jungle world of Malraux's *La Voie royale*; the
animal menageries of Bernanos; Camus's plague-ridden rats, dying
in hordes. It would seem that Aymé, in reducing the entire human
species to a particularly ferocious category of the animal kingdom,
had carried the symbol as far as it would go. But Pierre Gascar, one
of the better postwar novelists, of the same generation as Camus,
used it in an entirely different way. In his *Les Bêtes* (*Beasts and
Men*), a book of rather eerie short stories, the animals, as pitiful as
man himself, escape from man's control with disastrous results for
man and beast. Gascar's subsequent work, starkly realistic and
powerful, remains somewhat isolated, outside the main currents of
contemporary fiction.

The development of the bum is even more significant. An obvious
descendant of Duhamel's Salavin, Céline's Bardamu, Kafka's K,
Camus's Stranger, and Sartre's Roquentin, in the postwar novel he
carries the material and spiritual destitution of his forebears to
almost impossible extremes. The bum, as he appears in Jean Cayrol's
trilogy, *Je vivrai l'amour des autres* (I Shall Live the Love of
Others), 1947, is drawn from his creator's experience of a concentration camp. This sense of destitution is most apparent in the first
volume of the trilogy, *On vous parle* (Someone is Speaking to You).
The "someone" is a nameless derelict in Paris. Once he has established the patterns of total solitude and misery, Cayrol, a Catholic
believer, discreetly attempts to lead his hero back to life through the
power of love, as Christ raised Lazarus from the tomb. But the last
two novels of the trilogy, which are constructive in intent, lack the
power of the first, and the same is true of all Cayrol's subsequent
work.

It is Samuel Beckett, Irish by birth and a friend of James Joyce,
who gave the bum his most powerful reincarnation since Dostoevski's *Notes from the Underground*. And, in a sense, it was with the
publication of Beckett's trilogy—*Molloy*, 1951, *Malone meurt*
(*Malone Dies*), 1952, and *L'Innommable* (The Unnameable), 1953

—that French fiction started to move in a new direction. At least one trend in the novel had remained "pure" and uncommercialized. This was the really "metaphysical," non-Sartrean novel, heir to Mallarmé's *Prose pour des Esseintes* as well as to the surrealist "anti-novel." Esoteric, deliberately destined for the few, the "metaphysical novel" on the whole assumed the visible universe to be but the outer shell, or threshold, of another invisible universe which must be sought, even though it may never be reached. The quest, the voyage, the expedition into strange lands are its main themes. Daumal's crystalline *Mont Analogue* (*Mount Analogue*), 1952, Masson's weird *Les Tortues* (*The Tortoises*), 1956, Gracq's *Le rivage des Syrtes* (*The Coast of the Syrtes*), and Blanchot's *Aminabad* rely in different ways on the creation of an intensely mysterious, obscurely dangerous atmosphere, rich in mythical suggestion. Beckett's trilogy, to which he later added the utterly unorthodox *Comment c'est* (How It Is), 1962, managed to combine the themes of quest and dereliction, fusing them into a concrete yet paradoxically elusive whole. Beckett's fictional universe is probably the most singular and powerful to have appeared in the past decade.

Beckett's name was first made famous by his play *En attendant Godot* (*Waiting for Godot*), 1952, performed in 1953. It drew attention to his novels. These, whether originally written in English (*Murphy,* 1938, and *Watt,* written in 1942–44 but published only in 1953), or, like the later novels, in French, cannot be considered separately. Beckett's work, from the very start, contains a quasi-Rabelaisian parody of all the rhetorical devices and logical processes by which, like Mahood, the "man in the jar" in *L'Innommable,* we attempt to draw over our heads a tarpaulin "waterproof only in spots." Beckett's bums never tire of describing their curious activities; they endlessly count, examine, discuss. Through them Beckett destroys, with ferocious humor, all our past and present attempts to "think" our human condition, to impose an orderly structure upon our environment.

Beckett's bums all wear the uniform made famous in *Waiting for Godot*: the shabby bowler hat, the long clown's overcoat—a manner of grotesque human garb handed down from the past and never really made for them. They start off, in a Dantesque landscape, on strange quests which come to nothing, falling into all the ditches along their way. Time, in Beckett's novels, is the gradual, never-ending disintegration of the body. All his characters have legs that stiffen, shrink, and become useless. And their journeys from one illusory shelter to another reveal their way of dealing with our inevitable progression in time: strange crawling tactics, improbable uses of bicycles that fall to pieces.

In his first novels and short stories, written in English—*More Kicks than Pricks, Murphy,* and *Watt*—Beckett used the traditional third person form of an omniscient narrator to set up the increasingly unorthodox adventures of his characters. For his trilogy, originally written in French, he adopted the subjective "je," drawing from this much-used form ambiguous and disconcerting new effects based on the spoken language. His last work, a novel in three parts which tells the adventure of a character crawling along in the mud, seems to have pushed them to their extreme limits.

Beckett, though he is counted among them, is really quite different from the "new novelists" who appeared in France during the mid-fifties. These deliberately set out to counteract both the standardized commercial novel and the novel of political commitment. They found a willing publishing house in the "editions de minuit" (midnight publications) founded in 1942 in Occupied France as a clandestine press. This is why the group is sometimes referred to as the "midnight novelists." The movement, started off by Beckett, got under way in 1953 with the publication of the first novel of Alain Robbe-Grillet, *Les Gommes* (Erasers), and of Michel Butor, *Passage de Milan,* an untranslatable title alluding both to a back street and to a bird of prey, the kite. By the sixties the "new novelists," as they were called, had made an impressive showing. The best known among them, along with Robbe-Grillet and Butor, are Nathalie Sarraute, Marguerite Duras, Claude Simon, Claude Ollier, and Robert Pinget.

Butor, Robbe-Grillet, and Sarraute feel no hesitation about fully explaining their widely divergent aims and methods and a lively critical literature has developed around the "new novel" in France and abroad. But theory has not interfered with practice. Since *Les Gommes* Robbe-Grillet has published a novel every other year with clock-like precision: *Le Voyeur* (*The Voyeur*), 1955; *Jalousie* (*Jealousy*), 1957; *Dans le labyrinthe* (*In the Labyrinth*), 1959; and, in 1961, the "roman-ciné" *L'Année dernière à Marienbad* (*Last Year at Marienbad*), the scenario of the much-debated prize-winning film. Butor has produced four novels since *Passage de Milan*: *L'Emploi du temps* (Passing Time), 1956; *La Modification* (*Change of Heart*), 1957, his best known novel; *Degrès* (*Degrees*), 1960. Nathalie Sarraute's prewar *Tropismes* (Tropisms) was republished in 1957, following upon *Martereau*, 1955, and *Portrait d'un inconnu* (*Portrait of a Man Unknown*), 1956. Sartre, in a preface to this last novel, called it an "anti-novel," a term sometimes applied to the "new novel" as a whole. *Planétarium* (*The Planetarium*), 1959, further elaborated the principles that Nathalie Sarraute had set forth in her essay on the novel, *The Age of Suspicion*.

Marguerite Duras, a prewar novelist who has also written a film scenario, *Hiroshima mon amour,* joined the group with *Le Square* (*The Square*), 1955, *Moderato cantabile*, 1958, still the best known of the short novels she has published, and *Dix heures et demi du soir en été* (*10:30 on a Summer Night*), 1960. The latest Duras novel is *L'Après-midi de Monsieur Andesmas* (The Afternoon of Monsieur Andesmas), 1962. Claude Simon, whose first, prewar novel had been ignored, brought out, in rapid succession, *Le Vent* (The Wind), 1957, *L'Herbe* (Grass), 1958, *La Route de Flandres* (The Flanders Road), 1960, *Le Palace,* 1962.

Critics could argue about it, catchwords could come and go: the "new novelists" were off to a fresh start. No one label could be applied to them all: "new realism," "new objectivism," "thingism," "aliterature" were all inadequate, referring only to minor aspects of very different novels. "In Search of the Novel," a commentary appearing in the literary review *Les Cahiers du Sud* (April 1956), rather well summarized the main trend. "The novels of today no longer attempt to set up complete inventories; they no longer present us with an image of complete destruction. The novel today has become once again an *education*. And perhaps it is more than ever alive and essential, because it is through the novel that a man tries to enter into contact with the world, that a moralist tries to discover a meaning and that all writers try to penetrate the world of literature; because through the novel . . . our novelists try to perceive a true order of relationships between the world and themselves. An order within man's situation. . . . For they have at least one ambition in common: to base the novel on man's position in the world. . . . To make the novel an instrument of recognition, of the reconquest of the self and the world, the means to a true reconciliation."

As of today, the better novelists are still hesitant; they still tend to limit their novels to carefully circumscribed situations. But a period is now apparently closed. The "new novel" is more concerned with discovering the real nature of human life than with explaining its ultimate meaning, with consent rather than with revolt, with exact formulation rather than with poetic or lyrical interpretation. The great novels of psychological investigation, of metaphysical or ethical revolt and of intellectual assertion have played their part and played it well. But the young writers seem to feel that this type of novel has now reached a dead end. Not that the novel is moving toward a facile and blind serenity. It has merely for the time being abandoned the great urge to unify, to be all-encompassing, to explain as might the Creator himself, to attempt the gigantic *summa* of a Proust. It is not surprising that during this transitional period many insignificant novels have appeared and that the novel, as a whole, seems like a broken mirror, reflecting only fragmentary images of our time. The trend toward the direct statement of experience is nonetheless manifest. The novelists are trying to express the new sense of reality which they have found in their new relations to the world.